CW00551874

Macmillan Building and Surveying Series
Series Editor: Ivor H. Seeley
Emeritus Professor, The Nottingham Trent University

Macmillan Building and Surveying Series
Series Standing Order ISBN 0-333-69333-7

You can receive future titles in this series as they are published by placing a standing order. Please
contact your bookseller or, in the case of difficulty, write to us at the address below with your
name and address, the title of the series and the ISBN quoted above.

Customer Services Department, Macmillan Distribution Ltd
Houndmills, Basingstoke, Hampshire RG21 6XS, England

Social Housing Management

A Critical Appraisal of Housing Practice

Martyn Pearl

MACMILLAN

First published 1997 by
MACMILLAN PRESS LTD
Houndmills, Basingstoke, Hampshire RG21 6XS
and London
Companies and representatives
throughout the world

ISBN 0–333–62835–7

A catalogue record for this book is available
from the British Library.

This book is printed on paper suitable for recycling and
made from fully managed and sustained forest sources.

10   9   8   7   6   5   4   3   2   1
06 05 04 03 02 01 00 99 98 97

Printed in Hong Kong

This book is dedicated to the memory of my parents and to my wife and children

Contents

List of Figures and Tables

Figures

Tables

Preface

This book is not intended as a standard reference work for practitioners to look up the 'right' way to manage housing. There is sufficient variety in the types of housing organisations, the breadth of expectation and the ideological differences amongst controlling factions for such a task to be both impractical and undesirable. Housing management has been subjected to such radical change over recent years that any attempt to offer a purely descriptive work in the Macey and Baker style would be of limited value. Even if technically correct, it could only hope to provide a snapshot in time and offer a broad generalisation of housing practice. Whilst it is incontrovertible that all local authorities are bound by legislation and government decree, and housing associations by Housing Corporation guidelines, there remains such a gap between interpretation and implementation as to make any study of the legal and technical requirements a backdrop rather than an analysis of the main issues.

For observers of social housing management, whether students preparing to be practitioners of the future, or existing practitioners, the real issue is how to provide a consistently high quality of performance when faced with often seemingly impossible conflicts, constraints and dilemmas. For those involved in the pursuit of educating and preparing students for future practice, one demand constantly made by students is the need to know about and gain experience of the *real world*. However, having been involved in social housing for many years, I have yet to be convinced that such a thing actually exists. Getting to grips with what might actually constitute reality is a largely illusory pursuit. To experience a global reality is impossible, because one person's version of reality is unlikely to correspond with another's. For those with the task of managing housing, the challenge of their reality is to coordinate this vast range of realities into something approaching a coherent matrix of policies and practices satisfying a range of conflicting as well as complementary requirements.

Perceptions of reality are often formed by the randomness of chance. There are a multiplicity of influences which affect the experience of an individual or a household in their role as consumers. They are as diverse as the political and ideological differences between local authorities and as ephemeral as personal moods. Officers are only human, having 'off' days on which they may be less sympathetic, patient and compassionate. They are also merely agents, exercising their skills and expertise in delivering the policies of other more remote bodies.

Reality is served best by the ability of individuals to stand back from a situation and reflect, and approach new experiences with the openness and confidence that comes from self-awareness. Years of hands-on experience mean little without the opportunity to broaden horizons and question and learn from mistakes. Most of us have worked with fellow officers who may have years of service, but very little good experience. The best practitioners are those with the sensitivity and awareness to understand that perceptions of 'reality' often need to be questioned, and a deterministic approach taken to influencing change, where needed. Although neither people nor circumstances fit into the neat categories contained within academic books or training manuals, it often helps to know that a body of views and advice exists which might help in making difficult decisions. It is hoped that this book will contribute to such a body of advice.

It has proved a more substantial undertaking than I originally envisaged, and it is due to the help and support of a number of key individuals that it has been brought to fruition. Foremost in this list has been my wife who has offered support and read through the transcript, correcting grammatical errors and offering stylistic suggestions. Wendy Spray, with whom Chapter 5 was co-written, offered knowledge, experience and insight into the tenants' movement which far exceeded my own. I would like to thank Stephanie Al-Wahid, Director of Development at Waltham Forest HAT, for her time, support and information. Andy Jennings and Vic Baylis both were invaluable in providing material for the CCT case studies. Richard Peacock and Martin Walsh from Oxford City Council both gave time to explain another perspective on CCT. Jon Passmore from Moat Housing Group and Mike Longman from Ridgehill Housing Association provided material relating to their organisations. Jon also took the time to share his thoughts on the future of housing, along with John Palmer from Stonham HA, Charles Waddicore, Director of Housing and Social Services at LB Sutton and Rosemary Prince from Gloucester HA.

Others who have offered invaluable help and advice on drafts of various chapters have included Roy Darke from Oxford Brookes University, Peter Williams from the Council of Mortgage Lenders and Dave Ashmore from Oxford Citizens Housing Association.

I am particularly indebted to Ivor Seeley, the Series Editor, who has meticulously read through the material sent to him, offering advice, suggestions and supportive comments along the way. My publisher, Malcolm Stewart at Macmillan, has been the epitome of patience. And finally, all my colleagues and friends who have offered emotional, professional and moral support to keep me going when my enthusiasm began to flag.

MARTYN PEARL

List of Abbreviations

ADC	Association of District Councils
ADP	Approved Development Programme
ALA	Association of London Authorities
AMA	Association of Metropolitan Authorities
BES	Business Expansion Scheme
BS	British Standard
CHAC	Central Housing Advisory Committee
CIH	Chartered Institute of Housing
CITB	Construction Industry Training Board
CCT	Compulsory Competitive Tendering
CPD	Continual Professional Development
CRE	Commission for Racial Equality
DLO	Direct Labour Organisation
DoE	Department of the Environment
DSO	Direct Service Organisation
EA	Estate Action
EMB	Estate Management Board
GDDF	General Government Financial Deficit
GLC	Greater London Council
HA	Housing Association
HAG	Housing Association Grant
HAMA	Housing Associations as Managing Agents
HATs	Housing Action Trusts
HIP	Housing Investment Programme
HIT	Housing Investment Trust
HNC	Higher National Certificate
HRA	Housing Revenue Account
IoH	Institute of Housing (predating award of Royal Charter)
IT	Information Technology
KFTRA	Kirklees Federation of Tenants and Residents Associations
LSVT	Large Scale Voluntary Transfer
NFHA	National Federation of Housing Associations (changed to National Housing Federation)
NVQ	National Vocational Qualification
PATH	Positive Action for Training in Housing
PFA2000	People for Action 2000
PEP	Priority Estates Project
PFI	Private Finance Initiative
PPI	Published Performance Indicator
PSBR	Public Sector Borrowing Requirement
RICS	Royal Institute of Chartered Surveyors

SNU	Safe Neighbourhoods Unit
SRB	Single Regeneration Budget
THFC	The Housing Finance Corporation
TPAS	Tenant Participation Advisory Service
TMC	Tenant Management Cooperative
TMO	Tenant Management Organisation
TQM	Total Quality Management
TUPE	Transfer of Undertakings (Protection of Employment)
VCT	Voluntary Competitive Tendering
WFHAT	Waltham Forest Housing Action Trust

1   Introduction

'Three human needs – food, clothing and shelter – are so fundamental
that our life cannot continue without them.'

(Ward, 1985)

This is a book about housing management. It is an occupation which
closely touches the lives of both those delivering the service and those
who receive it. As Colin Ward observes, housing is so fundamental to
ensuring quality of life, that its distribution and control lies at the very
core of a welfare society. Without a secure base, few other benefits of an
advanced society can properly be enjoyed. This work is not intended to
be a policy analysis of the success or failings of social housing, nor a
technical evaluation of the costs of delivering the landlord function. Each
has been undertaken elsewhere within the recent past. Instead, the perspective of the book is that of the practitioner. Whether employed as a
front-line housing officer or a director of housing, the role of individual
housing staff is often as critical to the manner in which services are delivered as the policy framework within which they operate.

Much has occurred during the 1980s and 1990s to change the face of
public housing, opening to scrutiny a number of fundamental principles
which have traditionally embodied the very basis of the welfare state in
Britain. The right to welfare services based primarily on need has been
roundly challenged by the ascendance of the New Right, particularly during the 1980s. Housing has borne the brunt of this challenge, in the form
of swingeing expenditure cuts and a reduced role for the public sector in
favour of private sector enterprise. Across the public arena, the protection
offered by professional autonomy has been dismantled on a platform of
increasing rights and choices for consumers, or customers. In parallel, the
Audit Commission, having announced that the management of council
housing was in crisis (Audit Commission, 1986), have been involved in
implementing a major overhaul of structures and services. The resulting
programme of performance measures has substantially altered the face of
social housing. While radical change has resulted in perceptible improvements in the management of services, the burden of implementation has
fallen squarely on the shoulders of housing officers, many of whom are
front-line staff. They might, if consulted, have conceded that change was
overdue and having occurred has shaken up a profession in danger of
becoming complacent and insular. However, relatively few would have
chosen the methods adopted to achieve it.

The catalyst for many of these changes was the perception of an inefficient and nepotistic public sector cushioned by the virtual monopoly position

1

enjoyed by some inner-city local authorities. There is little doubt that such criticisms were valid in part, with housing staff clearly implicated in a catalogue of poor performance. However, it would be wrong to locate the blame for such a position exclusively at the door of professionals. A cocktail of poor systems, underfunding and political ideology, combined with a somewhat sheltered existence, provided a perfect environment for underachievement. Huge reductions in government spending have served to increase public demand for fewer services, leaving greater levels of unmet need and professional frustration. In many areas, the only option has been to 'fire fight', avoiding catastrophes where possible. The history of social housing management has therefore often been characterised by a mixture of misplaced paternalism and committed professionals producing extremely competent work under difficult circumstances.

Yet the picture is not consistent across all localities, functions or organisations. For each negative perception of policy or practice, there is often a contrary opinion. What appears good for inner-city organisations, may be irrelevant or unenforceable in rural communities.

For practitioners, the difficulty is often in making sense of their surroundings, and negotiating a sustainable path though the minefields of day-to-day practice. To succeed, they must be aware of political ideology, the power of personality, national and local circumstances, popularity and self-interest, all of which will impact on their working environment. The following chapters will examine the major influences on social housing management with particular reference to these variations in practice and the scope of choices open to individuals.

The New Right Agenda for Change

The First Phase: 1979–87

Much has been written about social housing and its management in recent years. A 'market' has developed in the study and analysis of housing management which had little currency during the 1960s and 1970s. During those boom years when local authority housing construction reached levels of 200 000–300 000 new dwellings per year, very little guidance or analysis was produced about the process of management. However, the development of an environment dominated by resource constraint, value for money and performance monitoring has located housing management firmly within the sphere of resource management. Prior to the creation of the Audit Commission in 1983, housing management reports evaluated the scope and effectiveness of services rather than the organisational context within which those services were delivered. Reports such as CHAC's *Councils and their Houses: Eighth Report* (HMSO, 1959), the Cullingworth Report (Cullingworth, 1969), Housing Services Advisory Group, *Organising a Comprehensive Housing Service* (HSAG, 1979) examined housing management services and structures primarily in the context of delivering effective services to meet housing need.

Much of the council housing produced during this time was in response to political commitment to 'the numbers game', i.e. constructing the largest number of dwellings in the shortest time. Housing management arrangements were largely developed 'on the hoof' in response to huge, badly designed and poorly constructed estates which flowed regularly from the conveyor belt. Because of the sheer scale of activity, a rather mechanistic approach to housing management emerged based on 'the obsessive emphasis on property rather than people' (Power, 1987). This was coupled with a societal culture in which the relationship between the state and its citizens was much less interactive than has more recently developed. Consumer expectations of influencing and participating in strategy or policy were low, undermined by the paternalistic and distant behaviour of professionals and elected members alike. The legacy has been a widespread support for government policies which have been aimed at reducing the power and involvement of town halls in the provision and management of social housing. This has been evidenced not only in the success of the Right To Buy (in which personal financial gain is a compelling incentive), but also of initiatives such as Large Scale Voluntary Transfers and the growth of the tenants' movement. Each has in its own way promoted change in both the style and nature of housing management.

By the 1980s social housing management had reached the stage of pleasing no one. Pressures for change became irresistible as the result of combined efforts from both left and right of the political spectrum. The New Right, neo-liberal policies pursued by successive Thatcherite governments perceived public housing as inefficient, monopolistic, dependency-forming and mollycoddling. This philosophy was founded on the anti-collectivist belief that state intervention was inefficient compared to the free market, working against the interest of the individual by reducing liberty and eroding incentives to achievement (George and Wilding, 1976; Clapham *et al.*, 1990).

Linked to monetarist austerity measures designed to reduce public spending and promote the private sector, reform of housing management was intended to loosen the grip of local authorities in providing for housing need. The government considered public provision ideologically unsound, when the market would be more efficient in providing the resources necessary to meet both need and aspiration. Equally important, in fulfilling their statutory homelessness function, local authorities appeared to have access to a blank cheque to pay the spiralling costs of bed and breakfast accommodation. Ministers believed that local authorities had a perverse incentive to encourage and exaggerate housing need. Greater levels of demand offered a platform from which to argue for additional public housing. The urgency for the government was therefore to curb the worst expenditure excesses of local authorities while in parallel offering potentially disaffected tenants the opportunity to purchase their dwellings or transfer to alternative landlords. Their belief was that such a pincer movement would

succeed in reducing the role of council housing departments to the providers of last resort, for those who could afford no alternative.

At the other end of the political spectrum, pressure was also being exerted
by the far left who believed that public sector housing management was
too paternalistic, oppressive and autocratic. Writers such as Colin Ward
believed that the growth of housing departments since 1975 had been
accompanied by the monolithic centralisation of control within large and
complex bureaucracies, removing services from the people they were designed to serve. Their view was that the control of housing should be
returned to its inhabitants, who were, after all, best placed to know their
own best interests and those of their households. Ward quotes Tony Judge,
Chair of the Housing Management Committee of the former GLC: 'The
impression, often confirmed as accurate on deeper examination, is of a
vast bureaucracy concerned more with self-perpetuation than with either
efficiency or humanity' (Ward, 1985). Their solution was therefore to devolve control to occupants, producing a more efficient and effective use
of resources as expenditure would be related to actual need.

The belief that council housing management had failed and required
radical reform was therefore a view shared by both right and left. Both
considered it to have proven a *dis*service, disabling effective control and
encouraging self-interested, bureaucratic control of resources rather than
accurate targeting to those in greatest need. Unsurprisingly, the consensus
ended here, marked by significant differences relating to the role of the
market, state funding support and the position of housing as a right rather
than a commodity. The change which occurred emanated largely from
outside of the housing movement. Initiated via the legislative reforms of
Conservative governments from 1979, it subsequently gained additional
momentum from community groups exercising their newly found rights of
citizenship. The catalysts have been both carrot and stick. The government wielded the heavy legislative stick while tenants have been offered
the carrot of huge financial incentives to purchase their council homes
under the Right to Buy. This initiative, introduced by the Housing Act
1980, has proved particularly significant in shaping housing management
for many local authorities. The sale of over 1.5 million better quality council
houses has resulted in many inner-city councils managing an increasingly
residualised and more expensive stock. The pepper-potting of owner-occupiers
amongst previously council-owned blocks or estates, has also demanded
new skills in reconciling tenant/resident expectations.

The 1980s therefore saw a series of battles between central government
and local authorities as the former introduced tighter expenditure controls
over all areas of public spending. Centralised control wrested away from
councils the traditional autonomy to raise and spend resources as they
saw fit. In many instances housing found itself in the familiar position of
being torn between two opposing approaches: one, a local need-based
perspective reflecting statutory responsibilities, against a national perspective of resource constraint, value for money and privatisation. While all

public services experienced reduced resource allocations, housing took the brunt of expenditure cuts: 'In 1980 the government announced expenditure plans in which at least 75 per cent of all planned reductions were concentrated in the housing programme' (Malpass, 1992). The resulting economies, both in revenue and capital expenditure, inevitably affected the manner in which services were delivered.

The Second Phase: 1987–1996

Despite its initial success, the Right to Buy did not significantly dent council stock holdings in the inner-city areas where the problems of poor repair and deprivation were most acute. It had run its course even before the property slump at the end of the 1980s. The desire to introduce fresh impetus to the programme of reform resulted in the publication of a 1987 White Paper entitled *Housing: The Government's Proposals* (DoE, 1987a). Within it, the government's stated intention was: 'First, to reverse the decline of rented housing and to improve its quality; second, to give council tenants the right to transfer to other landlords if they choose to do so; third, to target money more accurately on the most acute problems; and fourth, to continue to encourage the growth of home ownership' (DoE Cm 214, 1987, p. 1). These proposals were implemented by the 1988 Housing Act which further extended Right to Buy discounts, and introduced Tenants' Choice and Housing Action Trusts (HATs). In addition, new financial regimes were introduced for both local authorities and housing associations. Their effect was to force rents to rise steeply, to a position more in line with the private sector, directly reflecting the actual costs of providing and managing the stock. Each of these was a intended as a further nail in the coffin of social housing and to diminish the role of local authorities in managing housing stock.

By pursuing this course, ministers expected that the vast majority of council tenants would chose to opt either for home ownership or alternative renting arrangements. However, they were mistaken in the belief that most council tenants shared a conviction that local authorities were bad landlords. More to the point, the familiar devil offered more security than the unknown quantities of both housing associations and the private sector. Many tenants continued to harbour fears of a return to the private sector abuses of Rachmanism, with its accompanying insecurity and rent increases. To some, the differences between housing associations and private landlords had never been clearly explained. The introduction of assured tenancies and market rents under the Housing Act 1988 therefore raised once again the spectre of potential exploitation. While local authorities were clearly not perfect, they represented a known and secure option with democratically elected control. The strength of feeling in favour of council control was demonstrated by the total failure of the government's proposals to create six HATs on estates constituting some of the worst housing across the country.

For the government, the strategic importance of HATs was intended to be a further demonstration of the impotence of local authority housing management. Their plan was to remove from local authority ownership those estates representing the most obvious management failures and place them within the control of a private sector organisation which would subsequently have access to substantial sums of public money for improvements. Despite portraying the initiative 'as a way of rescuing tenants from incompetent local authorities' (Karn, 1993, p. 75) and diverting £125 million over three years towards the designated areas, local tenants overwhelmingly rejected the proposals. In all six areas, Tower Hamlets, Southwark, Leeds, Sunderland, Sandwell and Lambeth, tenants voted to remain with their local authority despite the loss of a unique opportunity to secure a programme of upgrading and refurbishment of their estates. However, a much altered HAT model was subsequently introduced, discussed further in Chapter 8.

Yet even such a vote of confidence could not disguise the fact that a feeling of widespread disaffection remained amongst many tenants. A groundswell of discontent and dissatisfaction over the shortcomings of housing management provided the platform for change. This has been particularly strong within inner-city environments where poor quality housing and multiple deprivation increasingly demanded a new approach. The alienation felt by many is reflected by Cole and Furbey (1994, p. 117): 'Had council housing conferred on its occupants extensive citizenship rights, had it offered autonomy to each household, a genuine choice of dwelling, opportunities for mobility, and a trained, efficient, responsive and accountable management, then it is possible to imagine opposition to state withdrawal from direct housing provision in Britain.' The fact that this did not happen reflects the dominance of a public sector management culture which was largely dismissive of consumers and non-professionals. There are indications that this is now changing, in response to the opportunities and consumer rights more recently conferred upon tenants. Whether such change has occurred too late to reprieve council housing departments in the wake of Compulsory Competitive Tendering (CCT) remains to be seen.

For housing associations, the position has been quite different. The Housing Act 1988 offered a double-edged sword. It identified associations as the main providers of social housing, thus assuming the mantle previously worn by local authorities, with promised increases in development programmes. At the same time, it expressly located associations within the private sector despite their long-established public sector tradition. This involved the requirement to raise development finance from the private sector, to increase rents to market levels, and to offer assured tenancies rather than the secure tenancies previously awarded. The latter change, part of the ongoing decontrol of the private rented sector, was partly in response to pressure from private landlords to remove what was seen to be unreasonable restrictions on their ability to regain possession of their dwellings. Whilst not removing security altogether, the new assured tenancies dispensed with rent control and offered greater opportunities to grant short-term tenancies without long-term implications. To overcome the widespread concern felt by many housing association tenants at these new arrangements, the Housing Corporation issued the Tenants' Guarantee. True to its name, this document was intended to reassure tenants that housing associations would act responsibly in all matters relating to their tenancies.

Many in the movement felt that this new mantle represented little more than the emperor's new clothes. Whilst granted the opportunity for significant increases in size, housing associations acquired such an opportunity at considerable cost, increasingly operating at risk, without the security of government grants to bail them out in emergencies. Rents have reached such high levels due to the expense of private borrowing, that they are increasingly becoming affordable only to those on full housing benefit. Standards are being eroded as associations desperately attempt to keep development costs as low as possible. Associations are also losing any balance previously achieved in their tenant profiles. Increasingly, they are expected to rehouse the poorest, most vulnerable and deprived households in society, previously the task of local authorities. However, they rarely have access to the range of resources available to local authorities to provide an appropriate level of housing management. The price of becoming the main provider of social housing might yet prove to be the disintegration of the established housing association movement.

The Realignment of Social Housing Management

It has therefore been against the backdrop of such reform that a new interest in the analysis and debate about housing management has developed. Housing, alongside such other public services as social work, health and education, has been subjected to a systematic deconstruction of its professional values and orientation and a subsequent reconstruction along the lines of the private sector. The emergence of a new culture of public sector management based on the Audit Commission's trinity of efficiency, effectiveness and economy (1986) has created the foundation for the development of a new-style housing management, the nature of which is discussed more fully in Chapter 2. Social housing management is undoubtedly at a cross-roads following a decade and a half of radical reform by successive Conservative administrations. Terms such as 'council housing' traditionally used to describe subsidised housing has now given way to less specific nomenclature such as 'social housing' and 'affordable housing'.

Since its inception the Audit Commission has produced reports covering the full range of local authority activities, analysing the efficiency of services and the value for money achieved for public money invested. Many of these have been critical of public organisations and the apparent failure of many to deliver services effectively, efficiently and economically.

As a result, the government has introduced a series of measures which have had the effect of shifting the emphasis of social policy from being needs-driven to being determined instead by what is affordable. The political agenda is now dominated by a series of Treasury-driven imperatives including efficiency, economy, value for money and competition, harnessed to a manifesto commitment of consumer choice, the promotion of tenants' rights and citizen empowerment.

The antipathy towards local councils has been fuelled by the fact that the highest spenders, – reflecting the greatest deprivation –, are usually Labour controlled. The most notorious of these, the London boroughs of Hackney and Lambeth, have been consistently labelled by the media 'loony left', generating regular headlines of corruption and inefficiency. The belief that such local authorities would either have to improve their ability to manage or disappear when subjected to market forces (more likely the latter) has been at the heart of much of the government's legislative programme. This was implemented by the introduction of Compulsory Competitive Tendering in the 1980 Local Government Act, requiring specified local authority manual functions to operate at a profit. The ring-fencing of the Housing Revenue Account (HRA) within the Local Government and Housing Act 1989 further emphasised the intention that the price paid by consumers for the services they receive should reflect the cost, encouraging a greater awareness of value for money. It achieved this by restricting the ability of local authorities to subsidise the HRA from external sources, including the General Fund. Other than HRA subsidy paid by the DoE, the expenditure on landlord services had therefore to be largely balanced by rental income or efficiency savings.

While local authorities were the subject of vilification and constraint, housing associations had become the flavour of the month, enjoying an unprecedented period of growth and influence. Many senior staff in local authorities cast envious and covetous eyes towards new, highly paid jobs being created with both established and new Large Scale Voluntary Transfer (LSVT) associations (see Chapter 8). However, few managed to cross the rubicon, and a form of association elitism emerged in which the movement closed ranks to exclude those perceived to be deserting the sinking ships of local authorities. While the housing association rise to prominence has not completely faltered, much of the early promise has failed to materialise. Instead of the glut of funding opportunities envisaged by many, the reality has been that the major developing associations have been drawn into competition with each other with the weakest threatened with extinction. The catalyst has been the Housing Corporation pushing for more homes for less Housing Association Grant (HAG), with the carrot of increased resources for the most successful, and none for the least. This has led to the anomalous situation in which, on the one hand, associations have consistently warned the government of the dangers of reducing HAG rates on rent levels, whilst on the other, significantly overbidding for Approved Development Programme (ADP) resources. This apparent inconsistency has only been perpetuated by the wealthier associations, with large numbers of pre-1989 dwellings[1] significantly subsidising the rent levels of the more expensive, assured tenancies. However, no matter how rich the association, the time will inevitably come when the ability to cross-subsidise (rent pool) no longer exists because new regime dwellings exceed the older ones.

When the bubble finally burst following the announcement of huge expenditure cuts for social housing within the 1994 autumn budget, associations which had geared up for high levels of development activity found themselves overstaffed and over-committed. For many, the opportunities of the late 1980s turned into the disaster of the 1990s. The picture was less bleak for the very largest, national or regional associations with sufficient reserves and dwellings to cushion the impact of falling grant rates whilst retaining the confidence of the money markets. The legacy, however, has been a changed face for housing associations as the price for taking on the role of social housing provider. The trend has been for smaller associations to be subsumed within larger ones either by way of merger, takeover or integration into group structures. The result is that the traditional reputation of associations as small, specialised, responsive and accountable to their tenants has taken something of a knock. Similarly, the ability of associations to control their tenant profile, offering the opportunity to create balanced communities has also been severely undermined by their newly acquired responsibilities for housing the homeless and vulnerable. This has been highlighted by the report, *Building for Communities* (Page, 1993), which warns of the potential danger for associations of being drawn into developing the problem estates of tomorrow. Page indicates that already, classic local authority failures of high-density estates inhabited almost exclusively by vulnerable households was being replicated by housing associations. This has been further compounded by evidence that to reduce costs, more recent association development has been built to lower standards, in terms of both space and materials, than previously had been considered acceptable (Karn and Sheriden, 1994). There is growing concern, therefore, that faced with the demand pressures for their housing that local authorities had previously shouldered, associations may fall foul of similar housing management pitfalls.

---

1. Such dwellings were developed or acquired with the benefit of much higher levels of HAG (often 95%) under a residual HAG regime in which subsidy levels were locked into the objective of achieving fair rent levels for all new housing association dwellings. Post-1989 dwellings have been funded on the basis of fixed HAG levels, which have fallen as low as 48% of the development costs, the remaining finance being acquired from private institutions. These loans have to be repaid with interest, largely from the rental income generated by the dwellings themselves.

The seductive nature of development has persuaded a number of associations to invest the bulk of their energy and resources into generating expansion at any cost. The result is that in many organisations the structures and mechanisms for effective housing management are lacking. This is despite the potential implication of poor management, greater rent loss and excessive repairs, all of which are particularly serious for associations, who no longer have redress to the Housing Corporation to underwrite operational losses. Accountability has also emerged as an issue of equal concern to performance. The 'democratic deficit' has been a major criticism levelled at the housing association movement, i.e. the fact that members of boards of management are not, like local authorities, elected, but rather recruited by often *ad hoc* and unaccountable means. The effect is that those in control of associations may have little understanding of, or empathy with their chosen constituency. This is compounded by the fact that the larger developing associations tend to operate either nationally or regionally. This increases the potential logistical problems of providing local services caused by the remote location of power and control. Each of these issues will be examined further in Chapter 3.

Practising Housing Management

For practitioners, in addition to manoeuvring through political and professional issues, practice is a daily matter of squaring a circle when faced with endless conflicts and inconsistencies. The task often centres on the need to make intuitive personal judgements in taking other complex decisions. Whilst the majority of situations may fall within guidelines contained within policy and procedure manuals, significant numbers will pose dilemmas based on sensitive and often emotive issues, which require the resolution of conflicting attributes, such as:

- *Fairness/Popularity* It is often extremely difficult to maintain equity in the face of extreme pressure by consumers, members or colleagues to react expediently. This may be particularly true of pre-election periods. There is frequently a thin dividing line between pressure which is purely popularist, i.e. gains the backing of influential parties, and that which genuinely highlights a need for flexibility in response to manifestations of need.
- *Consistency/Flexibility* These two factors may be mutually exclusive. The exercise of discretion, which is the tool of flexibility, will result in decisions being taken on the basis of individual circumstances. By definition, this will imply that such decisions are extraordinary and will differ from case to case. Whilst such a facility may be warranted and specific decisions wholly appropriate and justified, the system clearly gives rise to inconsistency and potential abuse. At the other extreme, consistency in its literal sense would indicate that

all situations displaying identical characteristics would be treated exactly the same. Whilst this should be true, no two housing cases *are* identical and the process of prioritisation is normally based on some form of categorisation, i.e. generalisation. Rigid bureaucratic procedures can often produce inequity when applied unquestioningly to broad categories.

- *Comprehensibility/Comprehensiveness* There is almost always a trade-off to be achieved between an easily understood policy and one which attempts to be comprehensive by catering for all possible eventualities. A classic example is that of an allocation policy. The easiest type to understand and follow is the date order system, whereby allocations are decided by the date registered on a list, i.e. first come, first served. It is clear and unequivocal, yet offers little concession to housing need. At the other end of the spectrum are points systems which may be comprehensive, resulting in a position in which it is operable only with the aid of a computer. Decisions may be extremely equitable, but difficult to explain to anyone not directly involved in the process. In practice, the most successful schemes are those which achieve a balance between these extremes. However, crucially influential is that comprehensiveness and sophistication generally costs more to administer than a less sensitive system.
- *Efficiency/Effectiveness* In the public sector context, efficiency has become virtually synonymous with economy. Delivering services in the cheapest possible manner is often inconsistent with achieving objectives. This is discussed further in Chapter 2.
- *Economy/Demand* The trend towards capping finances has meant that, in practice, demand can only be interpreted within the context of available resources. This often results in inconsistent treatment of individuals if resources run out during a financial year. In such circumstances, access may be dependent on timing rather than indicators of need. An example is the resource-capped Social Fund.
- *Accountability/Competition* One of the features of the public sector has been the checks and balances traditionally forming part of operational mechanisms. Restrictions on absolute power and control residing with individuals has been the basis for avoiding corruption and bias in decision-making. However, such mechanisms are often costly and time-consuming, and sit uneasily with the competitive requirements of the private sector, imposed by CCT.

The effectiveness of housing management therefore invariably relies on the quality of judgement exercised by individuals. Yet many practitioners are often expected to work with insufficient guidance, inadequate training and inconsistent support from colleagues. This may not necessarily be the fault of either the individual or their employing organisation; the goalposts for measuring performance in social housing have moved so often that they have become almost a blur. The one constant in social housing management appears to be that of change. Chapter 2 examines the paradoxical question 'what *is* housing management?' in an effort to identify solid ground on which good practice can be sustained within an often unpredictable environment.

Housing, a Political Environment

Change may occur in a planned manner or, equally likely, result from unpredictable events. Housing staff in Ealing experienced major change during the 1980s as political control of their authority switched from Conservative to Labour and back to Conservative again. Each electoral change was accompanied by significant shifts in the style and organisational culture, translating into new policies and practices for the staff. Perhaps it was no coincidence that the Director of Housing under the original Conservative regime departed soon after Labour came to power, only for the director appointed under Labour similarly to lose tenure when the Conservatives regained control in 1990. Such occurrences serve only to highlight the political nature of housing in the public sector. More than any other service, it generates radically divergent views about its philosophy and context, translating into differences about how it should be provided, who should occupy it and on what basis.

For most housing practitioners, direct exposure to the political environment may be more limited, although equally intrusive, if less personally threatening. In many local authorities, elected members create policy via committee structures, leaving officers to execute their wishes on a day-to-day basis. In others, roles differ and members are more interventionist in their approach to service delivery. This may take the form of deciding housing allocations via a merit system, i.e. the applicants considered most deserving. In other circumstances, members may be active in running decentralised estates and influencing the expenditure of local budgets. In many instances, member involvement will complement, cooperate, and be in full support of officers. In others this may be less true, and relationships may be fraught. This is perhaps inevitable when so much is at stake in meeting local need and achieving political electability. The role of elected members is generally to create a policy framework within which manifesto pledges can be implemented, which can only be achieved with the cooperation and assistance of paid officers. Whilst such an alliance often works well, relationships can become blurred or unstable. This was highlighted in the well-publicised case of Westminster, where three senior officers were found guilty, alongside elected members, of gerrymandering, i.e. implementing policies based on self-interest rather than for the good of local people.

Facing Reality

To many observers, these scenarios merely represent a level of insecurity and flexibility already inherent to the private sector, which provides the competitive tension driving industry and commerce. For successive Conservative governments since 1979, the failures of the public sector have largely been as a result of ineffective management perpetuated by the lack of competition. Their exhortation has therefore been for professionals and bureaucrats to come out of their ivory towers and experience life in *the real world*. They believe that only by working within the harsh disciplines imposed by market forces can the public sector expect to offer value for money and service efficiency. This will be examined further in Chapter 7, i.e. the extent to which the introduction of market mechanisms via Compulsory Competitive Tendering (CCT) will influence service delivery.

However, whatever the efficiency merits of such an argument, it is important to examine what the *real world* actually means. For anti-collectivists and supporters of the politics of the New Right, the *real world* is one in which there is minimum state intervention, and individual citizens are forced or encouraged to make their way on the basis of their own skills and abilities. Any further movement towards developing the role of the state is considered to inhibit personal freedom and encourage dependency. This largely macho perspective characterised the Thatcherite governments of the 1980s, embracing the ideal of the survival of the fittest and offering succour only as a last resort to those patently unable to provide for themselves. This contrasts sharply with the more populist perspective of British society since 1948. Mass support for a welfare state has projected a *real world* in which each citizen should have the right to access public services for the purposes of health care, education and to some extent housing. Clearly therefore, reality achieves a different currency depending on which perspective one chooses to adopt.

The *real world* for housing practitioners relates to their working environment and the outcomes for which they are responsible and are instrumental in achieving. It is therefore critical that they are aware of the diversity of *real worlds* inhabited by both providers and consumers if they are to deliver quality and achieve performance targets. There is no reason why experience or aspiration should be the same for everyone. For those fortunate enough to be housed and employed, the real world will be quite different from the one for those without either a home or employment. For homeless households, the reality of long stays in bed-and-breakfast is a harsh one. Yet the reality, or outcome, of the homelessness process will largely depend on the location in which the application occurs. Some local authorities choose to adopt a punitive approach to homelessness, ensuring the process leading to refusal or acceptance is as protracted and rigorous as possible. They may also implement policies requiring all households accepted as homeless to spend time in hostels or bed-and-breakfast hotels. Other authorities may have a more sanguine approach to

```
┌─────────────────────────────────────────────────────────────────┐
│  ┌─────────────────────────────────────────────────────────────┐ │
│  │                     Lambeth Services                        │ │
│  │                     Chief Executive                         │ │
│  │                                                             │ │
│  │       Arguably, the toughest job in local government!       │ │
│  │                    Are you up to it?                        │ │
│  │                                                             │ │
│  │            Salary & terms - open & negotiable               │ │
│  │                                                             │ │
│  │            Why might you not want this job                  │ │
│  │                                                             │ │
│  │  This has to be the ultimate challenge. Look at the public  │ │
│  │  perceptions: one of the worst reputations of any local     │ │
│  │  authority in the UK; poor morale; poor services; and a     │ │
│  │  dreadful public image. We get the worst press; constant    │ │
│  │  negative publicity; anything good that we do never gets    │ │
│  │  reported; anything bad that happens always gets reported;  │ │
│  │  and on top of all that, we are now a 'hung' council        │ │
│  └─────────────────────────────────────────────────────────────┘ │
└─────────────────────────────────────────────────────────────────┘
```

Figure 1.1   Advertisement for Lambeth chief executive

homelessness, adopting a more supportive attitude towards homeless households.

The reality of everyday life for tenants living in poorly constructed systems-built accommodation which may be difficult to heat and have problems of water penetration, condensation, mould growth and insect infestation, is one of hardship. For other households fortunate to be allocated one of the many good-standard, low-density houses or flats in social ownership, the future may hold more promise. Yet how does even the former scenario compare with that of a single person forced to live rough because no one will house them? Comparisons are difficult and iniquitous. Yet for many housing practitioners, this reflects their working reality. The inevitable corollary of working within an environment in which demand so exceeds supply is the need to implement a system of rationing based on established priorities. Practitioners are therefore placed in the position of having to favour one person's reality over another's. Not only is this often extremely difficult, but may be accompanied by a liberal dose of threats, abuse and violence from an increasingly marginalised public already coping with problems of poverty, unemployment, illness and harassment.

In terms of their own employment, the reality for senior officers has been to command higher salaries in exchange for the constant threat of insecurity. Senior staff are commonly being appointed on fixed term contracts with added enhancements and performance related pay. This is a trend clearly borrowed from private sector management practices. Dismissal may hinge on the interaction of diverse and unpredictable factors. Careers may depend as much on the strength or absence of relationships with senior members, chief executives and other heads of department as on personal ability. Innovation and achievement may also be undermined by specific local factors, e.g. excess of demand over supply, availability of financial resources, support from tenants, etc. Some jobs are without doubt more difficult than others – the 1994 advertisement for Lambeth's chief executive (Figure 1.1) aptly illustrates this.

The *real world* is therefore not a single world at all, but rather a series of worlds, each reflecting the interaction of local personalities, issues and circumstances. Together these produce the outputs which give form to the individual reality of the providers and consumers of that service. The following chapters offer an insight into the issues which influence housing management, providing an overview of legislation, policy and practice which together create the framework for service delivery. The intention is to offer students and observers of social housing a broad perspective of housing management, whilst encouraging individuals, both as employees and professionals, to reflect on the implications of their actions and by so doing to learn from experience.

2 What Is Housing Management?

'There is no standard definition of housing management. This paper assumes that the activity centres on the landlord activities of the local authority.'

(DoE, *Competing for Quality in Housing*, 1992)

'At the moment, there are no universally agreed national standards for housing management services provided by social landlords. Indeed, there is no agreed definition as to what housing management is, or as to what kind or level of service landlords should give to customers.'

(Chartered Institute of Housing, *Housing Standards Manual*, 1993)

'There is no generally accepted definition of what constitutes a standard unit of housing management output and in practice there appears to be considerable variation in both range and level of services provided by housing authorities.'

(DoE, *Empirical Study into the Costs of Local Authority Housing Management*, 1992)

Although this book is about housing management, as the above quotes indicate, there has in the past been little clear consensus as to what such a term actually means. A growing emphasis on value for money via competition and contract specifications has more recently provided a focus around which a common definition has become established. It has concentrated largely on output-related landlord functions, crystallised within the concept of the 'Social Housing Product' (see Chapter 11) introduced in the 1995 White Paper *Our Future Homes* (DoE, 1995b). The motivation has been to develop a series of measurable performance standards which might appropriately be applied to an increasingly diverse range of landlord organisations. This has become particularly important in the light of the political commitment to promote housing companies and the potential extension of Social Housing Grant (the replacement for HAG) to private developers. A common set of standards would in theory allow the establishment of a level playing field on which services might realistically be compared, irrespective of the organisation delivering them. However, this has generated a growing concern amongst existing housing associations that the future allocation of grant may be heavily influenced by, or directly linked to, performance comparisons achieved by the production of league tables of measured output. The effect has been to further intensify competition, particularly in the service areas covered by these standards.

However, such an approach offers only a part of the whole picture.

Output statistics do not account for the variations in demographic, locational and socio-economic factors which ultimately dictate the nature and the complexity of the services provided. Later chapters will illustrate that such are the variations in the way organisations approach their landlord responsibilities that meaningful comparisons are extremely problematic. In many cases, like is not being compared with like and the basis for comparison is therefore flawed. At one end of the spectrum are the smaller housing associations and local authorities employing relatively few staff to carry out the minimum housing management functions. At the other extreme are councils such as Glasgow and Birmingham with over 100 000 dwellings, and the larger housing associations such as Home, North British and Anchor, each of which exceed 20 000 dwellings in management. While many smaller authorities tend to be minimalist in their approach, the larger urban authorities have generally opted for a comprehensive housing model. Nor are such physical differences the only variations between housing organisations. Equally huge ideological variations exist which are often major influences in determining the culture and ethos of organisational practice.

Recent trends (DoE, 1992a and NFHA, 1995c) have been to categorise social housing management as relating to those activities comprising the landlord functions of property management, i.e. rent collection, void control, repairs, etc. This corresponds with the framework imposed by central government for the separation of mainstream welfare support from landlord activities as part of the process of introducing competition. However, while such a definition may reflect national policy objectives, it does not reflect the scope of routine housing practice, representing a selective interpretation of the workload of many housing staff. It ignores the extensive expectations and pressures on social housing managers to provide services beyond those limited to bricks and mortar functions. In reality, the needs of tenants are central to the type of housing management implemented in the public sector.

Such a redefinition reflects the thrust of central government policy-making since 1980, designed to locate public sector practices within a more private sector environment. However, the motivation and core values of social housing organisations often differ markedly from those of the 'for profit' rented sector. While the future of the welfare state remains in doubt largely due to cost, the past impetus for social housing had a much wider brief. The provision of council housing, accessed on the basis of need, provided not only better quality accommodation, but also had the effect of 'extending citizenship rights through meeting the objectives of equality, freedom, democracy and community . . . and offers a touchstone by which it (and its alternatives) can be judged' (Clapham, 1989). Local authorities have traditionally provided public services founded on non-profit-making motivators which fulfil moral, altruistic and civic responsibilities. These have provided a clear distinction between the approach of the social sector and that of the private sector. Yet despite, or perhaps because of, such obvious differences, the social housing role has been steadily privatised by a series of legislative and policy initiatives introduced since 1980.

Each successive policy has been instigated by the government as part of a drive towards improving public sector performance. Indicators of success have related primarily to returns on investment, reductions in public expenditure and value for money, rather than to achieving social welfare objectives. In establishing acceptable levels of performance, the government has compared management costs across both public and private sectors. Inevitably, the costs of providing appropriate services to the most vulnerable in society will be higher than those required by the able-bodied and adequately waged. Analyses of past levels of performance based solely on cost criteria therefore show the private sector in a much better light. In the face of strong central leanings towards the perceived benefits of market forces, qualitative and non-financial performance indicators have been afforded much lower priority, fading in significance against those measuring financial and quantitive outputs. If this trend continues, it will represent a major step towards the final demise of social housing. In practice, it would offer little perceptible difference to the private sector, leaving little clear rationale for its continued existence.

With such a great deal at stake, it is perhaps surprising that until recently so little attempt has been made by social housing managers to mark out their ground, more clearly defining objectives and promoting achievements. It is highly significant that for decades, millions of dwellings have been managed at the cost of billions of pounds, and millions of households housed and serviced without the benefit of clear standards against which to judge local practice. The unfortunate result has been that public housing management has often acquired a poor reputation, which has been exploited and perpetuated by an often sensationalist media, fuelled by political rhetoric from central government. This image is largely based on an unrepresentative number of failures or *faux pas* which often bear little relationship to the reality of practice in the majority of social housing organisations nationally. However, its effect has been to fuel such political negativity that an irresistible momentum has been created, pushing social housing management practice inexorably towards that employed in the private sector. If the result is the demise of the social sector as we have come to know it, the headstone might read, 'here lies social housing management; it had the best of intentions, but was often misunderstood'. The housing profession may yet come to rue the fact that established standards, values and identity have been lacking for so long, despite current attempts to redress the situation. These have included the publication of a *Housing Standards Manual*, produced by the CIH (Chartered Institute of Housing, 1993) to introduce codes of conduct and guidance for practitioners as well as promote the viability of *social business*. The need for such definition has become critical to safeguard the core values of social housing which have been consistently founded (if not always delivered) on objectives of equity, equality and altruism.

This chapter sets out to examine the range of housing management approaches active within the social rented sector. Of particular importance are the changes occurring in light of competitive pressures and the growing influence of a performance culture. Being clear about motivation, expectation and objectives is crucial if housing practitioners are to be effective in what they do. This has been provided in the past by a public sector ethos which established common points of reference for core values, standards and attitudes. However, currently social housing management is on the cusp, poised between a more traditional, social welfare role and a new public service managerialism rooted in private sector genericism. Important questions therefore need to be asked. What is housing management in the new order? How are housing managers expected to behave? What does the future hold in store? Perhaps even more crucially, does such a function as housing management really exist, or is it an artificial distinction in the context of recent management trends? The answer to such questions holds the key to the future of the social rented sector.

Defining a Framework for Housing Management

The 1980s and 1990s have witnessed the continual erosion of boundaries which have traditionally separated and characterised professional working practices. The result has been the blurring of demarcation lines between the public and private sectors and across tenures, creating a bridge between different professions and the professional/non-professional divide. Whilst public housing has borne the brunt of expenditure cuts and government legislation, it is not alone in feeling the winds of change blow through its corridors. The introduction of initiatives such as Hospital Trusts, Grant Maintained Schools and fund-holding GPs are examples of reform in health and education. For housing, the pressures for change occurred initially in the late 1970s, by which time the failure of the housing management in many councils, particularly those in the inner cities, had become painfully obvious (Power, 1987; Cole and Furbey, 1994). Poor standards of construction, high levels of voids and rent arrears and a growing alienation from tenants was the legacy of a politically motivated drive for quantity rather than quality in housing provision. It was therefore inevitable that changes would have to be made in the way that housing managers actually *managed* rather than merely delivered services. By the time that it was set up by the DoE in 1979 to promote better estate management at a local level, the Priority Estates Project (PEP) found that positive initiatives had already been taken by a number of local authorities. Social housing management has not therefore been totally dependent on ideas imposed from outside of the profession. Many local authorities and housing associations have pre-empted government promptings for more stringent management practices, greater consumer involvement, and improved systems and techniques. While the framework for public service delivery has largely been founded on an often ideologically blind commitment to market supremacy, a significant contribution has come from an increasingly responsive and dynamic housing profession, supported by a rejuvenated CIH. However, one should not be carried away with too rosy a picture. Many housing organisations and practitioners have had to be dragged screaming and kicking into this new performance-related, customer-care style of working. For many, change is unwelcome, particularly if it diminishes power and increases scrutiny and accountability.

The *culture* and *nature* of the organisational context for housing management has also undergone substantial change over recent years. A major plank of government policy has been to achieve a position in which 'in the public sector the emphasis must be on greater consumer choice and more say for tenants. This can be achieved by offering a variety of forms of ownership and management' (DoE, 1987a, p. 1). The realignment of functions and responsibilities and the imposition of new performance criteria have forced both local authorities and housing associations to adapt to new styles and methods of working. Enormous pressures exist for committee members and practitioners alike to develop and deliver services in line with constantly shifting goalposts, normally geared towards increasing the constraints on public spending. Within such circumstances, it is perhaps inevitable that organisations will metamorphose from one type to another in an attempt to safeguard the interests of their stakeholders.

Thus, the dividing lines between local authorities, housing associations and the private sector are becoming increasingly blurred by hybrids such as Large Scale Voluntary Transfer (LSVT) housing associations, Housing Action Trusts, housing companies and private management contractors. Such an increase in diversity may prove to be of significant benefit to consumers over the long term, but the process of transition has implications on service delivery. This may potentially manifest itself in the form of changing staffing levels and conditions of employment, alterations to the range of service to consumers, and/or changes to service standards. Whilst such change may be wholly justified and appropriate, its potential effect needs to be appreciated, with both employees and consumers clear about what they might reasonably expect from each model. Once change has occurred, it cannot completely be reversed and the potential effects of getting it wrong can be devastating. This is particularly true in the current housing climate, in which there is considerable pressure to emphasise short-term gains at the expense of potential long-term implications. Illustrations of this can be seen throughout social housing. For example, the apparent advantages of LSVT have proved irresistible for some local authorities. The seductive proposition of escaping political control and expenditure constraints has been an attractive carrot for officers within a number of housing departments which have followed the opting-out route. For the council, the prospective benefits of expenditure savings, the generation of capital receipts and Council Tax savings have also proved a significant motive for transferring stock. However, the long-term implications cannot yet properly be assessed despite initial indications that the organisations themselves are relatively successful (see Chapter 8). There are concerns, for instance, about the ability of local authorities effectively to fulfil their homelessness responsibilities where a statutory obligation exists to ensure the provision of housing, but no direct control over lettings. Already tensions have begun to emerge between some LSVT housing associations and the transferring local authority, most notably between Sevenoaks DC and West Kent Housing Association.

Clearly defined statements of service standards and objectives are therefore essential for an assessment of both the victims and beneficiaries of change, particularly in an age of performance monitoring. The rationale for developing housing services is, after all, to meet the needs of a defined set of *consumers.* Social housing remains largely about providing an acceptable level of service, based on articulated characteristics of housing need, to those who are unable to afford alternatives. However, the agenda of the New Right, which has been at the root of much government policy since 1979, has reintroduced the moralising dimension of *deserving* and *undeserving* needy. This has resulted in the increased marginalisation of certain groups, e.g. single people and single parents, made public within the ill-fated *Back to Basics* campaign in 1994. In reality, despite the rhetoric, those dependent on personal subsidies, i.e. housing benefit and income support, have found their standards eroded by a succession of cuts in allowances and withdrawal of grants in favour of loans. This sort of radical change was perhaps inevitable, prompted by the constant analysis of public services within a framework of economic constraint.

Need has therefore become defined in terms of what can be afforded, rather than as absolute, necessitating the need to remove some groups or individuals from the priority equation altogether. In the context of financial austerity, housing policy has tended not only to focus on what should be considered 'acceptable', but also to question what housing management *should be,* for the not-for-profit housing sector of the future. What has become clear is that the government wishes to see a removal of the virtual monopoly exerted over rented housing by local authorities in some areas, and an equalisation of the costs of rented housing, whether publicly or privately owned (Sir George Young, LSE 1993). The move towards this has already begun with significant rises in rent levels in social housing since 1990. The effect has been to increase the social security budget, to create additional pressures for both housing staff and tenants, and to prompt calls for further service cuts to keep within government spending targets. Pressures for change have centred on the relationship between the three specific areas which are crucial to the effective management of social housing management, i.e. the management of:

1 people
2 property
3 resources.

In the past it has been the critical interaction between these three elements which has distinguished the management of social housing management from that carried out in the private rented sector (not including housing associations). Crucially, there is a question mark over the extent to which such a distinction can be maintained against a growing emphasis on resource constraint. The emphasis is shifting from the previous priority of managing the delivery of services based on *need*, to one of managing need based on available *resources*. As such, the locus has been shifted from service control, to resource control. Whilst there is little dissent from the view that public sector housing management differs markedly from that delivered by estate agents, property management companies, etc., there is less than universal agreement about the need or desirability of such a demarcation between public and private. There is a growing view that efficient, cost-effective bricks and mortar management should benefit everybody equally, irrespective of personal needs, which should be accounted for separately. In such a scenario, there is little support for the notion that the management of social housing organisations and functions differs, or need differ, from that practised in any private sector organisation.

The Distinctive Nature of Housing Management

One of the characteristics of housing management to date has been the diversity of activities and range of personnel involved in it. Many, such as architects and surveyors, are affiliated to established professional bodies other than the CIH and therefore follow the code, values and ethics of those professions. Planners, solicitors and accountants have also been major figures in determining housing policy and practices for both central and local government. Housing-related activity may have constituted a relatively small part of their total workload, and their judgements would have been located within the practice base of their own respective professions. This prompts the question, to what extent can *housing management* be considered a separate and distinct high-level, professional function? The answer could be critical in determining the outcome of the Compulsory Competitive Tendering (CCT) process and influencing the characteristics of any non-local-authority organisations bidding for contracts. Failure to prove the case will inevitably result in those private sector companies winning management contracts employing skilled, *generic* managers to perform the landlord function. This would undoubtedly result in a loss of professional identity and influence in service standards. If, however, there are distinctive attributes marking out housing management from other types, future competition for management contracts should reflect the training, skills and disciplinary codes distinguishing housing professionals from their counterparts.

Table 2.1   The extent to which housing management functions are located within departments other than housing

Housing management function	Within housing %	Outside housing %
Allocations	100	0
Void control	91	9
Housing and/or welfare advice	74	26
Rent collection and arrears recovery	71	29
General administration	69	31
Managing accounts and planning capital programmes	67	33
Housing benefit administration	21	79
Community charge benefit administration	13	87

Source: DoE, *The Nature and Effectiveness of Housing Management in England* (HMSO, 1989).

The Location of Housing Services

In assessing the position of housing management in relation to other disciplines, one only has to take account of the number of non-housing practitioners involved in the provision of services to tenants of local authorities and housing associations. Table 2.1 indicates the extent to which certain functions are likely to be located outside of housing departments (DoE,1989). It is clear that certain functions forming part of the housing management process may be neither the exclusive domain of housing professionals nor even primarily housing functions. Financial control and administration heads the list, closely followed by legal and technical processes. Each of these has become an increasingly critical function to the effective delivery of housing services. As such, they have become seamlessly integrated within the structures and remits of comprehensive housing departments and larger housing associations. However, while the posts may be housing based, they are usually staffed by accountants, solicitors and surveyors whose training and professional backgrounds may not be housing specific. Training and personnel functions are also not exclusive to housing, nor the general clerical and administrative work which is a feature of almost all services.

Parallels may also be drawn for most other functions carried out as part of the work of a normal housing department: Citizens Advice Bureaux staff interview and advise the public; private estate management companies arrange the letting and rent collection for private lettings; policy and research is a feature of many other professions. Even the function of management is becoming less clearly housing specific as more and more housing managers obtain generalist DMS and MBAs in preference to recognised professional qualifications, and senior posts are increasingly occupied by executives with experience outside social housing.

Housing Management or Managing Housing?

Can it therefore be said that in the new public sector environment, *housing management* is anything more than public sector management with a housing emphasis? Clearly, the prevailing, central government view is rooted in the managerial perspective that a good manager can manage anything. However, not surprisingly, the Chartered Institute of Housing (CIH) insists that housing management is different: 'housing is different in the sense that it requires a considerable integration of different skills and knowledge . . . people who have a clear knowledge of that business and the motivation and commitment to achieve the aims of that business are absolutely fundamental' (Lupton, 1993). To those supporting this view, a housing professional embodies a range of knowledge and skills which both links together properties and people and coordinates the input of specialist functions enabling this to occur. They believe in characteristics which elevate the process to the level of sophistication and complexity which justifies the label *professional*, setting housing management apart from any other kind. However, evidence exists that such a belief is not universally held (Pearl, 1993), with many within the profession leaning increasingly towards the managerial model.

Wherever the balance lies, there can be little doubt that the culture and nature of housing management has changed. The greater emphasis on resource management ahead of accounting for need is relatively recent, applying a veneer of increased legitimacy and professional status over the image of the public sector as amateurish, bureaucratic and moribund. Many would acknowledge that such a change has long been overdue. This is particularly so for consumers, for whom the experience of housing management has often been perceived as a controlling function rather than a facilitating one; and for whom the decisions of administrative and bureaucratic gatekeepers have often been arcane and inconsistent.

An enhanced management approach does not necessarily signal the demise of housing management. However, there is a critical balance which must be achieved between the roles of manager and that of a social housing professional. At the root of this lies a professional commitment to the core values, aims and objectives of social housing as distinct from an approach which primarily seeks the technical achievement of resource management. It should be remembered that many consumers of public services are unable fully to exercise their rights as customers because of age, frailty, language, culture or marginalisation. It is therefore essential to safeguard the interests of the more vulnerable sections of society, who might be considered *clients* rather than *customers*. This has been a commitment which has to date characterised the professional altruism of social housing management, although many would argue that it has so far achieved only limited success. It is from such a base that the distinctiveness of housing professionalism has been founded and developed. Whilst sound resource management is crucial to the achievement of such an objective, it is in the balance between efficiency, economy and competition as against effectiveness, equality and equity within which housing management will retain its identity.

Housing Management: The Framework for Implementation

There is no single, correct way to manage social housing. The nature and style of housing management will be the result of complex and dynamic interactions between national, local and organisational factors. Although the approach of recent governments to policy-making has been very much 'top-down' (Means, 1993), their success in achieving prescription at an operational level has been limited. Since 1980, the stranglehold exerted over social housing finance has been highly effective in constraining the level of social house-building, and directing limited capital and revenue resources to types of expenditure considered acceptable by government ministers.

However, despite an ever-increasing raft of centralising measures designed to bring local authorities in particular in line with central policy objectives, the effectiveness has been patchy. Although there were swingeing expenditure cuts in the 1980s, many local authorities embarked on ambitious decentralisation programmes designed to increase their accessibility and popularity, while at the same time improving services (Cole, 1993). Councils have established something of a tradition of developing innovative mechanisms to circumvent constraints imposed upon them.

The result has been the emergence of a situation in which a common framework for housing management has been developed, but within which there is significant scope for manoeuvre. Even within the requirements of CCT, arguably the most standardising of all policy initiatives, there is considerable scope for local perspectives to be enshrined within contract specifications (see Chapter 7). Over the following sections, the range of issues influencing organisations' approach to housing management will be examined within the context of governance and legislative frameworks.

Local Variations on a Housing Management Theme

Local authorities are controlled by councillors elected on a political manifesto. Thus, although statutory requirements may be common to all councils, the practices adopted in Fenland District Council would be both unacceptable and inappropriate in the London Borough of Lambeth. It should be no surprise that Conservative-controlled councils, in the main, have a more constrained view of their role as service providers than Labour and Liberal Democrat-controlled councils. Nor is it a coincidence that most deprived, inner-city areas and regions of high unemployment and economic decline are Labour controlled, whilst the more affluent, suburban and rural areas in southern England were more likely to be Conservative although in recent years there has been a marked swing to the Liberal

Democrats. Differences in political ideology therefore play an important part in determining the nature of the housing service, dictating either a minimalist, reactive approach or a comprehensive, proactive approach, or a compromise between these two.

The nature of the locality, including factors such as demography, tenure profile, and the rural/urban split, also influences the way that authorities work. In the mainly non-metropolitan district councils, there are often much lower levels of housing need, and much smaller stocks of council housing than in large urban authorities. In such situations, there is often no separate housing department, the landlord functions being distributed between other council departments such as finance, engineers, solicitors, etc. in conjunction with a small housing section. In contrast, many larger, inner-city authorities operate comprehensive housing services covering a wide range of functions and many thousands of dwellings (see Chapter 8). While housing associations are not affected by political control in the same way as local authorities, they will be influenced in some degree by the political approach of their local authority partners. It would also be naïve to eliminate completely political motivation from association management committees, albeit manifesting itself in a personal capacity rather than being party influenced.

The approach to housing management will therefore strongly reflect the characteristics of individual landlord organisations. Even in the delivery of day-to-day housing functions, there are marked differences between the range, level and extent of services which might be experienced by consumers. Residents of the London Boroughs of Lambeth and Wandsworth will pay different levels of rent and council tax and receive substantially different services even though they may face each other across the same road. The quality of housing services experienced by applicants or tenants will often be dictated more by their location than by their particular circumstances. Significant levels of discretion exist within most housing functions, allowing officers to exercise personal judgement, which may prove either positive or negative influences on service outcomes. However, despite this, housing managers do not operate within a vacuum, and both local authorities and housing associations are bound by legislation or dictum which define the requirements for delivering specified functions and standards.

External Influences

Whatever services organisations might like to provide, their discretion is considerably tempered by central control imposed by the government. The DoE and Housing Corporation have exerted an increasing influence over the nature and style of housing management through the imposition of a number of controlling measures, including:

- *Performance monitoring* The growth in performance indicators (many of which are prescribed by central government and/or funding institutions) against which outcomes are evaluated has resulted in a trend towards more explicit expectations in the delivery of levels and standards of service. This has been an important development for both officers, who are now more aware of the expectations placed on them, and consumers, who increasingly have objective criteria against which to judge the quality and quantity of the services they receive.

- *Financial control/contract management*   The introduction of competition has become an integral theme of public sector management. It has resulted in a shift towards a performance culture, requiring the specification of all public sector services, against which tenders will be priced and contracts awarded. The result is increasing prescription in the role of professionals, not only in housing, but in other, traditionally autonomous professions, e.g. health, legal and social work. While this has not completely removed the ability of housing organisations to exercise choice in services provision, the imperative for economy creates an inexorable move towards standardisation.

  This promises to be a particular problem for smaller local authorities, not having access to the skills necessary to draw up CCT specifications. The temptation will be to purchase specifications 'off the shelf', thus adopting another authority's standards irrespective of whether they are really appropriate. A similar dilemma also faces housing associations. Increasing dependence on private sector finance and the shift of HAG (Housing Association Grant) from rented housing to shared ownership has placed many smaller associations at risk. Not only do they lack the necessary asset base to sustain a large, privately financed development programme, but they are also unable to afford the salary levels commanded by qualified and experienced financial managers. This offers a stark choice between atrophy or merger with a larger, more secure association which can offer the necessary security. This trend has already led to the demise of many small, specialist and black housing associations, undermining one of the great traditional strengths of the housing association movement, i.e. flexibility, responsiveness and specialisation. The 'small is beautiful' lobby have certainly lost the present battle, if not the war.

- *Customer care*   The enhanced status of the consumer bolstered by the Citizens' Charter and a series of Housing Act rights, has encouraged a more outward-looking approach to service users and their views. It has resulted in a greater inclination towards achieving consumer satisfaction rather than the traditional paternalism previously practised.

- *Quality assurance*   Both local authorities and housing associations have been forced to tighten their procedures to ensure that they are producing intended quality levels. Accreditations such as BS5750 (ISO 9000) and the Charter Mark have often resulted in organisational change to meet required standards.

Each of these criteria is examined in further detail in Chapter 3, with Chapter 7 devoted to Compulsory Competitive Tendering (CCT).

The Regulatory Framework

Legislation has also been critical in contributing to the framework within which both local authorities and housing associations operate. Key statutes such as the Housing Acts 1980 and 1988 have introduced radical changes such as the Right To Buy (1980) and Tenants' Choice (1988). There has also been, within recent years, a growth in the production of supplementary guidance material promoting good practice and establishing acceptable standards. These tend to be issued by bodies having an interest in the housing activities of organisations and/or practitioners. They include: CIH, Association of District Councils (ADC), Association of London Authorities (ALA), Association of Metropolitan Authorities (AMA), National Federation of Housing Associations (NFHA),[2] Tenants Participation and Advisory Service (TPAS), Priority Estates Programme (PEP) in addition to guidance material issued by the DoE and Housing Corporation.

Yet even the existence of minimum statutory standards does not always guarantee entitlement for all who might be expected to qualify for services. There remains considerable room for flexibility in the interpretation of key legislative requirements, which partly explains the diverse, inconsistent, and often contradictory standards implemented both nationally and locally. This lack of clarity often results in the courts being asked to intervene, giving rise to a substantial body of case law. However, such a route often adds considerable expense and delay to the process of service delivery, generally working against individuals.

The implementation of statutory duties is likely to be conditioned and influenced by a range of factors, many of which may be subject to constant change. For example, the treatment of a particular homeless applicant may be affected by the timing of their application, i.e. whether appropriate accommodation was available or due to become available. Other factors such as how articulately they present themselves, the values of the interviewing officer, and expenditure levels on temporary accommodation may also play a part. Legislation is therefore generally unable to provide anything more than a basic framework within which the law is interpreted. Even highly explicit guidance is often unable to cover all possible eventualities. As a result, it is possible that even acting within the letter of the law, an organisation can take unreasonable decisions, against the best interest of their consumers. Paradoxically, it is also possible that organisations may, in good faith, step outside the law to pursue policies which they perceive to be of benefit to local residents. This rather odd state of

---

2.   Changed in 1996 to National Housing Federation.

affairs is one of the consequences of the complex interaction between central and local government, and political left and right.

Managing Property or People: Welfare versus Contractual Frameworks

'Associations are torn between the commercialism of the private sector and the ethos of public service. There is nothing intrinsically wrong with growth or competition. But it must be balanced against the more intangible notion of community control or at least influence.'

(Brown, 1995)

The balance referred to in this quote has found a focus in the debate about the location of social housing management within either a *contractual* framework or a *social* one. The contractual framework 'seeks to eliminate "social objectives" from housing management; here, it is concerned solely with property management functions' (CIH policy briefing note, undated). Within this orientation, social needs are attributable to individuals, whatever their tenure, rather than to the housing they occupy. Thus the expectation is that any 'social service' will be provided independently by the statutory social services or voluntary agencies. The social framework on the other hand 'recognises that social welfare is very much part of the landlord role' (ibid) whilst accepting that the costs of any social welfare element may be high, resulting in unfavourable comparisons with the private sector.

These two models present social housing practitioners with very real dilemmas. The contractual model is flawed in two main respects. The first is that it assumes that an individual's personal needs can generally be satisfied within a vacuum, i.e. within the confines of their own dwelling. It allows neither for the relationship between behaviour and environment, nor the considerably differing tenant profiles in terms of poverty, vulnerability and deprivation between the social housing sector and the private rented sector. The private sector discriminates against these groups either actively or indirectly, resulting in high concentrations of acute need within social housing. The second is that Social Service Departments have also faced a considerable squeeze on resources and have priorities which often differ from those of housing officers. It is unlikely that they would be in a position to fill any tenant support role left vacant by a reorientation of the housing function.

The social model also has its drawbacks. Increasingly housing officers operate within an environment which demands greater economy and efficiency via reducing public expenditure and the imposition of performance monitoring. At the same time, they are often faced with intractable problems which are both time-consuming and resource-intensive. This is usually the direct result of managing a housing stock which has become increasingly residualised, containing poorly built and difficult to manage estates, higher levels of poverty amongst existing and new tenants, and increasing vulnerability and dependency due to care in the community. In many situations housing staff are expected to deal with a range of problems over which they have no direct control, such as lack of employment, high crime rates and erratic behaviour from disturbed individuals. In implementing a social model it therefore becomes extremely difficult to draw lines of demarcation, leaving housing managers vulnerable to increased consumer expectations and greater levels of responsibility than might be reasonable.

However, national housing policy has not been neutral on the issue. Virtually all pressure from central government during the 1980s and 1990s has been towards the contractual model, squeezing the resources, planning and coordination of welfare support. Many housing practitioners have therefore been left with the task of delivering a welfare role informally with little or inadequate training or support. This problem, which is examined further in Chapter 6, has become particularly significant following the introduction of Housing Revenue Account ring-fencing within the Local Government and Housing Act 1989. Within the regulation of this new financial regime local authorities are required to account separately for those housing services which directly relate to the management of its stock, i.e. landlord services. The purpose was to be able to accurately calculate the costs incurred in the provision of landlord services, thus ensuring that tenants paid a realistic rent, reflecting actual (without external subsidy from the General Rate Fund) expenditure. The rationale was to make tenants more aware of the value for money, or lack of it, received for rental payments.

As might be expected, grey areas emerged as to what might legitimately fall within the category of landlord services and what should fall outside. Issues such as the role of wardens and hostel workers, community centre expenses, play areas, etc. do not neatly fall into either category. This ambiguity resulted in a judicial review of the 1991/2 rent increase applied for by a tenant of the London Borough of Ealing (*Regina* v. *London Borough of Ealing* (1992)). This was on the grounds that certain elements of the warden service should not be paid for from the Housing Revenue Account as they were of a 'care' nature, therefore falling outside of the ring-fencing criteria contained within schedule 4 of the 1989 Act. The Court of Appeal's decision, although inconclusive, indicated that some elements of the work of wardens 'went beyond a strictly landlord function' (Thompson, 1993) and that in such cases the costs should not fall on the Housing Revenue Account. The DoE draft circular, *The Housing Revenue Account Ring-Fence* (DoE, 1994a), further clarified the accounting position for welfare services: 'housing authorities [may] account for welfare services in the HRA if they wish. Before doing so, authorities will need to distinguish between essential care services more akin to the work of, for example, district nurses or health visitors, and other welfare services.'

Table 2.2   The social role of housing managers, as defined by the CIH

- debt counselling and benefits advice
- racial harassment prevention
- dealing with aspects of alcohol and drug abuse
- liaison with social services over community care, children at risk or the mentally ill
- dealing with environmental problems such as dogs, traffic or litter
- helping to develop community projects such as play schemes or 'good neighbour' schemes
- arranging adaptations for people with disabilities
- wider aspects of neighbour disputes
- working with police to improve security or deal with anti-social behaviour
- welfare aspects of wardens' work
- supported accommodation
- community alarms
- community development

Source: CIH, *More Than Bricks and Mortar* (undated).

Concern remains over the practical distinctions of what constitutes 'special needs' and what might be considered routine work for wardens and housing officers. Increasingly, the needs of the very vulnerable in social housing are placing significant, regular demands on housing professionals. If these roles do not form part of the housing management function, who will take them on? While there are many other agencies and organisations with an interest in these issues, none has the same type of involvement as housing staff. In addition, the reality of resource constraints has hit all parts of the public sector in recent years. 'The pressures in prioritising staff time is such that social work departments, for example, are increasingly concerned with crisis intervention in child care cases, with little spare capacity for their wider role' (CIH, undated). The CIH believes that housing management does and should have a social dimension, the nature of which is defined in Table 2.2.

In reality, the concern amongst many housing practitioners is not whether they are required to undertake *either* a contractual *or* a social welfare role. The worst scenario is that they will be formally expected and funded to act as the managers of bricks and mortar, but drawn into performing a wider role. There are few current indications that Health Authorities or Social Services Departments are either eager or prepared to take on the degree of intervention appropriate to 'care in the community' programmes. The probability is therefore that housing officers will continue merely to 'firefight' rather than be able to plan adequate and effective services designed to sustain both communities and their homes.

A Clash of Cultures: The Five 'E's

'The concept of performance is difficult and complex and not universally accepted. The concept itself has been seen as having three distinct yet related elements: economy (the purchase of resources at lowest cost consistent with a specified quality and quantity referred to as inputs), efficiency (a specified volume and quality of service, throughputs, using the least resources capable of delivering the specification, outputs), and effectiveness (providing the right service to enable the organisation to implement its policies and objectives, outcomes). Whilst others have argued that further 'E's should be added equity, efficacy or electability – or that the language should be extended to include concepts such as acceptability.'

(Walker, 1994)

The dynamic between the welfare and contractual models illustrates a growing tension in the move towards a commercial/performance culture, while consumer need continues to grow. Increased demand often requires additional expenditure which is usually problematic during a period of public sector austerity. Such expenditure can generally only be afforded by raising rents to fund services. With an increasingly residualised public sector, social housing is therefore in danger of becoming a service paid for and delivered exclusively to the poor and vulnerable.

The growing emphasis on competition has led to a growing compartmentalisation of public services. Within organisations, there is a split between purchaser and provider, and between services there has been a shift away from a culture of networking and interdisciplinary coopera-tion to a more contractual relationship in which liaison and interaction is carefully costed and controlled. This is exacerbated further by concerns over commercial confidentiality and market position for contractors. In particular, the separation of services within the context of policy develop-ment fails to recognise the interdependence of one public service on all others. For instance, if levels of housing management are reduced, there may be immediate implications for Social Services in having to provide additional support for elderly and disabled tenants. Similarly, policy deci-sions by Social Service Departments and Health Authorities may affect the daily work environment of housing officers. The tendency, however, is for such interactions to be considered not within a strategic framework, but as distinct and separate, with funding and accountability located within different government departments. The inevitable consequence is that policies such as community care, dependent on interdisciplinary cooperation for their success, are compromised.

Increasingly, performance indicators set by government and the Hous-ing Corporation place emphasis on quantative and financially based measures of achievement. In this respect, there has already been a perceptible shift towards the *contractual model* of housing management. The key influ-

Table 2.3   The 'E's within the welfare and contractual housing management models

Social model	
Equity –	Are systems just and fair?
Equality –	s71 Race Relations Act 1976 – consistency
Efficiency –	Value for money; demand-led
Effectiveness –	Meeting strategies
	Achieving social objectives
Evaluation –	Performance monitoring
	Accountability
	Government scrutiny
Contractual model	
Efficiency –	Linked to economy
Effectiveness –	Meeting contract requirements
Evaluation –	Extent of profitability

ences in this area have been the E's identified by the Audit Commission (Audit Commission, 1988a), i.e. efficiency, economy and effectiveness, with particular emphasis on the first two. While it is indisputable that both efficiency and economy have crucial roles to play in housing services, there are real dangers for strategic planning if they alone become the driving force behind service delivery. Table 2.3 illustrates that efficiency and economy can play a crucial part within the welfare model as it does with the contractual one. The difference is that in the former, it is interpreted within a more balanced approach to value for money, i.e. calculating the implications of *not* implementing particular services. An example of the hidden costs of cutting debt-counselling services may be an increase in rent arrears and the additional expense of recovery. The contractual model potentially loses the ability to recognise such linkages by separating tenant-related aspects of the service from property-related ones. In addition, the emphasis on economy as the driving force behind service provision, has the potential effect of undermining effectiveness in that policy objectives may be seriously distorted and compromised. Yet funders of social housing often interpret success via those indicators located at the performance/contractual end of the continuum, resulting in indicators of demand increasingly becoming interpreted in relation to available resources rather than being needs-led.

Achieving a Middle Ground

This might suggest that concepts such as efficiency and effectiveness will always be at odds with each other. If this were true, housing management would always be about providing services, no matter what the cost or how well they are delivered. Such a position is clearly untenable, although some might interject that this has not been far from the truth in the past. What is important is to achieve a balance between tight control over resources expenditure and the adequate provision of services which achieve their objectives. This process is likely also to make reference to a number of other, non-Audit Commission 'E's such as equity, equality and electability. The task for managers is to determine the point at which housing management reaches an optimum balance between achieving efficiency and effectiveness.

Any discussion about efficiency and effectiveness cannot take place without reference to the third Audit Commission 'E', economy. Over the past decade all public services, but particularly housing, have operated within an environment of severe spending constraints. However, the indiscriminate squeeze on social subsidies for house building and rent levels has had serious results. In many areas the government's imposition of absolute economy measures, irrespective of the potential consequences, has undermined and seriously flawed policy initiatives, e.g. the introduction of a means tested grant regime in 1990. There is little merit in delivering services which are so flawed by underfunding that they deliver none of the benefits originally intended, serving only to divert resources from other requirements.

For social housing management, the inexorable transition into a performance culture has posed a number of key questions about the process of achieving targets:

- How can they properly be measured?
- Are the measurements common to everyone?
- How are criteria determined?

Without such basic reference material, it is impossible adequately to assess performance or judge whether adjustments need to be made to service delivery or resource allocation. In the past, the tendency has been for both public and private sectors to develop performance indicators which reflect the performance which the provider thinks the consumer wants. This is often based on a limited understanding of the criteria and lifestyles which might determine consumer demands for services. Situations will also arise when consumer demands will conflict with other pressures on service delivery, such as politically motivated actions, legislative requirements, corporate policies, and funding requirements. Social housing services will often be the result of compromise negotiated between a range of interested parties. However, inevitably some groups will fall outside of the negotiated service and understandably feel aggrieved. Such groups are often non-tenants who have the least bargaining power either individually or collectively. In general, they lack the collective voice of tenants' groups and associations, and are often disparate and possibly itinerant. In terms of exerting power, they are therefore limited in their influence. The pressures to gear services towards tenants are therefore overwhelming, including:

- political pressure – organised tenants' groups are more likely to exert influence, particularly in marginal wards
- funding issues – tenants pay directly for the bulk of housing department salaries and services, or for the repaying of private loans by housing associations. In contrast, non-tenant services are in direct competition with other council services for funding from the General Fund and are therefore less likely to receive priority
- local authorities in particular are concerned about the opportunities for their tenants to opt out of their management
- housing associations are required to involve tenants in order to continue to qualify for HAG.

Effectiveness is therefore not necessarily a standard approach to the same issue. No two organisations will take the same position over an identical issue. Not only might perceptions differ, but considerations relating to value for money and returns on investment will also vary. For example, a policy on the point at which rent arrears should be written off may not be as simple as setting the costs of collection against the amount outstanding. The image that might be created by writing off such debts without taking action is also important. This might not only send the wrong message to tenants who are erratic payers, but there is also the moral/public outrage at the loss of consumers' money amongst tenants who do pay their rent. At what point therefore do political factors outweigh purely financial considerations? The answer can only lie within each specific organisation. It must also be appreciated that some organisations start with more difficult tasks than others, a position appreciated by the DoE: 'neither the efficiency nor the effectiveness of housing management can be assessed in isolation from the difficultly of the context in which it was produced' (DoE, 1989). Objectives can also be achieved in the end, but in ways which might not justify the means. When things get too difficult, managers may resort to manipulating circumstances to produce results: 'success may, of course, be partly achieved through restrictive policies, such as restricting the number of offer refusals' (DoE, 1989). Closing homeless persons units for periods during the day, limiting access to advice staff, etc. are all tactics which can be utilised to restrict demand and achieve specific targets. Measuring effectiveness in any meaningful way therefore becomes difficult in isolation from the overall objectives of an organisation.

One thing is clear, that effectiveness, efficiency and economy have to coexist within the same environment. Where they complement each other, scarce resources are more likely to be wisely spent and targeted towards those most in need. However, public services have become primarily financially driven, placing efficiency and economy at the forefront and restricting effectiveness to a supporting role. In this latter scenario, 'E's such as equity and equality are likely to suffer most. They require the sort of sophistication and flexibility which may be resource intensive, demanding open attitudes and flexibility which organisations under severe resource constraints are rarely able to offer.

Equity and Equality

Issues of equity (social justice) and equality are, of course, crucial in all walks of life, not just housing. However, the unique role of housing as a foundation for virtually all other social necessities needs to be understood. Without adequate housing, health and educational potential will suffer. Social behaviour is often conditioned by the adequacy or otherwise of one's housing conditions. Without housing it is virtually impossible to find employment or to become enfranchised. It can therefore become a key which can open up not just a series of vital social and economic opportunities, but the reality of citizenship itself.

There is insufficient space here to detail the body of evidence which exists to prove the discrimination and disadvantage experienced by large sections of the population in Britain. Studies (CRE, 1984 and 1985; Watson and Austerberry, 1986) consistently indicate that women, black and ethnic minority, gay and lesbian, and people with disabilities are all treated badly by the institutional mechanisms in British society. Lack of employment opportunities for all of these groups have limited their economic strength, thus inhibiting the ability to exercise choice in selecting housing. The result is that social housing provides the only practical option for many households marginalised within a property-owning democracy. The vulnerability and dependence of these households places housing officers in a powerful position. As the gatekeepers to social housing they are uniquely placed either to perpetuate or contribute to the reduction in disadvantage. In most situations social landlords will use needs-based allocation systems in an attempt to house those people in greatest need. However, few of these systems are so comprehensive as to eliminate officer discretion. It is in the grey areas of flexibility and expedience that discrimination most often occurs. Usually this is due not to overt racism or sexism, but to ignorance or institutional discrimination.

Equal-opportunity policies are crucial tools with which to identify and eradicate discrimination. However, they can only be effective in circumstances where an organisation is open to critical review of its performance in the light of empirical evidence. Many organisations continue to take the view that they are colour and gender blind when taking decisions about service delivery and employment processes. They are convinced that outcomes are based on merit alone, with no element of personal or professional bias and prejudice involved. For this reason, they say that there is no need to monitor activity and performance. However, such a position would not be accepted for activities such as void control, rent collection or repairs, all of which are regularly monitored to ensure standards of performance. It can be argued that equal opportunities are even more important to monitor because of the insidious nature of discrimination.

It is the responsibility of housing managers to be aware of such issues and to redress inequality where it is within their power to do so. Equality is not about treating everyone the same; it is concerned with recognising, appraising and prioritising a range of needs which are extremely diverse. Prioritisation is inherently discriminatory, inevitably placing one set of needs above another. However, this only becomes problematic when priority is awarded for spurious or inequitable reasons. Housing managers alone can not redress the effects of a fundamentally unequal society. Deprivation results from a wide range of factors outside of a housing remit, e.g. unemployment, poverty, racism, violence, drug abuse, etc. However, the effects of these ills are often disproportionately manifested on housing estates and amongst social housing tenants. There is therefore a compelling argument that housing management does have a role to play in promoting initiatives designed to reduce the impact of these problems.

Equality and equity can positively coexist alongside the more business-oriented efficiency and economy. There are many ways in which these concepts can be implemented with little or no extra costs, particularly with regard to attitude and approach. There are also areas where good equal-opportunity practice will increase efficiency and thus generate savings in the long term. However, they are not cut-price options. Where cost saving is the primary consideration, this creates an environment in which strategic social objectives invariably take a back seat to commercial-style managerialism.

Summary

Having examined a variety of approaches to social housing management, we may still be no closer to establishing an accurate definition. The contrast between management driven primarily by financial considerations and competition, compared with an holistic and coordinated approach, is clear. The former limits the profession to property management in its strictest sense, while the latter embraces a wider, community development and welfare role. The former scenario offers the prospect of social housing as the sector of last resort, its management constrained largely to damage limitation. The alternative envisages a more dynamic role, based on a developing and collaborative process, responsive and sensitive to local needs. While not all public landlords welcome the latter style, many have been at its forefront, pioneering good practice in customer care and tenant participation.

If housing management were to focus purely on bricks and mortar, with little or no social content, it would be difficult for housing managers to claim that distinctive *housing* skills or expertise were required. With cost and competition becoming major influences, the most likely outcome would be that the landlord function would then become a generic commodity management process, employing practitioners skilled primarily in resource

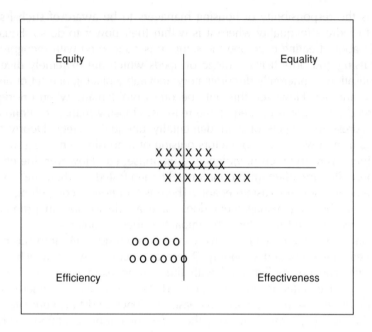

Figure 2.1   The equity–efficiency matrix

management. However, the expectation that social welfare agencies, divorced from day-to-day control over the domestic environment, can replace the housing welfare dimension is flawed. It is unrealistic, within the severe resource constraints experienced by other public sector disciplines, to expect that they will suddenly take on additional responsibilities at no cost. It is also unreasonable to assume that such a fragmented approach would offer the service quality that a coordinated approach to property and people can provide.

Nor is there any clearly argued service rationale for such a development. In fact, previous analyses of the public rented sector (Cullingworth, 1969; Audit Commission, 1986; DoE, 1989) have favoured the development of a comprehensive housing service, bringing functions together within a single, coordinated span of control. The fragmentation of management tasks into purchaser/provider responsibilities has the potential effect of de-skilling and reducing the breadth and variety of training for housing managers. Already, one impact of the lead-in to CCT is that local authorities are becoming more cautious about training budgets and staff development.

The establishment of a successful framework for social housing management lies in the balance between the 'E's. This is illustrated diagrammatically in Figure 2.1, in which the styles of operation are clearly differentiated between social and private landlords. Social housing organisations (x) are more likely to operate with reference to all E's, i.e. at, or around the centre of the grid. Private landlords (o) are likely to be driven more by effectiveness and efficiency towards the bottom part of the grid. This relative location of respective core values probably represents the most accurate illustration of the differences between the for-profit and not-for-profit sectors. It is this difference which has characterised the public sector ethos but which is in danger of being lost in the drive for competition.

This chapter has examined the pressures for change on housing management across a broad canvass. Key influences such as community care, CCT, and tenant participation will be developed in future chapters. There can be little doubt that future social housing management will include significantly higher levels of resource and person management than has previously been the case. Few would lament the loss of the image of the housing manager as well-meaning but rather profligate and aloof. However, whilst the private sector offers housing solely on the basis of ability to pay, social housing must continue to provide a safety net for those unable to afford economic or market rents. The major difference between the public and private sectors is the 'bottom line' which motivates organisations to operate in the manner they do. Private housing organisations are in business to make as large a profit as possible, and their services and standards will be tailored to achieve this end. Social housing organisations also have a motivation to keep costs down and to generate surpluses, but services are based on the dual premise of meeting need and providing value for money. Social housing management must therefore continue to be a union of skills, disciplines and styles. It must adopt the best private sector management practices to ensure that organisations are run in the best possible manner; it must be cognisant of the needs and desires of its consumers, whether tenants or applicants; it must be prepared to change as needs, constraints and opportunities change; but underlying all of these practices there must exist a foundation of social justice and fairness.

3 Housing Management in a Time of Change

'The housing service now faces the challenge of change. Change is both necessary and inevitable and it will not arise simply because of government policy but also through the changing expectations, demands and needs of the customers it serves. The challenges will arise on every front – the structure of the organisations, the attitudes underpinning them, the qualities and qualifications of staff, the roles to be undertaken, and even the type of organisation in which they work and people to whom they are responsible.'

(Provan and Williams, 1991, p. 225)

Whatever the fate of the organisations managing social housing, there can be little doubt that they have experienced unparalleled change in the decade spanning 1986–96. Government policy, as detailed in Chapters 1 and 2, has been designed not only to influence housing policy and practice, but to reshape the entire face of the rented housing sector. The effect has been the promotion of new structures and organisational types (see Chapter 8) and the modernisation of long-established ones, sweeping styles, cultures and attitudes into a new era. The bedrock of change has been the imposition of a series of key private sector concepts into the public sector environment. These have included competition, performance expectations, quality assurance, customer care, and the separation of the strategic role from that of provider. Certain elements of this largely enforced change have been widely welcomed, while others have been contentious, often generating significant resistance.

However, change as indicated by Provan and Williams is not solely about imposing external beliefs and values on unwilling victims. It is a natural and necessary process of evolution for organisations and services in response to the changing demands of consumers and external environments. Individuals and organisations resisting such a process tend to be insular, outdated and ineffective. They are more likely to adhere to practices which place procedures before people and which may be discriminatory (Stewart, 1988). Many practitioners, under fire from consumers, members and government alike, have in the past been reluctant to raise their heads above the organisational parapet, preferring the apparent security offered by anonymous bureaucracy. As a result, change has often been resisted irrespective of its potential benefits. However, political programmes of change during the 1980s and 1990s have pressurised the housing profession into adopting a more outward-looking approach to the delivery of housing management. This has corresponded with a growing recognition that specialist housing management skills alone are insufficient to ensure high quality service delivery. Increasingly, housing managers must possess an understanding of generic management principles such as objective-setting, performance-monitoring and quality assurance. The result has been a period of professional soul-searching and evolution set against the backdrop of dynamic organisational change.

Change brings with it both opportunities and threats, highlighting strengths and weaknesses within organisations and individual employees. It also presents a significant challenge to the traditional skills of senior managers charged with the task of implementing and controlling the process. Strategic organisational planning can easily be diverted and thus undermined by sustained staff resistance based on alternative agendas. The implications of mismanagement are far-reaching, competition having increased the stakes, with the ultimate price of failure being high. This is certainly true for organisations, threatened with lost development opportunities, management contracts, or even their total stock! It is also true for individuals, from whom much more is demanded in terms of budgetary control, risk management and innovation. This chapter examines the key components of change which have become pivotal to the realignment of social housing management.

The Agenda for Change

A Framework for Reform

The changes occurring within social housing have been located within a broader agenda of reform affecting the public sector as a whole. Such reform has had as its foundation the Thatcherite determination to 'roll back the frontiers of the state' and abandon notions of collectivism and state intervention in favour of a market-led, mixed economy of welfare. It has been further developed by John Major through the introduction of a series of Citizens' Charters, promoting customer choice in the public sector. The imperatives of success have therefore been rooted in, or at least borrowed from, the private sector. The effect has been that 'The public service, it seems, can only retain legitimacy by changing the way that it is managed, or appears to be managed, to reflect ideas about what constitutes good management, which will typically be based on private sector ideas' (Stewart and Walsh, 1992, p. 500). This has applied equally to local authorities and housing associations, resulting in significant shifts in the approaches to managing organisations and delivering services. The recognised glossary of social housing terms has expanded to include the regular usage of *business plans*, *total quality management* (TQM) and *customer care*, none of which would previously have been found within the operational plans of social landlords. Within some organisations, the transformation has been startling, with wholehearted espousal of the new styles of public sector management and reorientation towards more resource-based, performance-related outcomes. For others, the analogy of an oil tanker is more appropriate – leaden, lumbering and painfully slow to change direction.

There has been no shortage of guidance for housing organisations to follow to meet the new expectations placed upon them. Numerous reports, studies and manuals have been produced since the mid-1980s, often founded on the writings of American management gurus seeking the holy grail of excellence in the private sector. Virtually all have been biased towards resource management rather than a needs-based perspective. Although the customer has been a central consideration in this process, the nature of 'customer' has been premised on an ability freely to exercise unfettered choice. There must be doubt that such a model directly applies to the social housing sector.

The Audit Commission has been at the forefront of reform, influencing government in their programmes of policy reforms to public sector organisations and services. Although directed at local authority housing, the fall-out from the Commission's findings has been felt throughout the housing association movement. Having declared council housing management to be in crisis in 1986, it considered local authorities to be in the throes of a revolution in 1988, prompted by a changing identity and purpose. 'In any period of uncertainty and change, the well-managed organisation survives more successfully than the rest' (Audit Commission, 1988b). In the view of the Commission, the well-managed council will:

1 Understand its customers
2 Respond to the electorate
3 Set and pursue consistent, achievable objectives
4 Assign clear management responsibilities
5 Train and motivate people
6 Communicate effectively
7 Monitor results
8 Adapt quickly to change.

On face value, these characteristics are neither individually nor collectively contentious, offering a commonsense foundation on which to develop services. However, the sad story for local authorities has been that many had fallen well short of achieving even these basic principles. Change has therefore been inevitable, materialising in the guise of a new public sector management ethos.

New Public Sector Management

This new approach to management, labelled by some as 'new public management', was founded on the interaction of a series of key doctrines centred on 'contestability, user choice, transparency and incentive structures' (Hood, 1991) together with recently emerging attitudes towards business-type managerialism. They have swept away the traditional pillars of bureaucratic public services, opening up the previously inviolable authority of professionals and administrators to public scrutiny and challenge. However, while undoubtably achieving greater openness and accountability, the danger has been that along with the dirty bath water, the commitment to values such as altruism, voluntarism, equality, etc. have also been poured down the drain. Too far a swing towards a commercial culture and ethos would undermine the purpose of social housing, creating, in effect, a hybrid, socialised private sector.

Yet clearly there has been significant movement in this direction. The effect, according to Stewart and Walsh (1992), has been the promotion of public sector change based on a number of key themes:

• The separation of the purchaser role from the provider role
• The growth of contractual or semi-contractual arrangements
• Accountability for performance
• Flexibility of pay and conditions
• The creation of market or quasi-market
• An emphasis on the public as customer
• The reconsideration of the regulatory role
• A change of culture.

For local authority housing departments, the introduction of Compulsory Competitive Tendering (CCT) has been the focus of a number of these themes, introducing a market-led, contractual approach to the delivery of service. It has also been instrumental in promoting wholesale organisational restructuring to facilitate the client/contractor split, the nature of which is examined further in Chapter 7. A further effect has been the removal of any lingering expectation that employment in the public sector offered long-term security and a 'cushy little number'. Local authorities and housing associations have adopted more incentivised employment practices in tune with performance cultures. Fixed term contracts, performance-related pay, appraisal systems and the perks (company cars, medical insurance, etc.) more traditionally the preserve of the private sector are now common. For individuals, the personal benefits may be tangible; however, they have often been purchased at the expense of stability, access to training and personal development, and a commitment to equal opportunities. This should not deny the examples of organisations which have reaffirmed their commitment to good employment practice, subscribing to initiatives such as Investors in People and PATH (Positive Action for Training in Housing).

Competition has also had the effect of reconstituting the nature of relationships previously enjoyed both within and between public sector service departments. The requirement to develop contract specifications has resulted in a greater awareness of, and pressure towards, costing the corporate approach to service delivery. The realisation of the old adage 'time is money' threatens to reduce the priority afforded to the processes of consultation, liaison and evaluation of inter-disciplinary issues which may be essential to an authority's strategic planning. In achieving a competitive service the inevitable result will be a more self-interested and introspective contractor side. Even where contracts are won by in-house teams, the need to adopt commercial practices such as confidentiality and increased profit margins will become major influences on the style of service ultimately delivered.

There are also indications that a similar situation may be developing amongst housing associations. Their own costs for providing housing management services have always exceeded those of local authorities. This has now become a problem for some associations looking to mount credible bids for local authority CCT contracts, and others who consider that they might also have to tender services in the future. Already there are indications that a number of associations have begun to redress this imbalance by cutting their costs (see Chapter 7).

Economy is not however the sole indicator of positive achievement, even within a commercial environment. Alongside the pressure for customer-led service strategies and performance monitoring has been a drive to deliver *quality* within all aspects of an organisation's activities. Although uncertainty remains as to what might constitute a social housing definition of quality, there is universal acceptance that performance standards and the pursuit of excellence should be supported. In recent times initiatives such as BS5750 (ISO 9000) and the Charter Mark (described later) have become icons validating the achievement of quality standards within organisations. However, as with published performance indicators (PPIs), these kitemarks rely heavily on assessing administrative process rather than the quality of outcomes for consumers.

Whilst the concept of quality should clearly not be confined to the private sector, the direct importation of commercial interpretations of quality into public services has had major drawbacks, as described later. It has highlighted the need for a range of quality measures and indicators customised specifically for the services to which they relate. In housing management terms, they must recognise that catering for social need is quite different from producing a standard unit of manufactured output.

However, a movement towards a customer culture in the public sector has been heralded as a genuine increase in the rights and choices enjoyed by service consumers. Whilst there have been significant steps forward in this area, the substance must be placed into context. In reality, the public sector operates within a framework of *quasi-markets,* or internal markets, in which competition is often more notional than real. Such markets frequently remain provider- rather than consumer-led, continuing to impose on the public the professional perspective of what they might need. The effect of these changes has been to lurch social housing into an environment in which it has been forced to address a constant barrage of policy changes while in a state of constant flux. In some cases this has entailed returning to basics, to re-evaluate the very fabric of management, such as specific approaches to governance. In others, it is more about adjusting to new standards and expectations. However, overarching all of this has been an unquestioned need to review existing practices within a proliferation of quality indicators against which services have increasingly become measured.

Strolling Down Quality Street

Achieving quality has been one of the main clarion calls of the perform- ance gurus seeking to transform the social housing sector: 'Emphasis on the customer, quality, performance and value for money has never been greater. Both public and private sectors have recognised the real contribu- tion that quality management can make to the effective use of resources and to the reputation of an organisation' (NFHA, 1993, p. 1). For the government, 'The principles of making public services answer better to the wishes of their users, and raising their quality overall are the foun- dations of the Citizen's Charter' (Audit Commission, 1993a, p. 1). Similar expectations have been voiced by other interested parties, from the Tenant Participation Advisory Service (TPAS) through to the Housing Corporation. Performance standards imposed by the DoE, Housing Corporation and private funding sources have also contributed substantially to the quality debate. As principal financial stakeholders in social housing, each has a keen interest in the quality of financial management, strategic planning, performance monitoring and probity within and between organisations. Other stakeholders such as consumers and staff will be concerned not only with these issues, but with quality as it relates to employment prac- tices, service delivery, tenant consultation, fairness and consistency. The quality agenda is therefore exerting a major influence over operation of practitioners and their organisations.

Yet despite a unanimity of purpose, there is less consensus about how to define quality in the public sector. 'If it had been easy to define quality in public sector services, the management literature would now be full of criteria, measures, targets and indicators identifying levels of quality in an organisation or an individual's work, how it can be improved or increased, and resources and training needs . . . no such ready-made package exists' (Gastor, 1991). Currently, definitions tend to be derived from private sec- tor models and as such are biased largely towards outputs rather than outcomes (or efficiency rather than effectiveness). While attaining excel- lence is not the sole preserve of commercial organisations, private sector approaches have generally been afforded higher credence than their pub- lic sector counterparts. The result has been that in certain instances com- mercial approaches have been adopted, even when inappropriate. This is largely due either to an adherence to political dogma or a misguided interpretation of 'the inadequate language of consumerism' (Stewart and Walsh, 1992). As with the term *customer*, the literal transposition of an external concept directly on to social housing management is not always appropriate. The imperatives of a market-led system with a bottom-line profit motive presents a different dynamic from a socially oriented, not-for-profit service.

If quality is to be defined in any measure by the consumer, the special circumstances requiring local authorities to ration some services and impose coercion in others, requires quality assessment to be located within a sensitive framework. While in the commercial sector, 'quality is much more of a private issue between buyer and seller. In the world of welfare, there are other stakeholders' (Wilding, 1994, p. 58), social housing often performs a strategic, community-related function which should be judged on accumulated outcomes. This should not diminish the need for quality to be a central aim of all social housing organisations. However, it must be measured appropriately taking account of the constraints and objectives within which organisations operate. The concept of quality is therefore multi-faceted, reflecting attitudinal, contextual and product-related factors. The definition for car manufacturers will inevitably differ from that adopted by a housing association. Social housing has responsibility to consumers based on a relationship broader than purely ability to purchase. Services are generally expected to reflect the moral commitment of a welfare state to its citizens, with public sector perceptions of quality including reference to factors such as accessibility, acceptability, effectiveness, openness, equity, and accountability (Wilding, 1994). Housing services can only deliver quality by balancing both technical excellence and responsiveness to user demands (Walsh and Spencer, 1990; Catterick, 1992; Stewart and Walsh, 1989). The growing use of the term *social business* goes some way to illustrate the inherent tension in delivering a welfare product in a commercial environment.

The Mark of Quality

The emphasis on quality is perhaps inevitable given the context of increasing competition located within the framework of a performance culture. Quality indicators have become essential in assessing tenders, evaluating contract performance and achieving a balance between pure economy and effectiveness. This is crucial in the process of CCT, where the qualitative aspects of housing management (see Chapter 2) may not easily fit within a primarily qualitative contract specification.

However, ensuring that quality is delivered consistently is often a complex process. While most practitioners consider themselves attuned to such an objective, personal approaches often differ and conflict. Organisations require a corporate view of quality to be understood, shared and implemented by all staff. The quality chain is only as strong as its weakest link. To achieve this requires considerable investment in training, information systems and monitoring mechanisms for quality assurance. In recent years the trend has been for housing organisations to seek external recognition for the quality of service they provide. This has taken the form of registration for either the Charter Mark, or BS5750 (ISO 9000, internationally). Each is a recognised accreditation of the quality of processes involved in service delivery.

The Charter Mark is a government-sponsored initiative dovetailing with the principles promoted by the Citizen's Charter. The award is given in recognition of the achievement of excellence in customer relationships. The award of BS5750 is conferred by the British Standards Council as one of a range of nationally recognised standards covering all areas of organisational management and production. It recognises the ability of management systems to identify and implement good working practices by means of effective quality assurance measures.

Accreditation is a stringent procedure, involving considerable investment of time, cost and staff resources. However, the NFHA (NFHA 1993) promotes BS5750 on the basis of the following practical benefits for associations:

- cost savings
- improved service delivery to tenants and other service users
- consistency of service, ensuring equality of opportunity in access to and delivery of service
- better control over operating costs, achieved by a continual drive for error reduction and quality improvements
- elimination of gaps and duplication in working practices in a coordinated manner
- committed and well-trained workforce, who understand what is required and relate to the responsibilities and objectives defined in a clearly documented quality system
- tangible evidence of management competence and confidence in the association
- providing a sound base for all future initiatives.

In commercial terms, many government departments are reluctant to offer contracts to organisations not holding BS5750 accreditation, and for housing associations such recognition may also impress potential private sector lenders.

Despite the quality assurance guaranteed by these quality marks, they have shortcomings. The main problem is that they are largely process-driven and do not reflect the quality of output, or the relationship with consumers. 'BS5750 judges against the standards and specifications as laid down by the company itself . . . As such BS5750 offers a guarantee that the process will deliver the service or product in conformance with the specification; it does not guarantee the relevance of the specification' (Catterick, 1992, p. 38). Although systems undoubtedly improve under the new regime of quality control, there are serious concerns that processes may drive outcomes rather than a rational, sensitive and responsive approach to needs assessment.

Deciding the Characteristics of Quality

Within the established definitions of quality, few include any reference to aspects such as equity and equality. Without such indicators, there is a danger that quality becomes a selective term applied to a relatively few consumers able to afford the cost. Thus, services may fulfil quality criteria in their delivery, but may not achieve quality outcomes in strategic terms. In such circumstances, the integrity of such a *quality* definition would be seriously flawed. Specific aspects of quality which demand consideration, but suffer within a process-driven definition, are:

- *Strategic quality* – Are outcomes in line with strategic objectives? For example, one-bedroom flats may offer greater value for money in terms of cost per unit and dwellings produced, but may not reflect the housing needs of the locality or achieve a balanced community.
- *Equality* – Do services offer equality to all potential consumers? If households are prevented from accessing services because of poverty, household size, gender, ethnicity, disability, or any other factor which may be discriminatory, this cannot be considered to constitute quality.
- *Personnel quality* – Are the best people taking decisions based on the best information, equipment and training? Individuals present the greatest danger of derailing the quality train. Organisations need their employees to be equipped both personally and professionally to make decisions based on professional criteria and use sound judgement. Decisions influenced more by administrative considerations and financial constraint than the needs of consumers may lack overall quality.
- *Quality of vision* – Are the objectives of an organisation appropriate for one in its position? Are the methods used to decide priorities based on good practice and appropriate data, and does the organisation operate in the best interests of its consumers, employees, funders and the community at large?

These criteria all contribute to squaring the quality circle, offering a breadth of quality to an organisation's operations. However, perhaps the most important judge of quality should be the consumer or customer for whom the service is ultimately intended. This is to a large extent true in the private sector, where poor products tend to have short lives. However, the same has not until recently been possible in the public sector, where services have been delivered on a 'take it or leave it' basis. This approach does now appear to be changing, with *customer care* becoming a watchword for many local authorities and housing associations. To what extent it can be truly effective remains to be seen. As discussed subsequently, reference to a widespread emergence of a customer care culture in social housing must be qualified.

Customer Care: A New Approach or Window-Dressing?

'The emphasis on the customer of public services has the merit of forcing public organisations to look outward to those who use and receive their services. The danger is that the language of consumerism, with its emphasis on the customer, is inadequate to encompass the complexities of public action. Thus there are limits to the extent to which public services can regard those affected by the services as customers whose wishes are to be met.'

(Stewart and Walsh, 1992, p. 514)

'[a customer is] an individual or organisation who receives benefits from, or holds expectations about, an organisation and its performance.'

(Passmore and Fergusson, 1994, p. 2)

The perception of public services is now primarily as businesses (McKnight, 1977: Stewart and Walsh, 1992). 'This fact is reflected in the language employed. Professionals and their managers now speak of educational "products", health "consumers" and a legal "industry". Clients are defined as markets . . .' (McKnight, 1977, p. 69). In a housing context tenants are now referred to as 'customers' and the delivery of housing management linked closely to concepts such as 'customer care'. This has necessarily involved the elevation of consumers to the status of arbiters of quality, which, it is argued, is no more than exists in the private sector. While this may have been sadly lacking in the past, it must also be accepted that by necessity public services do not always perform functions perceived as beneficial to consumers, e.g. taking children into care, planning and environmental health notices, and homelessness decisions. Because of their controversial nature these decisions will never achieve universal consensus but nevertheless play an important strategic role in delivering services to the community as a whole. The notion therefore that the style of professional public services can mirror those offered in the private sector is spurious (Stewart and Walsh, 1992).

The notion of a true market in social housing is also somewhat artificial. The reality for many households if homeless or applying for housing, is that they have no alternative other than their local authority and/or housing association. Nor is there any choice of which local authority they approach, eligibility being dictated by geographical location. The term *customer* also indicates an active consumer of a service or product, i.e. an individual or household exercising a series of unfettered choices, constrained only by cost and availability. This may include deciding on factors such as the timing, content and cost of a purchase. Some such choices may be open to consumers of social housing services, although usually within a more constrained range of options. The growth of statutory rights for council tenants, and the development of initiatives for tenant control and participation, have undoubtedly increased the power of existing residents to influence the delivery of services. However, such influence is relatively limited in deciding their overall housing circumstances. Few social housing tenants have any control over the dwelling they eventually inhabit; some are lucky, others are not. If a household is forced to accept a flat on the 23rd floor of a tower block against their will, to consult on the frequency of cleaning communal areas or their preparedness to pay an extra 50 pence a week for additional caretaking services may not appear to constitute meaningful customer choice. In addition, choices are often so constrained because of prior decisions made by managers or politicians as to offer no real choice at all. Thus, referring to social housing consumers as *customers* often implies a status which in reality does not exist.

The term *customer* also has the distorting effect of creating an image of homogeneity of tenant bodies, implying that all require a similar type and level of service. As discussed in Chapter 2, this is untrue, and many less articulate and less assertive households, who cannot easily 'plug into the system', may find themselves disadvantaged and marginalised. This particularly applies to an increasing number of consumers who are vulnerable and significantly dependent on the support of others to enable them to live independent lives. The choices of these people may effectively be limited to the public sector because of constrained financial resources. Even within the public sector, they may suffer marginalisation because of a lack of personal skills and effective advocacy to ensure their personal needs and rights are met. The role of consumer is therefore, for many, passive, because of their inability, or perhaps unwillingness, to influence their housing circumstances. If the term 'customer' is to acquire any real meaning for the public sector, there must be a recognition that different types of customer exist, with differing needs and purchasing powers:

'Often, the problem for professionals is that, instead of having customers who know what they want, they have clients who cannot formulate their needs clearly in advance of professionals being called upon to meet them. A supplier–customer relationship is appropriate when customers know their preferences and can specify what they want; a professional–client relationship is appropriate when clients' needs are ill-defined and the prior tasks of formulating problems and devising ways of solving them must be undertaken.'

(Metcalfe and Richards, 1990, p.142)

New Skills, New Technology

Much of the change already discussed in this chapter relates to changing attitudes, cultures and practices in response to a new style of social housing. Functional changes such as consumer empowerment and enabling have demanded not only changed outlooks, but also the development of new skills, e.g. facilitation, promotion and devolution of power (see Chapter 5). Other new skills are also becoming increasingly important as local authorities and housing associations enter an era in which control of information is absolutely key to the success or demise of an organisation and the quality of the services delivered. Information technology (IT) has become a crucial area both for organisations and individual development: 'good quality IT systems will be the key factor in effective monitoring and service delivery' (Morris, 1994a).

Implementing CCT will place significant demands on housing services in terms of the specification, tendering and monitoring of contracts. Failure to succeed in any one of these three areas could seriously jeopardise the position of the in-house team resulting in the contract being unnecessarily expensive or poorly performed. To reflect this, an increasing number of posts have been created within the local authority client side for contract managers, i.e. officers skilled in understanding, formulating and monitoring contracts. These new functions are a recognition of a growing element of resource management in the execution of service delivery. Financial management is becoming an increasingly prized skill amongst housing practitioners, within both client and contractor sides of a local authority, or in development or management in housing associations. When so much rests on the successful control of expenditure, this is inevitable. Yet individual ability is insufficient in itself, only becoming effective when harnessed within a framework of finely tuned and well-implemented systems. Increasingly, such a framework has been built around computerisation.

Despite the crucial nature of IT, few housing organisations have really grasped the nettle and developed a strategic approach to its implementation. Historically, computers have been viewed with mistrust and suspicion by large proportions of housing management practitioners. Systems have traditionally been introduced with little clear strategic planning, poor staff consultation and often inadequate staff training. In addition, they have usually been controlled by the financial function of the organisation, thus invariably reflecting an accountant's perspective of data management. To compound these hurdles, older mainframe systems appear 'down', i.e. out of commission, for longer periods than they work, providing only the information the software is prepared to divulge – very much a case of the tail wagging the dog. The legacy has been a housing profession which has not readily made friends with IT or properly investigated its potential: 'many housing departments have put IT very low down on their priorities...many housing staff do not understand it, are barely computer-literate and have failed to build up a rapport with their IT colleagues in other council departments' (Morris, 1994). In a survey carried out in 1994 by Coopers & Lybrand, the inadequacy of local authorities' information systems in readiness for CCT was revealed in the following data:

- only 20 authorities had integrated information systems in place
- over half of councils had no formal IT strategy or were still in the process of formulating one
- over half of councils felt they were poorly placed to maximise their use of IT
- more than half of housing managers indicated that they did not feel confident that they had the skills to manage their IT resources effectively.

What is becoming increasingly clear is that such an uninformed approach to data management is completely inappropriate for both local authorities and housing associations required to cope with the future challenges set by CCT and business planning. Nor is time on their side, with impending deadlines the cause of major concern.

Developing Strategies for IT

It would be a mistake to believe that developing an IT strategy is simply a case of ensuring proficiency in keyboard skills or working knowledge of a few software packages. Such an approach would merely constitute tinkering around the edges. New technology often involves considerable expense and if it is ever to be embraced by staff throughout the organisation, repaying the investment of time and cash, it requires a change of organisational culture. An IT culture is one which:

- has clearly defined objectives for the collection, analysis and use of organisational data. Careful consideration will have been given to what management information is needed and in what form it should be presented. This must then be fed backwards to the points of collection, where staff are made aware of the exact nature of the information required and its purpose. Inaccurate, incomplete, irrelevant and out-of-date information is of little use.
- includes *all* members of the organisation. IT operates on a range of levels, including resource management, trend forecasting, automating routine manual tasks and recreation. The more that individual members of staff are exposed to IT in a positive and nurturing manner, the more likely they are to value, trust and utilise equipment to its fullest capability.
- offers proper, on-going IT training to all staff, with comprehensive and user-friendly manuals which act as a reference when needed.
- understands the potential of IT for both the organisation and the ser-

vices it delivers. This calls for innovation, integration and vision. 'Specific examples include: the development of online customer information systems; the use of hand-held terminals to support work with tenants groups and door-to-door-rent collection services; and specialist software for the production of tenants' newsletters and form design' (Steele and Pollock, 1993).

Successfully adapting to the changing environment and achieving effective service delivery can only realistically be attained by the skilled management of performance data. This is true for all aspects of organisational output, whether related to efficiency, economy, effectiveness, equity or equality. The success or failure in achieving objectives in these areas is crucial to all organisations and their stakeholders – IT skills are essential.

The development of robust systems is crucial not only for housing organisations charged with the direct delivery of services. It is also fundamental to the effective formulation and implementation of strategic plans designed to cater for local housing needs. Such a role has always been expected of local authorities but has become even more significant following the Housing Act 1988. Since then, council housing departments have become totally dependent on their ability to implement an effective strategic, or *enabling* role in order to achieve their desired outcomes.

A New Role for Local Authorities: Enabling Councils

'The role of the local authority will no longer be that of universal provider . . . it is for local authorities to organise, secure and monitor the provision of services, without necessarily providing them themselves . . . authorities will need to operate in a more pluralist way than in the past, alongside a wide variety of public, private and voluntary agencies.'

(Ridley, 1988)

What is Enabling?

Although all local authorities are expected to become enablers, there is no single, binding definition of what such a role might entail: 'like many such beguiling terms, "enabling" is a rather slippery concept when placed under closer scrutiny' (Cole and Goodchild, 1995, p. 53). Nor is there any consensus as to what form a model of enabling might take. 'One of the reasons why the "enabling authority" has been in vogue is that it can be used by different people to represent different concepts and visions of the future of local government' (ADC, 1990, p. 4). At one end of the spectrum it can be viewed narrowly as a tool for emasculating local authorities as the direct providers of services. At the other, it offers an opportunity for local authorities to engage properly in the process of local *government*, rather than local *administration* (ADC, 1987); i.e. enablement is 'not defined so much by direct service provision as by enabling the community to meet the needs, opportunities and problems faced in the most effective way' (Clarke and Stewart, 1989, p. 1). The choice is therefore between a largely passive, reactive, regulatory approach to enabling against one which promotes an attitude of empowerment, partnership and proactivity such as the CIH model in Table 3.1. This 'shopping list' is by no means excessive, representing the minimum response for an authority committed to its strategic responsibilities.

The practice of enabling, i.e. delivering strategic housing outcomes through third parties, is not new to local authorities. Even through the 'golden years' of council house building during the 1960s and 1970s, when local authorities' energies were devoted to increasing the public housing stock, they implemented an important strategic housing role within their areas. This concentrated on: efforts to improve the private sector through maintenance and improvement grants; providing mortgage finance for housing ignored by building societies; and support for housing associations and voluntary organisations providing housing for special needs and single people. In this context, the enabling role was perceived as complementary, but secondary to the main function of local authorities, i.e. to build homes. This position clearly altered following the Housing Act 1988, when from being primarily providers, local authorities became exclusively enablers, with housing associations taking on the status of provider.

The ability of authorities to ensure sufficient numbers of appropriate dwellings are provided now falls outside of their direct control. They are only therefore able to achieve strategic objectives by facilitation and encouragement rather than by direct action. This has raised concerns about whether local authorities actually have the powers and influence to achieve their goals should external factors, e.g. reducing HAG or antipathy by local associations to specific policy objectives, create barriers. Many practitioners believe that for the enabling function to be effective requires a review of the powers available to local authorities. Without the necessary leverage, the strategic function becomes a hostage to the fortunes of potential partners. It is also important that the corporate function of coordinating and promoting social housing held by the housing department is maintained despite its altered role. This is particularly relevant in ensuring the most effective use of planning powers, 'where land availability and other policies need to fully reflect the assessment of local housing needs, and where the use of "section 52" and other powers can make a useful contribution towards meeting those needs' (IoH, 1990, p. 106).

The potential difficulties facing authorities in realising their enabling potential is broader than just power and purpose. The transition from providing social housing to an enabling role is a complex process. Its success is not solely dependent on the ability of an authority to provide or facilitate resources for housing associations or other partners. There is an implicit organisational and cultural change required to reflect the nature of the new functions to be undertaken. This will involve the development of

Table 3.1   The housing functions of the strategic and enabling authority

1. Assessing local housing situation and needs.
2. Developing strategies to meet housing needs, ensuring, as far as practical, that a full range of rented and ownership housing services is provided.
3. Liaison with local housing agencies, seeking their engagement in complementary housing strategies and services.
4. Set standards, and encourage good management, maintenance and rehabilitation of all housing stock in the area.
5. Ensure access to suitable housing for all households according to equitable rules and priorities, and facilitate transfers and mutual exchanges between occupiers of all types of accommodation.
6. Administration of the Housing (Homeless Persons) Act, 1977.
7. Provision of housing advisory services, in respect of all aspects of private sector housing services.
8. Administration of housing benefits scheme, and assistance in maximising income support for all households in connection with their ability to meet housing costs.
9. Ensure liaison and development of integrated services, as required, with local health and social services.
10. Provide advice and assistance to local housing associations.
11. Promote and assist the development of tenant participation.
12. Promote good race relations, and ensure equal opportunities are provided in respect of all local housing services.

Source: Institute of Housing (1990).

new skills, approaches and expertise to capitalise on the unique position of local authorities to coordinate housing activity, collate data, and promote and regulate good practice within their area. This attitude extends also to housing professionals, who 'require a sea-change in professional ethos and approach' (Cole and Goodchild, 1995, p. 54) to do justice to the new raft of activities which have traditionally fallen outside of the relatively narrow remit of local authority housing management.

However, the need for such change coincides with most local authorities having to cope with the effects of even more radical reforms in the shape of CCT (which is in itself a form of enabling) and, in some cases, local government reorganisation. Both impose substantial structural changes, and demand new working practices and organisational cultures. There is therefore a danger that enabling may be considered a distraction to the main issues facing authorities. Perhaps the only real enabling authorities are those which have followed the LSVT (Large-Scale Voluntary Transfers) route, disposing of their stock to one or more housing associations. In such cases both officers *and* members are left with a single focus: the provision of housing services through other agencies and organisations.

Housing Association Governance: Accountability or Competition?

As local authorities have been faced with a changing role as enablers, so have housing associations in terms of their 'promotion' to providers. Since the Housing Act 1988, associations have been expected to achieve rapid and often destabilising change in fulfilling their new role as the main providers of social housing. Many have undergone huge expansions in a relatively short time, in the process having to adjust to borrowing enormous amounts of private finance to sustain active development programmes. The competition amongst the largest housing associations for development opportunities has attained cut-throat proportions in some areas, exacerbated by the recent creation of 50 new, relatively large and affluent associations following Large Scale Voluntary Transfer (see Chapter 8).

For local authorities, this has presented an opportunity to broaden the base of housing association activity in their areas to ensure healthy competition and generate a wider range of options. While this has been handled in a measured and responsible manner by most authorities, some have been tempted by 'loss leading' offers of cheaper rents offered by associations seeking to break into an area for the first time. These bargains are often sustained by subsidies from reserves generated by existing stock and may subsequently result in housing developed to lower space standards to reduce costs (Karn and Sheriden, 1994). Not only is the prize of Housing Association Grant (HAG) at stake, but also the prospect of partnerships with local authorities, potentially leading to cheap land and further, local authority HAG.

The provider role has been acquired by the housing association movement at a substantial cost, accepting as its consequence a significant element of financial risk in the development process. This move towards a more business-like and competitive system, encouraged by both the government and Housing Corporation, reflects the trends generally sweeping through the public sector. Coupled with the Housing Corporation's increasingly stringent Performance Review standards, both staff and committee members have been forced to develop new and sophisticated methods of managing their associations. The ultimate legal control of an association rests with its committee members who have been thrust into centre stage, shouldering the burden of responsibility for any possible failures. This has been a substantial shift from the previous expectations placed on voluntary members, many of whom have found it hard to adjust.

Like it or not, associations wishing to remain active developers have had to face up to the reality that they have become multi-million-pound *social businesses*. This has involved a major shift in the manner in which voluntary committees conduct themselves and relate to paid officers of the association. The result has been the emergence of significant tensions both within committees and between committee members and the executive. A survey of fifty housing associations carried out in October 1993, indicated that a significant proportion (over 40 per cent) of the associations questioned had experienced major disputes between their chief executives and the management committee. In addition, '32% of chief executives felt that they did not receive adequate support from their management committee' (*ROOF*, March/April 1994). Although this appears to indicate that the majority of housing associations work harmoniously, a significant body of evidence (Anlin and Lush, 1994; NVCMF, 1994; Wadhams, 1994) suggests that roles and relationships remain volatile.

One of the main reasons behind this growing volatility is the changing composition of most management committees in response to their new responsibilities. Increasingly the tendency is for committees to operate in a more formalised manner, making increased demands to receive financial and technical information which in the past would have been considered to be the 'property' of the executive. This reflects a heightened awareness amongst voluntary members of the need to receive crucial operational information in order to exercise a level of control appropriate to the risks incurred. This has been prompted by recognition of the need to exercise *active* control, together with increasingly stringent requirements of lenders and the Housing Corporation. In addition to leading to a more complex and comprehensive set of management reporting procedures, these shifts have also had significant consequences on the culture and composition of management committees. There has been a marked trend towards recruiting new members with specific professional skills and expertise. In the past, a voluntarist motivation has been sufficient to achieve access to committee status. The well-meaning amateur has for many years been the hallmark of the voluntary sector, influencing and shaping the objectives and practices of housing associations and other voluntary organisations. However, the increasing demands on both time and expert knowledge has reversed this, shifting instead to a more technocratic approach to voluntary control. While having the effect of strengthening committee membership in terms of specialist skills, it has been at the expense of both local accountability and equal opportunities.

The Housing Corporation has pushed strongly for tenant representation on management committees to be increased. However, this has only been achieved to a very limited extent, usually taking a back seat to the recruitment of the members mentioned previously. In addition, there is concern that lending institutions might be less keen on having tenants (who may have self-interest in keeping rents low) represented to any extent on management committees. But this has not been substantiated and remains the subject of conjecture. Similarly, the racial and gender imbalance amongst the financial and technical professions currently courted by association committees also works against the promotion of equal opportunities. While there has been some improvement in achieving a more balanced committee member profile, it has been limited. There are also signs that the emphasis on technocratic control has brought with it a changing culture and social attitude which has created tensions between new and older committee members. Increasingly, key decisions are effectively being made by a small, influential caucus of committee members with the expertise and knowledge to interpret crucial performance information. The often articulated concerns about the lack of true accountability (the 'democratic deficit') of housing associations to their tenants and the community at large does have substance.

However, such tensions are not confined only to committees – officers are experiencing the fallout from such change. 'The new responsibility for risk-taking placed on committees and the emphasis by the Corporation that they should be in control appear to have undermined the notion of a partnership between chief executive and committee. Directors are finding meetings "more gruelling" and committees "more annoying" as committees sought to intervene in a more detailed way and made an explicit attempt to exercise control over them' (Billis *et al.*, 1994). Similarly, the lack of cohesion between committee members has also, in some cases, translated to senior members of staff. As the organisational culture changes, staff who had previously joined an association because of an affinity with its core values and objectives may find themselves at odds with the new regime. This, in turn, can foster an atmosphere of distrust between committee members and the executive which can only be detrimental to the manner in which the association operates.

This is further complicated by the lack of clear distinction between what might legitimately be viewed as the responsibility of officers and what should fall to the committee. At the core of this is the inevitable overlap between the involvement of staff and committee in identifying and setting the goals and working practices of an association. The neat division between policy setting and implementation does not, in reality, reflect the level of interaction between members and officers necessary to produce workable policies and practices. Members are often largely dependent on information provided by officers to be able to make strategic decisions and to monitor the association's activity. There is always an underlying concern that such a dependence places the committee in a vulnerable position which might be abused. Tensions often emerge between officers wishing to maximise the potential of their organisation to take up development opportunities and provide much-needed social housing, while members, although being sympathetic to such objectives, may be more inclined to take a more conservative approach. The reality is, however, that in most associations the relationship between staff and committee is largely positive. This has to be the case as staff are key to sustaining the organisation in practice, and a committee can only be as effective as the staff it employs.

At a time when housing associations have fallen under close scrutiny, in terms of accountability, performance, diversity and competence, the issue of governance is a major concern to the movement as a whole. Following sustained calls for a reassessment of the regulation of associations, the National Federation of Housing Associations (NFHA) responded in April 1994 by setting up an inquiry into housing association govern-

ance. The terms of reference for the inquiry panel were to make recommendations to the NFHA on good practice and potential changes to the
statutory and regulatory frameworks. The report of the enquiry, *Competence and Accountability*, published in March 1995, contained a code of
governance for housing associations and the Housing Corporation designed
to ensure high standards of probity, whilst adequately responding to the
demands of the working environment. In addition, as part of a broader
investigation into standards in public life, the Nolan Committee also investigated the running of housing associations. Its conclusions were generally favourable, finding that associations were 'well-regulated and generally
well-run' but pressing for further accountability to end-users via board
membership.

Managing Diversity: Ensuring Equity and Equality

One of the major issues raised as a result of the governance debate has
been the difficulty in maintaining commitments to equal opportunities and
community welfare in the light of resource pressures. The inexorable drive
towards competition and performance monitoring has placed substantial
pressures on organisations to provide clearly specified, low-cost, value-
for-money services (see Chapter 7). The potential effect is a tendency towards
standardisation and rationalisation. Services which can be shown to benefit from both economies of scale and keen pricing from competition,
may well be considered the most successful.

Generating cost savings should not necessarily prejudice housing standards. However, the rigid imposition of cost considerations in every cir-
cumstance may well do so. A common result of standardisation is that the
model against which standards are set establishes a 'norm' which may be
predicated on spurious criteria. There is widespread evidence of this throughout social housing, where dwelling design has in the past been based on
the needs of able-bodied, middle-class males of average height. This partly
reflected the status quo of architects working within the public sector; and
also most effectively uses the standard dwelling types and building materials produced by the building industry. The effect has been that substantial amounts of social housing have been built to inflexible specifications
with severely restricted usage. Recent attempts to establish *lifetime homes*,
i.e. dwellings flexible enough in their specifications to adapt to the changing needs of their residents, as an industry norm, have met with limited
success. This is due largely to the cost implications of building to higher
space standards, when current trends are in the opposite direction.

Shortcomings in the physical environment is but one example of the
narrow approach to service delivery adopted by many housing organisations. Adequate provision for the elderly, infirm, women and ethnic minorities is also prone to be overlooked in a myopic drive for efficiency.
Part of the reason has been the lack of representation within the workforce

of people able to bring alternative perspectives to those which have traditionally held sway. Although this most notably relates to gender, race and
disability, the list also includes a variety of groups whose needs and abilities are perceived by society to fall outside the 'norm'. Such an imbalance
does not solely relate to number, reflecting also seniority within organisations, or access to training or promotional opportunities. There are many
reasons for the perpetuation of this situation which include:

- *the 'in my own image' scenario* – in which traditionally white-male-
  dominated organisations continue to maintain such a position, whether
  intentionally or subconsciously;
- *the 'don't rock the boat' scenario* – in which a working environment
  is dominated by a particular group which makes life hostile for any
  newcomers of a different group. There have been well-publicised
  examples of this in both the fire service and police, where women
  have been harassed by their male colleagues. This is particularly true
  of those areas of work which have been exclusively male preserves,
  e.g. the construction industry.
- *the 'we always pick the best man for the job' scenario* – many organisations who decline to adopt equal opportunities policies often
  do so on the basis of believing that they operate fairly, appointing
  staff strictly on their merits. These are likely to be organisations who
  do not monitor the outcome of the recruitment process, being convinced they do not discriminate. Clearly, the failure to monitor means
  they cannot possibly be sure that this is true and also goes against
  the performance culture in which 'if it can't be monitored, it can't be
  managed'.
- *the 'we are an equal opportunities employer' scenario* – many organisations appear complacently to believe that simply by publicly
  supporting equal opportunities, it happens without any further action
  on their behalf. This is not only misguided, it is damaging to both the
  external image of the organisation and the internal morale of staff
  who might originally have been attracted in the belief that they shared
  the corporate values.

In an environment in which value for money and competitiveness are
all important, the effective management of staff resources, amounting to
the most important asset in any housing organisation, is vital. In this respect, the implementation of equal opportunities policies and practices
makes organisational, rather than ideological sense. The crucial issue is
that the best staff are employed in the first instance, and that they are
then enabled to perform at their optimum level while in the workplace.
Equal opportunities attempts to achieve this by removing artificial barriers
and encouraging a nurturing environment in which diverse skills are recognised, rewarded and capitalised upon.

A balanced approach to recruitment also has a direct bearing on the nature and quality of service delivery. Most social housing organisations attract consumers from a broad spectrum of backgrounds, cultures and social class who display a wide range of personal characteristics and aspirations. Few households share exact housing needs or aspirations for the future. Those organisations employing a workforce which manifests a similar diversity of backgrounds to their consumers, are more likely to be sensitive and responsive to local needs. They are also often those most able and prepared to change and to be dynamic in their operation. On the other hand, those erecting barriers to maintain and protect long-established cultures against external infiltration will find the management of change both alien and painful.

For the social housing practitioner, the task is to manage change so that the concept of social justice is embedded and that statutory duties towards equal opportunities are fulfilled. Any service which does not at least account for the varied needs within the community is inherently flawed. This does not mean that all needs can always be met. It is a feature of social housing that resource constraints continue to require the prioritisation of need as a means of rationing distribution. Equity and equality can still properly be addressed by ensuring that priorities are formulated so that no single group disproportionately suffers hardship and that constant dialogue is maintained to monitor changing needs over time. Of the greatest importance is that the assessment of need and the determination of entitlement is conducted in as transparent and comprehensible a manner as possible.

Summary

Managing change is often the single most difficult task facing any manager. This is true even when it occurs as consensual evolution over time. In practice, the opposite has been true in social housing where change has been imposed rapidly and without respite. The result has been that some organisations have gone to the wall, and many individuals have been sacrificed along the way in the name of progress. The evidence of this will be presented in later chapters which deal with the introduction of CCT (Chapter 7) and the changing face of organisational structures (Chapter 8).

One of the dangers of such a situation is that it becomes increasingly difficult to see light at either end of the tunnel, i.e. the path already trodden or the way ahead. Core values and objectives are therefore much harder to fix in a way which provides a suitable framework for future strategies and plans. Overriding pressures for economy have rarely been consistent with equal opportunities. While these two issues can coexist, there will inevitably be points of conflict where decisions must favour one at the expense of the other. The concern must be that such decisions are taken on the basis of short-term benefits which may reflect organisational or individual inexperience or insecurity. Nor does the pace of change show any sign of relenting. The growth of tenant involvement (see Chapter 5), the impact of community care, and threats to professional integrity all entail a significant reappraisal of the role of practitioners and their organisations. Similarly, the introduction of competition has imposed a reorientation of the relationship between employees and employers.

The most successful managers will be those who understand the dynamics of change and its effect upon the policies and practices of organisations. Those most able to control and manipulate their staff may not always achieve their objectives. Effecting change is as much about reflection and support as it is about direction and control. Staff often respond best when they are comfortable with change and are supported through the process. The same is true of customers, or clients, or whatever collective term is used to describe the consumers of services. The danger in a sustained period of change is that the organisation becomes more important than the people it serves. Even where such complacency has been overcome, the current dynamics of competition and resource constraint has threatened core public sector values such as equality and equity. Unless these are written indelibly into the cultural changes taking place, the language of the market will exclude them from the holy grails of excellence and quality.

4 Managing a Residualised Housing Stock

'Most "residualised" areas of council housing are large estates of low-income families, with high numbers of children. They may also be associated with poor location, high building densities, "utopian" design, a bad state of repair and ineffective housing management. But the common ingredients seem to be scale, poverty, a large number of children and an allocation system which places people where they do not want to be.'

(Page, 1993, p. 5)

Despite the sale of 1.5 million dwellings under the Right to Buy, local authorities and housing associations continue to manage in excess of 5 million dwellings. Many are of good quality, well designed and maintained to a high standard, proving extremely popular with residents. However, a sizeable number fall short of these standards, causing dissatisfaction amongst tenants and considerable management difficulties for housing staff. These difficulties are often manifested in problems such as high void rates, difficult-to-let dwellings and high levels of nuisance, crime and general unrest on housing estates. Each of these has become a recognisable feature of the residualisation of social housing. This chapter examines the implications of residualisation to the tenants and managers of the estates worst affected, identifying the resulting housing management issues, together with examples of initiatives designed to resolve problems and improve the quality of life.

In many of the very worst cases, residualised estates may appear to be beyond hope for all concerned. How can managers control the seemingly unmanageable? What do *sink estates* offer tenants who are often forced against their will to live in them with little prospect of improving their lot? There are numerous examples of inner-city estates where the quality of life is undoubtedly poor, and estate management becomes in reality little more than an *ad hoc* response to a series of crises. In extreme areas whole estates have become 'no-go' areas to anyone in authority, dominated by cultures of drugs, crime and vandalism. Many residents in such surroundings consider themselves to be written off or forgotten, imprisoned in often difficult to heat and infested dwellings, often too scared to venture outside their doors. Front-line officers are also placed in frequently impossible situations in which any meaningful action is outside the scope of their control and influence. Such estates represent an undeniable indictment of the planning system which conceived them and of the social

structure which continues to sustain them. However, set against this catalogue of disasters, is an increasing number of successes, where radical
approaches have broken the mould of apathy and neglect, resulting in
marked social and environmental improvements.

A Residualised Housing Stock

'Residualisation has been identified as a process whereby public housing "provides only a 'safety net' for those who for reasons of poverty,
age or infirmity cannot obtain suitable accommodation in the private
sector" (Malpass and Murie, 1993). Among other things, this "involves
lowering the status and increasing the stigma attached to public housing"'
(Clapham *et al.*, 1990, p. 66)

The effect of residualisation has been that social housing has increasingly
become perceived as the sector of last resort. This has partially resulted
from the success of Conservative governments since 1979 in achieving
their objective of producing a nation of home owners. A variety of incentives has generated an exodus of the wealthier and more economically
active tenants from local authority control, taking with them the better
quality stock from public ownership. This has been coupled with a major
downturn in the numbers of social rented dwellings being produced to fill
the gap. Various estimates (Whitehead & Kleinman, Audit Commission,
NFHA, DoE) have put the need for new social housing at between 75 000
and 150 000 units per year. With the virtual demise of local authority
building, the burden has fallen upon housing associations whose performance has consistently been well below this target. While many dwellings
in the social rented sector are non-estate, low-density dwellings in relatively good repair, the lack of mobility within the sector means that these
are less likely to become vacant. On the other hand, a much higher level
of voids occurs on the less desirable estates as households leave, often
out of sheer desperation. Even amongst new housing association dwellings, research has indicated a consistently marked reduction in standards
(Karn and Sheriden, 1994) and notable examples of poor location and
design (Page, 1993). The result is a social rented housing sector characterised by a disproportionately high percentage of economically inactive or
low-paid tenants, residing within a rump of often poorly designed and
less desirable housing stock, frequently in need of substantial repair.

As a consequence, the quality of life on a number of estates is often
poor, mitigated only by the relatively limited success of housing managers
in resolving apparently intractable problems. Often, only households lacking the ability (usually resources) to make alternative choices will become
tenants of local authorities or housing associations. For local authorities,
the almost complete absence of any direct building programme inevitably
restricts mobility within their stock. This generally means that tenants un-

fortunate enough to be allocated the least desirable properties will often face long waits before they are able to transfer to something better. Such tenants are inclined to say, with some justification, 'we have done our time in poor housing, let us move to something better and new tenants can have our dwellings'. This concept of *trading-up* does have a compelling logic, but can deny equal opportunities and present operational difficulties by generating additional voids.

Nor does this rather bleak picture only apply to local authority stock. While the legacy of 1960s and 1970s system building largely afflicts council housing, housing associations are increasingly experiencing many of the same problems in delivering mainstream housing services. The political and financial influences behind so many local authority disasters now threaten to overtake the association movement. The continual erosion of HAG since 1989 has reduced subsidy levels to the point where the future of development programmes is being questioned. To achieve financial viability, associations have cut back on many quality-related criteria. Space standards in particular have suffered (Karn and Sheriden, 1994), as have environmental works. Densities have tended to be at upper levels, and many associations have resorted to buying 'off-the-peg' developments at knockdown prices from speculative developers unable to sell during the recession. In addition, associations have been drawn into developing larger and larger sites, often in consortia arrangements, in order to unlock development opportunities and achieve economies of scale. This has resulted in the construction of a small but significant number of developments of five hundred units or more, extremely large by association standards but relatively small in comparison with the more extensive local authority estates. Whilst these measures have achieved short-term objectives of securing development funding and have 'produced' additional dwellings for social renting, the long-term implications for housing management are likely to prove significant.

Alongside deteriorating dwelling standards, associations have also experienced a radically altered tenant profile. Single-person households have risen from 27 per cent in 1981 to 38 per cent in 1993 (OPCS, 1995), and single-parent households have almost doubled. Correspondingly, couples with dependant children decreased from 27 per cent to 16 per cent, indicating a shift from the established profile of households renting social housing. The picture is similar across both local authority and housing association dwellings, with associations recording higher levels of single persons and elderly households. There are also further profile changes which reflect the priority given to homeless households. One of the most striking is the increasing percentage of households with children moving into social housing within recent years. Almost a half of all lettings during 1994 were to households with children, compared with 29 per cent nationally.

Social housing has also become the focus of greater levels of poverty and unemployment. Between 1977 and 1993/4, the percentage of tenants in employment dropped from 64 per cent to a position where 'Only a small proportion of new [housing association] tenants are in full-time work (twenty one per cent) and a further four per cent work part-time: the average [weekly] income of working households was found to be £158.27. But seventy five per cent of new tenants are not in either full-time or part-time work and fifty four per cent derived their incomes wholly from state benefits or pensions: the average income of those not in work was found to be only £72.38' (Page, 1993, p. 30). This is coupled with the fact that new tenants in work tend to earn less than existing tenants. In addition, more new tenants are within households which contain no employed member. These statistics are made all the more significant by the fact that both local authority and housing association rents have risen by 85 per cent since the new financial regime was introduced in 1989.

The focus on rehousing on the basis of *greatest need* has produced the most obvious effects of public sector residualisation. Statutory duties towards the vulnerable, elderly and young children, have generally prevented single people and childless couples from being actively considered for tenancies. Within current circumstances, greatest need inevitably relates to the most vulnerable households, having fewest choices and being least able to obtain adequate alternative housing. By their very nature they are more likely to be dependent financially on the state and on the support of others. The ability of communities to sustain themselves is severely compromised where such high levels of dependency exist. Areas of deprivation are also quick to be identified and stigmatised as problem estates with problem families. This may make it harder for residents to access the range of facilities open to other members of the community. In some of the more notorious estates in Britain's inner cities, milk will not be delivered, credit is hard to come by, and employment opportunities may also be undermined. As a result, the process of social exclusion becomes even more acute, leading to a spiral of decline.

The demands on housing managers has been exacerbated further by care in the community, which has required more complex and sophisticated methods of management. Greater levels of support are now needed to enable tenants to retain independence and coexist with their neighbours. Supporting the most vulnerable individuals in their own homes requires considerable time and effort, increasingly involving tasks for which housing officers have little training or authority (see Chapter 5). In practice, their function amounts to little more than to restrain, mediate and contain. The most vulnerable often fall prey to unscrupulous drug-dealers and criminals who take advantage of their limited means. Such volatility and criminality within social housing has resulted in increasing violence and abuse towards housing staff and other practitioners. On some estates, this has created a situation in which some blocks have become out-of-bounds to officers without stringent security measures. Attempts to address these problems have been undermined by the effects of continued residualisation.

Managing Problem Estates

The estates which display greatest problems are often those which have

'for many years been used by the local authority as a place to "dump difficult households" or households ejected for "unneighbourly behaviour" from elsewhere, there will often be a higher level of crime and fear. This will affect staff working there as well as residents. It will tend to create a beleaguered and distressing atmosphere, where no one has the confidence to contain disturbing behaviour. Sometimes the police, resident leaders, estate managers and housing caretakers have given up their attempt to "hold" the situation. A spiral of disorder can set in.'

(Power, 1991, p. 78).

Within this 'spiral of social disintegration and violence' (DoE, 1993b, p. vii) develops a culture of behaviour which owes little to the recognition or acceptance of social norms or niceties. Instead, a relatively small proportion of residents either deliberately or inadvertently make life extremely difficult for others and make estate management highly pressurised. It is often the behaviour of tenants towards each other which makes a difficult situation almost impossible, undermining the process of housing management. 'There have always been badly behaved tenants – people who play music all night long, keep vicious dogs or who verbally abuse their neighbours – but housing providers right across Britain are reporting big increases in anti-social behaviour on estates' (Kelly, 1995).

One of the manifestations of residualisation has been the increased incidence of anti-social behaviour. It is difficult to assess whether in reality people behave any worse than in previous years. However, what is certain is that more complaints about nuisance are received than ever before, with an increased likelihood of incidents getting out of hand, leading to threats and physical violence. In 1985/6, 1270 per million of the population reported domestic noise nuisance to environmental health officers. By 1989, this figure had risen to 1855 per million, and in 1990/91, to 2264 per million. Noise nuisance remains by far the commonest complaint, making up a quarter of all complaints (Figure 4.1).

In many neighbour disputes it is impossible accurately to apportion right and wrong. Tempers very quickly become inflamed and attitudes entrenched, with any vestige of reason being lost. In such circumstances there are relatively few options open to a landlord. Where such disputes are parochial, the intervention of estate staff is often resented. This has become particularly problematic as the result of the Right to Buy, which has often produced situations of council tenants living next door to owner-occupiers or leaseholders. In many cases tensions are generated by different expectations of lifestyle on the part of the owner, or part-owner, due primarily to an increased financial stake in their home.

The growth in nuisance complaints has also been caused by the increasing

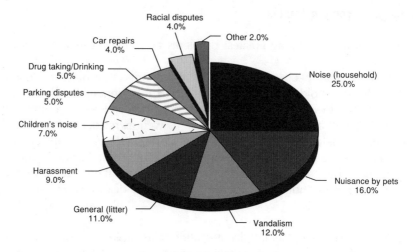

Figure 4.1   Types of nuisance caused by neighbours

numbers of vulnerable people housed by social landlords: 'they include the poorest and most deprived households, single parents, the elderly, small children, ethnic minorities, homeless people and those discharged into the community under community care policies. They are both more likely to be complained about by neighbours and less able to resolve problems for themselves' (Karn *et al.*, 1993, p. 7). Management staff are therefore increasingly drawn into highly complex negotiations between the complainants, the offenders and any supporting agencies. In reality, the substance of such complaints often relates more to differing percep-tions of lifestyle and patterns of personal behaviour than to situations of deliberate nuisance. Increasingly, in recognition of these problems, land-lords are using external mediators to achieve a negotiated settlement. Often a neutral third party will be more acceptable than the landlord, who may already have exercised sanctions against one or both parties involved. This method has proved increasingly successful, although it is only viable in situations where negotiation is possible. If one or more of the parties is not prepared to talk, other action may be required.

Anti-Social Behaviour – Perpetrators or Victims?

The dilemma for practitioners is balancing the needs of the locality against those of individual tenants. Many of those labelled as *problem tenants* are in reality tenants or households experiencing considerable personal prob-lems. Differing lifestyles may not be a problem where people can get on with their lives without directly affecting others. However, on high-density estates, in flats or in dwellings sharing facilities and amenities, this may not be possible. Noise travels easily in poorly constructed system-built blocks, as it does in any dwelling with poor noise insulation, which, in reality, pertains to many recent dwellings where noise insulation is often too expensive to be provided within development costs.

The same applies to the design and layout of social housing. Often conflicts between neighbours centre on issues which might, with hindsight, have been expected to have been points of contention. This may include the siting of children's play spaces, provision of car parking, locating elderly persons' accommodation immediately above or below family housing or unallocated open spaces. These all constitute 'fault lines', i.e. areas prone to generate conflict. They may prove completely innocuous to the many tenants prepared to make compromises and respect the needs of others. However, there are no clauses within tenancy agreements requiring patience, consideration and good humour, all of which are often prerequisites of harmonious coexistence.

The phenomenon of anti-social behaviour is not exclusive to social housing. Similar types of problems exist across all tenures, including owner occupation. Many of the most intractable problems are caused by 'personality clashes between particular individuals, whose anti-social behaviour is directed solely at each other' (Karn *et al.*, 1993, p. 20) often as the result of not seeing eye to eye over routine everyday events. Yet factors particular to, or more common within social housing create an increased vulnerability to nuisance. The likelihood of problems developing within social housing are heightened by several factors:

1 Households increasingly get little choice about where they live. If housed as homeless, they may receive one offer of accommodation which they are unable to refuse.
2 Households within social housing are more likely to be living under the pressure of unemployment and poverty.
3 As the result of care in the community, there are increasing numbers of tenants who display unconventional behaviour and for whom common patterns of living are not appropriate (see Chapter 5).
4 Accommodation may be in poor condition or unsuited to the needs of the household. Transfers within council and housing association stock has become increasingly rare due to the demands of homelessness.
5 Greater levels of racial intolerance and harassment.
6 The development of a culture of drugs and solvent abuse.

The result is often that one person's lifestyle proves to be another's nuisance.

Most housing officers are familiar with the term 'problem families'. It is often freely used to describe households who cause difficulties not only to their neighbours, but also to their landlord. Thus, on occasions, households proving to be awkward, difficult or challenging can be labelled a problem family even if they are not. This may be particularly likely of a tenant asserting their rights against the wishes of their landlord. In such an example, however, the 'problem' may relate more to the organisation than the tenant. Yet it is inevitable that some degree of stereotyping will occur, creating false impressions and labelling on the basis of subjective assessments. There is little doubt that societal images of certain groups, e.g. young black men, skinheads, or young single parents, are more likely to lead to them being labelled as problems than is the case with other groups. In addition, the lifestyle of poorer households may also attract attention as a result of domestic standards which do not correspond with the norm. While some individuals and households within these categories do create nuisance for others, there is a danger that issues become prejudged, potentially disadvantaging vulnerable households even further.

Racial Harassment

For some, the problems of living on unpopular estates are compounded by additional levels of disadvantage and marginalisation. While racial harassment is not confined to high-density estates or social housing, the levels experienced are likely to be correspondingly higher than elsewhere. Many households become virtual prisoners in their own homes as the result of threats and abuse from neighbours or gangs of youths on their estate. The nature of the harassment might range from verbal abuse to physical violence or pushing lighted rags through letter boxes.

The successful resolution of such circumstances is frequently difficult. The position of victims is often made worse because the harassment is usually for no other reason than the colour of their skin and cannot therefore be resolved. If the perpetrators have been identified, various courses of action might be open to housing managers, ranging from injunctions to eviction. However, few landlords have managed to construct a sufficient case to go through to eviction. Because racial harassment is not in itself a term recognised in law, landlords have often had to package legal action within a broader, nuisance context. Many have now included a clause in their tenancy agreement which cites racial harassment as ground for eviction, creating a more robust vehicle with which to pursue legal action. In many situations, however, evidence is neither available nor sufficient to take such action. The available choices are therefore restricted either to supporting the victims in their home, or to move them elsewhere. Providing adequate support in the home is often difficult, although initiatives such as Leicester DC's 24-hour emergency line connected to the local police station goes as far as it is possible to go. Other initiatives have centred on the local community in an attempt to raise awareness of the effects of harassment and at the same time encourage local support for the household.

All too often, the only realistic option is to move the victim, often causing disruption and distress. Having done this, a further dilemma arises relating to the resulting vacancy. Is it let to another black family if their need warrants it, exposing them to the same situation happening again? The consequence of deliberately not allocating the dwelling in this way may be that the perpetrators will achieve their objectives, creating a no-go area for black families.

Controlling Anti-Social Behaviour

'Households with few resources have economic problems and are under stress but that does not make them problem families. However, a very small minority of households have members who find it impossible to function within the normal bounds of civilised behaviour. The disruptive activities of two or three such households can affect a whole estate and can seriously impair the quality of life of others.'

(Page, 1993, p. 35)

For persistent offenders, there may be two possible courses of action. The first is to work with the tenant and their household in an attempt to re-solve the nuisance. In a number of cases a variety of factors such as poverty, alcohol or substance abuse contribute to disruptive and anti-social behaviour. Overcoming these accumulated problems often requires a supportive approach from the community in addition to the involve-ment of statutory bodies and support agencies, such as victim support, advice agencies and community groups.

The second option involves transferring either the victim or the perpe-trator elsewhere. Although this may appear the easier solution, it is often complicated by practical constraints. In many neighbour disputes there is no clearcut victim or villain. It may therefore be problematic to decide who to move if neither party wishes to go. Even when one party wishes to move, there may be support, employment or other social or medical factors which complicate the issue. Where problems centre on a single household causing widespread disruption to other residents, the most practical solution is to remove them, either by transfer to a different property, or to evict them and offer no further housing. The first option is potentially fraught with difficulties: 'In cases of anti-social behaviour, transfers, like evictions, merely move the problem to another place and expose a new neighbour to possible dispute' (Karn *et al.*, 1993, p. 20). There may be some justification in the view that where the lifestyle of a vulnerable indi-vidual is so eccentric as to cause significant distress to neighbours, it may be fair to move them elsewhere after a period of time. However, sharing the problem around, while potentially equitable, offers little comfort to the unfortunate residents forced to endure the consequences. In other cir-cumstances, transferring perpetrators may be perceived as rewarding bad behaviour, particularly where the family had already requested a transfer.

However, the alternative, i.e. outright eviction, is also a difficult route for other reasons. Firstly, there are practical issues in assembling sufficient evidence to convince a court to support this course of action. Where the nuisance is caused by a group of individuals, residents often live in fear of their actions. Giving evidence in court may result in the perpetrators being evicted, but the victims remain in the same dwelling, vulnerable to reprisals. Secondly, irrespective of an individual's actions, rendering a household homeless is an action which cannot be taken lightly. It may be one or two members in a household causing problems, for which the whole household is subsequently held responsible and punished. There is an increasing expectation that parents will take responsibility for their children's activities.

Probationary Tenancies

One response to the growing issue of anti-social tenants has been the proposal to establish probationary tenancies contained in the DoE White Paper, *Our Future Homes* (DoE, 1995b) and the Housing Act 1996. This follows pressure by a number of local authorities who have experienced increasing difficulties in implementing effective action to control persistent offenders. One of the main problems has been the time required to take the necessary court action for eviction. Manchester City Council have been particularly active in developing a model of probationary tenancies in an attempt to overcome this.

In introducing its proposals for probationary tenancies, the White Paper clearly sets out a context for their use: 'A secure tenancy is a valuable asset, providing a home for life. In the Government's view this has to be earned' (DoE, 1995c). The onus is therefore shifted on to tenants to prove their worthiness over the term of the probationary period. Within the current proposals, all local authorities and HATs have the discretionary power to grant probationary, periodic tenancies lasting up to twelve months, after which time the tenancy becomes secure. During this time, should the behaviour of a tenant or their household prove anti-social, they may be issued with a notice to quit followed by court action.

For some, the powers offered by probationary tenancies are long overdue. They are not, however, universally accepted as being either effective or desirable. In the first instance, they are limited in their scope, relating only to new tenants and offering no solution to long-standing problems. One concern is that an effect of this limitation might be to tip the balance of advantage in disputes in favour of existing tenants. Another is that existing tenants might create impossible difficulties for new tenants they dislike or wish to reject. There have been graphic illustrations in the past of the lengths some tenants on all-white estates will go to to prevent black families from moving in. There are also concerns that it offers too much discretion to the landlord which may be abused in certain cases. However, perhaps the most undermining criticism is that probationary tenancies will not offer a speedier solution to anti-social behaviour than the current mechanisms. The reversion to the issue of notices to quit may lead to a number of judicial reviews challenging the actions of the landlord. Such a process would be extremely slow, creating even longer time delays into achieving a lasting solution.

However, probationary tenancies do have their supporters, not least Manchester City Council. At their behest, North British Housing Association (NBHA) began, from March 1995, to let nearly 50 tenancies on the Monsall estate, in Manchester, on the basis of assured shorthold tenancies. If tenants indulge in anti-social behaviour, they may be evicted and deemed intentionally homeless. The effectiveness of the scheme remains to be evaluated over time.

Other Management Practices

In addition to the development of probationary tenancies, a variety of other practices have been developed across the country.

- Wandsworth have been at the forefront of implementing measures to counter anti-social behaviour on its estates. These range from commissioning a private security firm to police common areas, to the introduction of compulsory identity cards for all new tenants to prevent unauthorised occupation of its properties.
- Since 1993, Sedgefield has employed 11 uniformed ex-policemen equipped with radios and patrol vehicles to mount a form of neighbourhood watch over its estates. The authority believe that the crime rate dropped by at least 20 per cent.
- Many councils, including Sunderland and Southwark, have introduced a system of professional witnesses, who collect evidence to bring troublemakers to court. This overcomes the problems encountered in convincing harassed neighbours to give evidence when frightened of reprisals.
- There has been a growing usage of independent mediation companies in an attempt to negotiate a lasting and sustainable solution to neighbour disputes. It has often been found to be more effective to involve a neutral party to act as objective arbitrators.

In its *Housing Management Standards Manual* (CIH, 1993a) the Chartered Institute of Housing stresses the need for landlords to adopt an effectively implemented and coherent strategy in relation to neighbour disputes. This should include reference to: preventive measures, through the design, layout and management of dwellings and their surroundings; ensuring that suitable legal remedies are available if required; involving tenants' and residents' groups; briefing of residents (both tenants and home owners) on expectations of them; careful allocations, etc. In addition, inter-agency and inter-departmental cooperation are also important, linked to a programme of officer training, proper record keeping and clear practice guidance which sets timescales for action, avoiding unnecessary delay which could lead to an escalation of problems.

Strategic Approaches to Problem Estates

Many of the problems caused by anti-social behaviour or nuisance are dealt with on a reactive basis to situations as they develop. While the most effective officers will succeed in resolving some problems and keeping a lid on others, the process is inevitably time-consuming, expensive and frequently frustrating. Clearly, a preferable approach is prevention rather than cure.

There have tended to be two main approaches to devising strategic programmes of action:

1 an environmental determinist approach – where the focus is on the influence of design and the physical attributes of an estate
2 a human/control approach – where social mix and housing management techniques are considered to be the most important elements.

A third approach is to highlight the critical interconnection between the two approaches (Page, 1993). David Page suggests that there are four key factors in achieving a satisfactory development:

1 Choice of site (location)
2 Design and layout
3 Tenant selection and allocation
4 Estate management.

To varying extents factors 2–4 are also relevant when considering strategies towards solving problems on existing estates. However, the most fundamental changes become difficult to implement retrospectively. Thus, introducing new estate management methods may be relatively easy, whereas fundamentally redeveloping an estate will be harder and significantly more expensive. It is, of course, impossible to change the location. Page points out that poor decisions relating to any of these four factors will diminish the effectiveness of the scheme and potentially result in tenant dissatisfaction. However, it may be that an inappropriate decision at one stage may be compensated for by corrective action in another. What has become increasingly evident over time is that decisions taken in the first three stages will have a direct bearing on the ability of housing managers to perform effectively.

Building for Communities (Page, 1993) highlighted the increasing problems experienced by housing associations in their new role as mainstream housing providers. Its effect has also been to expose the divisions which have emerged between the development and management functions of housing associations. In pursuing development opportunities, often regardless of their implications, many associations are storing up major future management problems. Examples include developing isolated sites, those in unpopular areas and the creation of very large estates. The hiatus between the development and management process has also been at the root of many local authority problems, with layouts designed by architects and planners in isolation from the potential residents or managers. For local authorities, the lessons have been learned by bitter experience, but a small number of housing associations appear to be following the same path.

What then can be done to resolve the problems of the most difficult social housing estates? Clearly the measures to combat anti-social behaviour previously described are one way of responding on a daily basis. However, these measures alone are insufficient to address the more fundamental issues which lie behind the problems. If Page should prove right, the answer lies within the four key factors detailed previously.

Developing Sustainable Environments

1. Location

The choice of location for new sites is of paramount importance. It is, after all, the one irreversible aspect of a scheme's attributes and is therefore the foundation of success. An ideal site will be one which is well positioned in terms of:

- access to amenities, i.e. schools, shops, health facilities, etc.
- good public transport
- proximity to employment opportunities
- aspect
- size – appropriately sized, i.e. not too large to be overwhelming, but large enough to be viable
- price – to enable the scheme to stack up financially.

In reality, such opportunities are few and far between, and in an increasingly competitive market, associations are bidding against other, commercial users. The competition would increase even further should HAG be made available to private sector developers as indicated in the White Paper, *Our Future Homes* (DoE, 1995b).

In practice, development sites are often compromises based on a mixture of opportunism, partnership and entrepreneurialism. The constant pressure is to procure land at a price which is financially viable generating sufficient rental income over the life of the scheme to repay the loan. An immediate trade-off for many associations is therefore that of affordability. The more expensive the cost of a scheme, the higher the rents will have to be, thus limiting access to the dwellings to those either in well-paid employment or in receipt of full housing benefit. Although the effects are often lessened by rent pooling, which may initially depress rent levels, this can only be sustained by cross-subsidy from existing surpluses which are finite. The result has been the creation of 'benefit ghettos' where only tenants in receipt of housing benefit can afford to pay the rent and which have been fraught with problems.

To overcome this, associations have had to resort to measures to reduce costs as much as possible. The main opportunities for savings usually relate to land costs and density, which directly affects space standards. Inevitably, cheaper sites are those not in prime locations, often having significant disadvantages, such as poor soil conditions, planning constraints or difficult site layout. The exceptions are sites in the ownership of local authorities, for which associations often do not have to compete. As local authority land holdings begin to dry up, housing associations will increasingly rely on the open market for their source of development opportunities. However, the financial constraints placed upon them will make the acquisition of suitable sites increasingly difficult. This may result in the continued emphasis on short-term development savings at the expense of long-term management and maintenance costs.

The other locational issue for associations relates to proximity to the management base. The more dispersed a stockholding becomes, the more difficult and expensive it becomes to manage. It may be feasible to open a local office if the number of dwellings to be served would support such a move. In the absence of such a facility, estate managers find themselves severely stretched, often spending large amounts of unproductive time travelling between destinations. The potential revenue costs of developing in isolated areas often remain hidden, being rarely accounted for in capital costings for new schemes.

2 Development and Design

As with location, major amendments to development and design will usually relate to new-build developments. The costs and logistical difficulties involved in decanting and redeveloping are often prohibitive in all but the most severe situations. However, it is an indictment of past mistakes that a significant number of poorly designed and constructed tower blocks and deck-access blocks have been demolished because of their obvious failure. Many had become impossible to let and maintain, becoming virtually derelict and constituting hazards to health and safety. Notable examples have been the Quarry Hill estate in Leeds, Ronan Point in Newham and the Stockbridge estate in Hackney. At present Hulme in Manchester is also undergoing major refurbishment, described later in this chapter. In almost all cases, failure has resulted from a combination of poor design, inappropriate management and insensitive lettings.

One view is that design is first and foremost the defining factor in creating livable environments and that problem estates can be improved by rectifying perceived faults. Alice Coleman is one such proponent, asserting that residents behave according to their surroundings and that large, flatted estates, with little defensible space were destabilising and doomed to failure (Coleman, 1985). While few might disagree with the contribution of design in creating problem areas, the emphasis on design alone has been extensively challenged in recent years. The Mozart Estate in Westminster is one example, where the Safe Neighbourhood Unit (SNU) evaluated the effectiveness of a major programme of works based on the Coleman methods. The findings of the unit indicated that 'to look at design on its own is misleading' (Brimacombe, 1989), and that many of the contributory factors were related to economic and social factors. Indeed, further findings indicated that the some of the specified works had not only failed to have any effect, but had actually worsened the situation and went against tenants' wishes.

Many of the individual design criteria recommended by Coleman have proven sound advice. However, her rather zealous approach has in some ways replicated earlier mistakes of planners and architects in imposing a professional view on those who live with the consequences. It also ignores the substantial expertise that local people have in the way they live their lives and their housing requirements. A more responsive method of achieving a sustainable improvement to poorly designed housing has been the development of the more consultative *community architecture* within recent years.

The concept of community architecture is simple but was radical in comparison with what had gone before. Quite simply, it involved extensive consultation, seeking the input of tenants in the refurbishment of their homes. One notable example of this process is Lea View House in Hackney, where local authority tenants were fully consulted and involved in the rehabilitation of their homes. The initial results indicated a major success. Before renovation the estate displayed all of the characteristics of a run-down, inner-city environment with high levels of crime, poor health and vandalism. After renovation 'crime and vandalism were virtually eliminated, common areas remained spotless, people's health – both physical and psychological – improved dramatically and there was a new-found sense of community spirit' (Wates and Knevitt, 1987). While this level of improvement has not been sustained over the longer term, the estate has not returned to its earlier depressed state. The personal investment that tenants have in the scheme has created the feeling of homes within a community, rather than a disparate collection of individuals living in unsuitable dwellings. This approach to consulting tenants and residents has now been widely accepted as producing much higher success rates than the previous methods adopted.

Estate Action

A further environmental initiative designed to redress design faults and facilitate improvements on estates was Estate Action. Introduced in 1985, using money top-sliced from Housing Investment Programme (HIP) allocations, Estate Action has provided funding to enable the problems on unpopular estates to be tackled. The proposal was that money (£34 million

Table 4.1   An evaluation of Estate Action schemes

Management indicators	Increased %	Decreased %	No change %	Not known %
Outstanding transfer requests	18	44	22	16
Average time to re-let the dwellings	5	57	28	10
No. of dwellings (still) difficult to let	0	58	26	16
Current tenants with rent arrears	19	57	18	6
Management costs per dwelling	56	0	7	37
Vacant dwellings	15	57	22	6
Incidence of crime	2	62	30	6
Incidence of vandalism and graffiti	2	63	29	6

Source: Pinto (1995).

in 1986/7, rising to £314 million in 1995/6) would initially be targeted in such a way as to allow local authorities 'to develop and implement strategies for the comprehensive regeneration of larger more run-down estates' (DoE, 1991). However, money would also be available for smaller-scale schemes aimed at reversing estate decline.

The impact of Estate Action appears to have been positive, although the mechanisms involved have not been popular. In practice, the process has had the effect of removing capital allocations from local authorities, requiring them to undertake a complex bidding process to receive some additional funding back, which then has to be used as directed by the DoE. Notwithstanding this further example of centralised control over local authority spending, Estate Action funding has been granted to over a thousand schemes, securing improvements to over 450 000 dwellings.

In his evaluation of the impact of Estate Action, Pinto (1995) concludes that 'EA is having a positive impact on council housing management' (Pinto, 1995, p. 139). This is substantiated by the improvements experienced in a number of critical performance indicators, detailed in Table 4.1.

What emerges from this experience is that significant improvement can be made to housing stock which in the past has proved difficult to manage. However, this cannot be achieved without significant levels of investment, in terms of both capital and revenue resources. The almost universal benefits experienced by those authorities using Estate Action money has been achieved at considerable cost, i.e. the doubling of management costs per dwelling. However, the consequent savings in the expenses generated by inadequate management indicates a sound investment.

3. Allocations Policies

Increasingly, the spotlight has been placed on allocation policies and practices as both contributory factor and potential solution to problem housing. Since the introduction of the Housing (Homeless Persons) Act 1977 local authorities have had a duty to house priority homeless households. In many inner-city areas in particular, the levels of homelessness have grown to such an extent that virtually all new lettings are to households by this route. Measures within the Housing Act 1996 will result in this situation changing, with all new homelessness acceptances being routed via the housing waiting list. The effect of the new measure will need to be evaluated over time. However, priority lettings to date include disproportionate numbers of single parents, vulnerable households, and those on low incomes, resulting in the creation of highly dependent communities. This has prompted a strong lobby (Page, Power, Coleman) for the sensitive control of allocations, particularly on to large estates. The rationale is that while housing need may be an important factor in deciding priority, the management of the estate should ultimately take priority. They call for the practice of dumping the most difficult families on the most unpopular estates to stop. Instead, local managers 'should have the power to prevent households that absolutely cannot cope with estate conditions or have a history of seriously disruptive behaviour from moving onto the estate' (Power, 1991b, p. 87). Similarly, the unquestioning concentration of families with few resources and often with young children on to estates should also be modified in the light of the problems which have ensued.

For housing associations, the position is complicated by their relationship with local authorities within their provider role. In developments benefiting from public subsidy, associations are bound to offer councils at least 50 per cent nomination rights to vacancies. In many recent examples, local authorities have offered HAG and land packages on the condition that they receive 100 per cent of subsequent nominations. The result has been that associations are exercising progressively less control over their ingoing tenants, being largely in the hands of housing departments. 'Almost every association . . . had a story to tell about local authorities using nomination rights in order to rid themselves of problem tenants who included perpetrators of racial harassment and those with a history of violence and disruptive behaviour against their neighbours' (Page, 1993, p. 35). Many associations are therefore finding themselves having to manage increasingly volatile environments.

The problem is indisputable. Virtually all of the most difficult-to-manage estates have displayed high levels of child density, tenants in receipt of benefits, and single-parent households. The solution is much less clear. What may be required are policies which consolidate existing communities, encourage as balanced a resident profile as possible (including the mixing of tenures) and offer the opportunity for personal investment into the area. This may include the development of local allocations policies which include: opportunities for applicants with relatives on an estate to receive preference (sons and daughters policies); the balance of allocations between homeless, transfer and waiting-list applicants; and the ability for existing tenants to transfer within the estate to larger dwellings when required. In addition, the ability to veto potentially disruptive tenants, particularly when the area is already sensitively balanced, would be an additional tool. Many estates where such policies have been put into practice do show a marked improvement in terms of reduced turnover of dwellings, lower levels of crime and vandalism and a more settled community (see PEP later in chapter, and case study of HAT in Chapter 8). However, while such an approach can certainly be effective, it is not without disadvantages.

One potential difficulty is in implementing an allocations policy which is sensitive enough to create the balance ideally required but which is also administratively sound. There are no exact formulae which prescribe 'balance', and judgements are therefore inevitably value loaded and depend heavily on discretion. In such circumstances, decisions may be unfair, discriminatory and inconsistent. There may well be situations where allocations are determined on the basis of existing circumstances rather than on the housing need of applicants. Thus black households may be disregarded for certain properties or estates because there has been an undercurrent of racial abuse or harassment. Single parents with young children may also suffer as the result of negative perceptions of their lifestyle: 'They've caused a lot of trouble, so they're not really suitable for the offer . . . in this road there are some owner occupiers and there has already been trouble . . . so we don't really want another problem family in there causing more trouble. So I'm not going to sign this one (the offer). I shall send it back to the other area and say we can't have this family' (Karn *et al.*, 1993, p. 29). Far from helping to create a balanced community, harmony is often achieved by homogeneity rather than diversity.

One answer is to segregate different groups with different needs. A major source of neighbour dispute is where elderly tenants are placed in close proximity to families with young children. The noise generated may reflect perfectly normal behaviour by the children, but be completely disruptive to someone who is frail and elderly. However, paradoxically, many elderly people do not like being isolated from the community at large and derive much pleasure from observing children at play. Similarly, the problems of noise caused by young, single people who are more likely to have parties and play loud music might also be lessened by creating a lettings policy which segregates them from tenants who are likely to be sensitive to noise.

The process of social engineering via 'sensitive' allocations is therefore fraught with dangers. However, there are clearly many who would say that all else has failed, and that it is a pragmatic approach to a desperate problem. If it is to be used, it must form part of an overall strategy which offers a balanced service to all service users. It goes against the spirit of equal opportunities and its effects must therefore be closely monitored to ensure that discretion is neither abused or works against particular groups. 'It would be both inequitable and illegal to allow prejudice and stereotyping to determine the choice of housing people receive' (Karn *et al.*, 1993, p. 29).

4. Management Strategies

The last of Page's four key factors is housing management. Although featuring at the end of the development process, it is important that consideration of good housing management practice informs decisions made earlier in the process. Failure to ensure adequate dialogue between management and development officers in establishing development parameters will inevitably result in the potential for major catastrophes. Many of the most notable failures in social housing have occurred where estates or blocks have been designed and developed in isolation from those who would either live in or manage the dwellings. It is a sad indictment that many of the council dwellings of the 1970s and 1980s which won design awards have been the first to be demolished.

In the main, housing managers have historically been passive recipients of the dwellings they are expected to manage. There have been signs that this has started to change within recent years, but the seductive short-term benefits of a development-oriented approach against the realities of long-term housing management continues to exercise a strong influence for many housing associations. The result is that managers are often placed in the position of having to devise innovative practices to overcome physical and environmental deficiencies and deliver an effective service to their consumers.

For local authorities, the problem has a long history. By the end of the 1970s there was a growing recognition that in solving one set of problems in replacing pre-war unfit housing, another set had been created in the shape of 'sink estates' and 'ghettos' in property less than twenty years old. The effects of poorly designed and insensitively managed property were coming home to roost with large numbers of empty, hard-to-let properties, particularly on high-density estates, difficult-to-manage estates and difficult-to-maintain dwellings. It was against this backdrop that a number of the larger, urban authorities recognised the need for change in the management of these types of dwellings. Rather than continue to manage more problematic areas from a distant, centralised housing base, decentralised services were developed. The 1980s was notable for the growth in decentralised structures, starting in Walsall in 1981, and continuing within most urban authorities (see Chapter 8). At the heart of these initiatives was a growing recognition that a combination of greater responsiveness, localised expertise and control and resident involvement offered the best chance of improving poor estates. In the fifteen years between 1980–1995, many different models of localised housing management were implemented, ranging from a token presence to full-scale devolution of power and financial control. They have varied in terms of effectiveness and achievements. The Priority Estates Project (PEP) is an example of such an initiative, working with local authorities throughout this time to develop a particular style of localised service, based firmly on tenant involvement.

Priority Estates Project (PEP)

PEP was set up in March 1979 jointly by the DoE and local authorities, to run three pilot schemes in Hackney, Bolton and Lambeth. The brief was to experiment with new, locally-based housing management and tenant involvement in an attempt to restore the fortunes of unpopular estates. At the same time, other initiatives to improve hard-to-let estates were also going on elsewhere, independent of PEP. Twenty such projects were surveyed in 1982, with the intention of documenting experiences and monitoring long-term change.

In implementing its programme, PEP has adopted a distinctive view of the kind of decentralisation appropriate for local housing departments. Many local authorities have decentralised to neighbourhood offices which cover broad geographical localities, often much larger than a single estate. However, for PEP the essential focus is the estate, or where appropriate, a part of an estate.

An estate office must be provided on each estate, which can comprise up to a maximum of a thousand dwellings, run by a project manager responsible for the performance in delivering the landlord function. 'Each local office will have to put together with the local authority the working system to cover the basic functions of estate management, rents, lettings, repairs, environmental maintenance, and welfare. Estate based management will only work if a number of key elements are carried out within the local organisation' (Power, 1987, p. 3).

Over the life of the PEP projects, there has undoubtedly been some improvement in the quality of the estates involved. A DoE report, evaluating the cost-effectiveness of PEP, found, 'The overall management performance of the priority estates was better ... even though they started from worse positions' (DoE, 1993d). It also indicated that tenant satisfaction tended to be higher on priority estates even without evidence of service improvements. However, revenue and capital costs were between 15 and 35 per cent higher, indicating, as with the Estate Action experience, that improved performance is often only achieved by substantial levels of investment.

However, localisation does not always deliver the improved performance expected of it. There are a number of disadvantages inherent in the process, including the remoteness of local offices from the centre, greater expectations by tenants, problems of information flow, pressure on resources, the need for a tenant-centred culture, and cost. Brent is one authority where in-house local management on certain estates has failed to perform adequately and external consultants have been brought in on a management contract (see Chapter 8). For all of the success of the priority estates in achieving results, there are an equal number of inner-city estates which have experienced local management without the necessary structures, training and resources required to enable them to work. For both staff and tenants, poorly delivered estate-based management can prove significantly worse than a centralised system. Not only are expectations falsely raised, but staff are often forced to take the brunt of complaints which may be beyond their control.

The Limitations of Housing Management

There are also other limitations even to properly delivered decentralised management. No matter how effectively and efficiently dwellings are maintained, allocated and developed, the result does nothing to reduce levels of unemployment, poverty and hardship experienced by many tenants in social housing: 'better housing is not enough if communities have no hope' (Joseph Rowntree Foundation, 1995). While the condition of dwellings may be improved and void levels reduced, the social deprivation experienced by many tenants on estates continues to increase. Between 1981 and 1991 the priority estates surveyed by PEP displayed the following characteristics:

- a doubling in the proportion of single parents
- a substantial increase in black and ethnic minority households. On seven estates black families made up the majority; overall the average was 26 per cent, over four times the national average
- levels of unemployment reached 34 per cent, compared with 10 per cent nationally
- the proportion of children under 16 was 31 per cent – over double the national average (Power and Tunstall, 1995).

Such a scenario amounts to a potent cocktail of social polarisation and disadvantage.

What can housing organisations do to combat these social issues and regenerate unpopular estates, making them better places in which to live? While selective allocations may present one option, they do not address the root of the problem. Poor, vulnerable and dependent households have to live somewhere. The answer more logically lies in a more holistic approach to housing management which recognises that living environments cannot be separated from the needs of their communities. The problem is that this goes against the contractual model of housing management promoted by central government (see Chapter 2). However, community regeneration is being successfully implemented, and Housing Action Trusts (see Chapter 8), Single Regeneration Budget schemes (see Chapter 9) and Housing Plus initiatives (see Chapter 9) all provide good examples. Each is founded on the integration of good quality housing management with the development of community facilities and the promotion of job training and employment initiatives.

In *Developing Communities*, the follow-up to *Building for Communities*, Page addresses the process of consolidating tenants into coherent communities, thus providing the basis for long-term stability. He takes the view that the first line of defence against anti-social and disruptive behaviour should be the community itself, acting in a policing role and discouraging wrong-doing. However, in order to get the community to take on such a role, it must first enjoy an environment which offers social stability and quality of life. Factors which Page considers contribute to this include:

* adequate social infrastructure – i.e. shops, health facilities, schools, transport, etc.
* space standards – offering adequate circulation and storage space as well as good-sized living accommodation
* affordable rents – geared to avoiding the worst effects of the poverty trap
* a variety of tenures – greater social balance will most likely flow from a variety of tenures, including owner occupation and shared ownership, rather than having large concentrations of social rented housing (Page, 1994).

Initiatives designed to empower communities by providing training for employment and management are further described in the study of Waltham Forest HAT (Chapter 8). Overall, these measures are geared to a vision of proactive and productive housing management rather than one emphasising the suppression of daily problems and crises.

A More Radical Alternative

Despite management innovation and resident involvement, there will inevitably be situations in which even the most innovative approach will be ineffective: situations where a combination of the social and physical fabric of an estate has deteriorated to such an extent that a radical change is required to make it work. Where this occurs in council-owned housing, there is considerable pressure on authorities to dispose of the dwellings to alternative landlord(s) in order to generate sufficient investment to carry out works. One of the main problems for local authorities wishing to retain such estates is that usually the capital costs of repairing them far outreaches available resources.

A number of models have already begun to emerge providing appropriate vehicles with which to achieve disposals. These tend to fall into a number of categories:

1. Transfer to existing housing associations   This is largely a housing-led option, influenced by the resources on offer via associations and the potential benefits of diversifying housing management styles. An example is Holly Street, an estate of high-rise dwellings in the London borough of Hackney. Five housing associations have been involved in acquiring and redeveloping the estate – Newlon, Circle 33, Kush HA, Samuel Lewis and North London Muslim HA. The redevelopment scheme is due to be completed over seven years, at a cost of £78 million. When complete, the new estate will offer housing to over 1000 households, of which 600 will be housing association tenants.

Holly Street is part of Hackney's Comprehensive Estates Initiative (CEI), introduced in 1991 to address the problems experienced by five system-built estates in the borough 'by tackling a comprehensive range of housing, social, community and economic problems, in partnership with other public sector agencies, private companies, housing associations and voluntary groups, residents, and using innovative management techniques' (LB Hackney CEI Progress Paper, 1994). Following its success, consideration has been given to transferring a further 19 estates, comprising over 12000 units, or 20 per cent of its stock, to consortia of housing associations and private sector companies.

2. Transfer to new, social housing organisations   The creation of a new model of urban regeneration organisations reflects a broad approach to tackling inner-city decay. Housing is but one element of a wider strategy covering employment, training and community development. Examples of such organisations are:

- *HATs*, where estates have been removed from the ownership of local authorities for a period of time, during which both the housing and community is redeveloped and revitalised. As indicated in the case study of Waltham Forest HAT (see Chapter 8), such an arrangement can be highly productive, but the financial cost is significant. However, supporters of the programme argue that without such investment, the long-term costs of social and environmental decay would be even greater.
- *Joint venture companies, e.g. Hulme Regeneration Ltd*   Following initiatives such as City Challenge and the more recent Single Regeneration Budget, considerable resources have been allocated to fund projects where the public sector can be seen to work closely with private enterprise. One example of this is Hulme Regeneration Ltd which is a joint venture company established by Manchester City council and AMEC plc.

   The company is to invest over £37 million in regenerating the Hulme area in terms of housing, employment, economic development and improvement of the local physical and social environment. It has adopted a vision statement based on creating sustainable regeneration in partnership with the City Council, local residents, the private sector, government and other agencies. As with the HAT model, this approach to urban renewal takes a holistic view of what contributes to a successful environment. In Hulme, housing management alone had already proved insufficient to establish and maintain a dynamic community within an acceptable environment. Even if housing standards could have been improved, the underlying social decay would undoubtedly have continued to render the task of housing managers ineffective.

3. Transfers to the private sector This third option relates to the direct disposal of council stock to private developers. This usually results in demolition of the existing dwellings and redevelopment of a very different kind. Alternatively, if the dwellings have not suffered serious structural deterioration and are well located, they may be refurbished and re-let as private lettings. The popularity of this option has diminished with the downturn in the property market since 1989.

Further impetus to transfer was contained in the Government White Paper, *Our Future Homes* (DoE, 1995b). It contains the commitment that 'Over the next ten years, we will tackle the problem of the most deprived areas' (DoE, 1995b, p. 35), by improving the physical quality, encouraging tenure diversity and improving economic and social conditions on these estates. This will be achieved by a two-pronged approach of attracting private investment by transfers of estates, or parts or estates, and the use of the Single Regeneration Budget (SRB), which has incorporated 'Estate Action' funding. In addition, in December 1995, the government announced the creation of the Estates Renewal Challenge Fund, worth in excess of £300 million over three years. This initiative was launched to 'improve the remaining poor quality estates by speeding up their transfer to housing associations and other new landlords' (Gummer, 1995).

The rationale is that 'the best way of tackling the estates with the worst social, economic and housing problems' (DoE, 1995b) is by a focused approach which encourages mixed, sustainable and dynamic communities. Whilst such an objective is clearly laudable, there remains some cynicism in housing circles about the extent to which private sector involvement can produce the numbers of social housing units needed to cope with demand. In addition, experience of the SRB is that housing projects have fared poorly in the number of successful bids. The effectiveness of this new policy is therefore open to scrutiny.

Summary

The problems facing housing managers in dealing with unpopular estates are not new. A 1946 book about housing estates in Bristol identifies issues such as 'social maladjustment' and 'the many difficulties in the way of developing a balanced community' (Jevons and Madge, 1946). However, growing evidence of residualisation on many less popular estates throughout the social rented sector has heightened the pressures. There are undoubtedly more reports of anti-social behaviour and violence, many of which are caused by a combination of phenomena which include:

- high concentrations of disadvantaged households with young children
- poorly designed and constructed estates
- inadequate and/or insensitive management policies and practices
- high levels of unemployment and social deprivation
- absence of adequate social infrastructure
- lack of tenant involvement.

Many of the worst estates to manage have suffered years of neglect and abandonment. The least popular housing often quickly becomes identified as a dumping ground for the most vulnerable and difficult tenants. A point is reached after which only those households with no choice or bargaining power will accept such housing. When this point is reached, there is little hope for effective housing management or of quality of life for tenants.

There are those who attribute this situation to bad design of both dwellings and environment. While being a significant factor, the physical environment cannot take full responsibility for the malaise on many social housing estates. If this were the case, neighbour disputes would not exist as they do amongst owner occupiers in terraced street properties. Nor would the success achieved on some estates without major structural alterations, have been possible.

The well-documented path trodden by PEP has provided significant evidence that localised management which involves tenants can improve difficult situations. On the majority of the 20 priority estates monitored since 1982, there have been significant improvements in the quality of housing management and in the tenants' perceptions of their dwellings. Yet it has also become clear that housing management can only achieve a limited success in isolation. Sustainable environments must be populated by balanced communities. A coherent community will not only breathe life into the physical environment, but will also exercise its own level of control over anti-social behaviour, racism, crime and vandalism. While not all communities achieve this level of sophistication and development, in most instances people are prepared to behave considerately to other people.

In reality, the tenant profile on many estates is far from balanced. Racial harassment is a fact of life for many black and ethnic minority families, who live in constant fear of physical and/or psychological abuse. There is also evidence of a growing drug and gang culture amongst the young who are often without any hope for their future. How then can such a situation be altered, so as to bring life back into seemingly abandoned areas? Experience has shown the answer lies not just in managing housing and improving the environment, but also in supporting residents and developing the social and economic infrastructure.

One of the major failings in past attempts at tackling problem estates has been a tendency to adopt fragmented and short-term solutions. Housing solutions have often been seen as separate from economic regeneration, health policies, youth and education initiatives and social work strategies. Thus, while mechanisms such as Estate Action have undoubtedly improved the fabric of estates, they have done little to regenerate an area and provide employment and training opportunities. The fundamental causes of crime and vandalism are often therefore left unaddressed, whilst concierge and other security systems offer some comfort by suppressing such behaviour around certain localities. There are, however, signs that this is beginning to change. The lessons learned from the early HATs have provided some indications that a holistic, project approach to regenerating estates may offer a greater chance of success. Further examples of good practice have also emerged from housing associations pursuing the Housing Plus approach. However, such programmes are hugely expensive and can only apply to a relatively few estates. For cash-starved local authorities the only way they are able to deal with their very worst problems is either to decant and demolish, or to dispose of the dwellings to other landlords to carry out the work they would otherwise do themselves. This course of action has not always met with the support of tenants who are often wary of a new, unknown landlord.

For the majority of social housing, the situation is less dire. Nuisance and anti-social behaviour occurs in all types of housing from terraced street properties to sheltered accommodation for the elderly. However, in such cases firm, sensitive action may contain the effects. Whether this difficult job will be made any easier under a regime of CCT is debatable. To resolve such problems often calls for a coordinated approach based on constructive dialogue between officers within and between organisations. For local authorities, there are indications that this may become more difficult to achieve following a client/contractor split (see Chapter 7). For all social housing, the future looks bleak if the approach to managing problem housing is based solely on a strategy of reaction and containment. Short-term measures can only offer temporary expedients, resulting in progressively worsening conditions for both tenants and housing managers.

5 The Role of Tenants in Managing Housing
with Wendy Spray

'We recommend that any Government considering re-organisation of the local authority housing function must first give consideration to structures which increase the say of housing consumers in how the service is provided.'

'Local Authorities should devise structures which encourage rather than deter the involvement of tenants in taking decisions about their properties.'
(IOH, *Preparing For Change*, 1987)

A growing body of legislation, policy and practice has been developed within recent years, designed to encourage the active involvement of tenants in the management of social housing. Its motivation has been derived partly from the objective of loosening local authorities' grip on social housing, and linked partly to the growth in the power of citizens and consumers. It has also mirrored a policy progression within many social housing organisations, recognising the importance of tenant participation in meeting their objectives. This has been particularly true of the inner city where strategies to improve run-down and unpopular estates have depended on empowerment and partnerships with local communities (see Chapter 4). However, despite the establishment of a framework for tenant participation implementation has proved patchy, practical difficulties having emerged both for professionals and tenants themselves alike.

While greater consumer involvement has generally been welcomed, it has often encountered significant barriers. For housing managers and their organisations, greater tenants' influence can be viewed as threatening and disruptive. The prospect of having 'unprofessional', self-interested and potentially disruptive individuals with power over the running of social housing has been a difficult pill to swallow. Where a paternalistic and confrontational approach to management has previously been adopted, the prospect of professional power being substantially diminished may prove particularly difficult. The culture of professional control over services and resources is long established, and will inevitably take a long time to change. Even now, many less progressive local authorities and housing associations continue to view tenants as passive recipients of service rather than active partners in the process.

However, tenants' problems do not relate solely to the interface with professionals. Years of being dictated to over all important decisions affecting their lives has left many tenants feeling disillusioned, cynical and apathetic. They may, understandably, question why their involvement is now courted at a time of diminishing resources, having been ignored when major choices were being made about developing and managing housing stock. Apathy is often an excuse used to explain the lack of active tenant involvement in an area. While many tenants do not wish to be involved actively in determining services, others are effectively marginalised due either to personal or domestic constraints, or because the available mechanisms of participation prevent them from becoming involved. The effect is that tenants organisations may be unrepresentative of the communities they serve. Least likely to be represented are the most vulnerable groups including single parents and black and ethnic minority households.

Nor are the needs of tenants likely to be homogeneous. The most spectacular tenant participation successes often occur on inner-city estates, where tenants are spatially concentrated and often have major grievances which become catalysts for action. At the other end of the spectrum, tenants in rural locations find such contact virtually impossible, particularly if they have no access to transport. For policies intended to generate tenant involvement to be effective, they must be geared towards empowerment. Thus inner-city tenants may require the provision of crèche facilities, support workers and adequate training. Rural tenants may need all of these, with the addition of a meeting location appropriate to a dispersed community and access to transport if required. The key to both circumstances is that landlords must be prepared to listen to the needs of tenants and respond positively to them.

This chapter examines the various forms that tenant involvement in housing might take, outlines available options and constraints, and evaluates the prerequisites for tenant involvement to operate effectively. Many of these issues are illustrated in the later case studies: Hornsey Lane Estate Tenants Association and Estate Management Board and Kirklees Federation of Tenants and Residents Association. These are two amongst a number of major success stories which demonstrate the benefits which can accrue from consumer involvement. However, the inescapable conclusion to be drawn from past experience is how unrealistic it is to expect tenants (and residents) to generate and sustain participation on their own. Housing organisations have a responsibility to provide a supportive and receptive environment, creating the foundation for effective tenant involvement.

What is Tenant Involvement in Housing?

Tenant involvement is important. It is the process which allows tenants to become actively involved in decisions about their homes. Owner occupiers would not expect to have the colour of their front doors chosen for them and nor should residents in social housing. A tenant can be involved in decisions over what kind of caretaking should be provided on

Figure 5.1   Tenant involvement ladder

Source: Labour Housing Group

their estate, or whether rents should be increased. The Chartered Institute of Housing and Tenant Participation Advisory Service provides a definition of tenant participation as: 'A two-way process involving sharing of information and ideas, where tenants are able to influence decisions and take part in what is happening' (CIH/TPAS, 1994c, p. 19).

This definition and much of the following chapter uses the term 'tenant'. However, tenant involvement can be broadened to include owner occupiers and shared owners. Resident involvement is becoming increasingly important with the development of multi-tenure estates and the large number of dwellings sold under the Right to Buy legislation. For simplicity, and because tenants represent the largest group of participants, the term 'tenant involvement' will therefore be used in a generic sense throughout this chapter.

There are many levels at which tenant involvement can and does take place. This can be represented on a Ladder of Tenant Involvement (Figure 5.1) which spans a range of options from passive and inactive through to highly involved (Labour Housing Group, 1989).

Legislative and policy changes since 1980 have generally had the effect of pushing housing organisations up the ladder in their approach to tenant involvement. However, many still remain on the bottom rungs. In research published in 1993, the DoE examined the extent to which tenant participation had progressed across social housing (DoE, 1993a). They found that 'the promotion of tenant participation remained relatively undeveloped in many housing associations and local authorities' (ibid, p. xiii) and that tenant membership of committees was not widespread practice. The research also indicated that support for tenants' groups was more likely to be forth-coming amongst larger social landlords than smaller ones, and marginally more likely to be provided in housing associations than local authorities. The overall picture, therefore, despite some notable, albeit limited success, is generally one of inaction and complacency. Many organisations face a steep and rapid climb if they are adequately to respond to the demands of competition with the full support of their tenants.

What Are the Options for Tenant Involvement?

Tenants and residents associations cover an area or estate. They are the bedrock of tenant involvement, usually constituted to campaign on housing issues and often to organise social activities. Some areas have developed tenants' and residents' federations, which operate as umbrella organisations for a number of tenants' and residents' associations. They act as support groups for their members and also as consultative bodies for local authority-wide, or housing-association-wide issues. In a number of cases, tenants' groups have negotiated formal agreements with their landlords, including estate agreements, whilst federations will seek a broader remit.

Other structures for consultation include consultative committees, forums, customer panels and area committees. These have become increasingly important in the local authority sector, as the introduction of compulsory competitive tendering (CCT) has created additional requirements for tenant input. Local authority tenants can also be non-voting members of housing committees. Housing association tenants have the dual option of being involved in their housing association boards of management and/or by purchasing a share, becoming voting members of their association. This offers the opportunity to exercise an individual or collective voice at the association's annual general meeting. Greater levels of tenant involvement can also take place through the establishment of tenant management organisations (TMOs). These include estate management boards and tenant management cooperatives, described in more detail later. At the greatest level of tenant control are ownership cooperatives.

Estate Agreements

In practice, many tenants have little desire or motivation to take on the responsibilities and demands of running a TMO. Most, however, value some degree of influence over the way their homes are managed. This has led a small number of local authorities and housing associations to develop Estate Agreements. These are negotiated arrangements between landlords and tenants which specify the standard of services to be delivered. Performance targets are regularly reviewed and both tenants and officers have a clear understanding of consumer expectations. Estate Agreements have been in operation since 1990, first developed by the London Borough of Camden. The introduction of CCT will have a similar effect of involving tenants in specifying services. However, the evidence from existing Agreements indicates that benefits can go much further than this, creating greater cohesiveness within communities and an improved relationship with their landlords.

Why Have Tenant Involvement?

The strongest argument is the moral one. Tenants should have a right to a say over how their homes are managed and developed. They have to live in them and with the consequences of decisions taken. Tenant involvement can draw on the body of knowledge and expertise the residents have about their own housing. Tenants will also have a much greater commitment to sustaining their community and maintaining their dwellings in good condition; vandalism will more effectively be controlled and requests for transfers will be reduced. 'Landlords with all their resources cannot protect their investment without the support of tenants, because they live there and landlords don't' (Goss and Rosser, 1996). Tenant involvement is generally a good route to achieving the Audit Commission's aims of efficiency, effectiveness and economy.

Increasing tenant involvement is one area of housing policy which appears to have cross-party support. Their motivations may be different, but each of the three main political parties favour greater consumer participation. Conservative Party support derives from their desire to increase 'choice' and they see it as a potential vehicle to break up local authority housing. Liberal Democrat support emanates from a commitment to community politics and the Labour Party's from its commitment to the empowerment of tenants. This consensus in an often divided political environment is one reason why progress has been made in encouraging housing organisations to step up the ladder of tenant involvement.

Prerequisites for Effective Tenant Participation

Prerequisites for Tenants

To be effective or sustainable tenant participation depends on a pool of available, committed tenants, without which it is unlikely to succeed. To achieve such a situation, landlords need to be both supportive and responsive to their needs. Complaints of apathy and lack of enthusiasm amongst tenants often stem from having to struggle against an unwelcoming environment, in spite of, rather than with assistance from their landlord organisation.

It must be recognised that, unlike officers, tenants do not have the natural focus of a fully-equipped workplace. It is therefore necessary to provide adequate resources, in terms of rooms to meet in; access to telephones and photocopiers; funding for expenses, including visits to other tenant groups and social activities; and access to independent advice. These needs are articulated within the 'Tenant Participation Charter' (1992) launched jointly by Tenant Participation Advisory Service (TPAS), the National Tenants' and Residents' Federation and the National Tenants' Organisation.

Tenants also need relevant training to enable them to contribute effectively within an environment dominated by highly trained professionals. In many situations, common sense, local expertise and persistence are qualification enough to enable an effective contribution to be made. However, as financial and other complex issues play an increasingly important part in influencing available options, additional training is becoming necessary. To be effective, tenants need to develop a range of knowledge and skills. Training courses should ideally be varied, some specific to their housing and delivered locally, others delivered externally, offering the opportunity to mix with tenants from other areas. Key developmental requirements include: interpersonal and groupwork skills; committee work; finance; administrative; communications; computer; and presentation skills. Tenants also need to increase their knowledge of housing in general and their local situation in particular.

Unlike officers, whose job is to manage housing, tenants are voluntary, giving up their time despite many other personal and occupational commitments. It is vital therefore that they are provided with administrative back-up and support. It is unreasonable to expect tenants alone to carry the burden of administration between meetings and ensure that issues are properly progressed. The best solution is a paid worker, able to service the group or association and thus lighten the load on tenants. Where groups have enjoyed such a resource, it has often proved successful – however, the majority do not. The work then inevitably falls on a few tenants with the time and expertise to commit. Few have both, and the most likely outcome is that many issues are not sufficiently followed through, little happens between meetings, members get disillusioned and attendance eventually drops off.

In order to make informed judgements tenants need access to information. However, in the past, they have often been ignorant of crucial intelligence which would have enabled them to influence key decisions. This situation has now begun to change, helped considerably by recent legislation. Knowledge alone however is not enough – tenants also need the appropriate skills to understand how to interpret the information at their disposal.

Tenants must also be motivated to get involved. Often this is generated by an issue or series of issues about which there is strong local feeling. It is essential that initial levels of commitment and enthusiasm are maintained for a tenants' group to have a chance of long-term survival. It is important that the group is seen to be effective and that meetings are enjoyable. This is particularly true of single issue associations, which may be susceptible to either despondency when things are going badly or complacency when they appear to be making headway.

Prerequisites for Housing Managers

As stated in the introduction, tenants cannot participate in isolation. Participation is essentially a partnership which needs willing partners. Officers used to operating in a traditional environment need to become more open and flexible to the potential for tenant involvement. Many of the old, paternalistic attitudes will have to change. Professionals have to be ready to listen to the views of tenants, to empower tenants and in some cases to adapt to being employed by tenants. This may entail retraining for some housing managers. It also demands a new approach to the meaning of 'professionalism' within housing (see Chapter 10). In the past, housing professionals have assumed a position of power underpinned by expert knowledge. The new professional must be prepared to use his/her expert knowledge to empower others.

The facilitation of tenant participation does not rest on the shoulders of individual officers alone. Organisations need to change the ways in which they work to provide suitable mechanisms for tenant input. Structures need to be democratic and accountable, taking account of equal opportunities. Tenants need to be aware of the options open to them, from tenants' associations to tenant management cooperatives. For such options to be viable, the mechanisms by which different organisations can set up should not be so complicated and protracted that members drop out along the way. The Right to Manage legislation was an example of where mechanisms have been developed for setting up a TMO. However, it remains unclear whether or not it has succeeded (see later).

The prerequisites described in this section are fulfilled within some housing organisations. However, in most cases, they are not. If they are absent, housing organisations should develop awareness, provide training and identify the funds to ensure that they are put in place. Start-up grants to tenants' associations, and specialist tenant participation workers are part of the answer, but as the Director of TPAS has suggested (Hood, 1995), more than this is required. Organisations have to develop a culture of participation throughout. If this does not happen, there is a danger that participation becomes a 'bolt-on' extra, supplementary to the core values of the organisation. In such circumstances, it is unreasonable to blame tenants for apathy and failure to get involved. For most tenants, the more active the tenant group, the greater the personal expense in terms of time and energy expended. Few people are prepared to continue to make such a personal sacrifice with little or no prospect of reward through achievement. It is therefore incumbent on housing organisations to play their part by providing an environment which nurtures and sustains tenants in contributing to the process of housing management.

Legislative and Policy Context

As if to underline the relatively recent mainstream development of tenant participation, virtually all relevant legislation has occurred since 1980. Initiatives had taken place within individual housing organisations, but these were isolated examples rather than widespread practice. However, even now considerable differences remain between landlord organisations in their interpretation of legislation and approach to involving tenants in the management of their homes.

The first major piece of legislation to effectively empower tenants was the Housing Act 1980. This introduced the *Tenants' Charter*, which conveyed a series of rights, including access to information and to be consulted, which tenants had not previously automatically enjoyed. Although a major development, these rights were conferred on individuals rather than collectively, doing little substantive to promote tenant participation.

The terms of the 1980 Act were subsequently consolidated within the Housing Act 1985, with additional measures under s104, requiring local authorities to provide written information relating to: tenancy conditions; statutory rights; councils repairing obligations; arrangements for consultation; and the mechanisms for inspecting personal records. In addition, s105 required councils to consult tenants on proposals for changes in housing management.

The Housing and Planning Act 1986 extended the right for local authorities voluntarily to transfer all or part of their stock, but only after consultation with tenants. Although there was no obligation to hold a ballot, the Secretary of State had to be satisfied that the majority of tenants were not opposed. This Act also empowered councils to delegate the management of housing to other bodies, offering the opportunity for the development of tenant management organisations such as estate management boards. Once again, before pursuing such an option, councils were required to obtain the approval of the majority of tenants.

The third main measure under this act was the establishment of s16 grants, to be distributed by the DoE to encourage tenant participation, and promote training and education in housing management. These fell into three categories:

1 Promotion Grants – for advice agencies promoting tenant participation;
2 Feasibility Grants – for agencies working with tenants' groups to assess the options for tenant participation; and
3 Development Grants – for tenants' organisations wishing to develop a tenant management coop or estate management board. The grant can be used to employ staff or engage consultants to set up a programme for development. To be eligible, the landlord must commit to providing 25 per cent of development costs.

Similar grants are available from the Housing Corporation for housing association tenants, under s87 of the Housing Associations Act 1985.

The Housing Act 1988 introduced 'Tenants' Choice', which enabled tenants to vote for an alternative landlord approved by the Housing Corporation. This might either be an organisation set up by tenants, or an existing one invited by tenants to submit a proposal. Transfers could proceed if more than 50 per cent of eligible tenants had voted, and less than 50 per cent of those entitled to vote indicated a preference to stay with their existing landlord. Those tenants voting against the transfer could opt to remain with the council even if the transfer proceeded. However, a measure which was introduced primarily as a privatising measure proved largely ineffective, resulting in only 981 dwellings being transferred from council ownership. Of these, 918 were on the Waterton and Elgin estates in Westminster which transferred to Waterton and Elgin Homes, a tenant-led housing association. The policy was often costly, with Torbay DC spending £750 000 on promoting a transfer of the council's stock before it was rejected by tenants. In repealing the legislation, the Housing Minister acknowledged that the scheme 'no longer served a useful purpose . . . [being overtaken by] other more effective initiatives' (*Inside Housing*, 19 Jan. 96) such as Large Scale Voluntary Transfer (LSVT) and Estates Renewal Challenge (see Chapter 4).

Tenants may also play an active role in the formal council decision-making process. Under s101 of the Local Government Act 1972, councils have powers to delegate functions to committees and sub-committees. Under s102, non-elected members of the council may be members of such sub-committees, even making up a majority.

However, the Local Government and Housing Act 1989 introduced restrictions on the role of such tenant members, removing their ability to vote. The only exemption to this is if the sub-committee is not responsible for setting the council's annual budget, and/or is responsible for no more than 1500 properties or no more than a quarter of the council's stock, whichever is the lesser amount.

This act also introduced the requirement for councils to furnish tenants with annual reports, containing information about performance over the previous year (s167). Guidance accompanying the legislation emphasises the need to keep information relevant, up-to-date and easily assimilated in order for it to be effective. The objective for the reports is to 'provide useful, up-to-date information for tenants about the performance of their housing authority, to promote their interest and involvement' (DoE, 1989, s167). Tenants of housing associations do not have the same statutory rights as those in local authorities, but are served by similar requirements contained within the *Tenants' Guarantee* (Housing Corporation, 1994).

In addition to the statutory measures, and the terms of the Tenants' Guarantee, both of which are binding on housing associations, they are also expected to work within the guidance set out in *Performance Audit Visit Manual* (Housing Corporation, 1995). This is a comprehensive manual which lays down the minimum requirements for association practices and

levels of performance. Section 5, 'Accountability to Tenants', sets out requirements for the publication of information, participation and means of
accountability.

Tenants have also gained additional influence as the result of the introduction of CCT. Under the terms of the Leasehold Reform, Housing and
Urban Development Act 1993, councils entering into any contracts or
other management agreements must consult tenants and take their views
into account when making decisions. Tenants must also have the ability
to comment subsequently on the standards of performance, and to be
informed of action being taken in response to those comments. However,
as explained in Chapter 7, tenants do not have a veto over their landlord
either going to tender or choosing a particular contractor.

The 1993 Act also introduced the Right to Manage, detailed in the
following section.

The Right to Manage

Section 132 of the Leasehold Reform, Housing and Urban Development
Act 1993 is an important piece of legislation which merits close inspection.
Since April 1994, 'recognised' tenants' organisations in local authority housing
have been granted the right to form Tenant Management Organisations
(TMOs) for the purpose of managing their own housing. The ownership of
the housing remains with the local authority but day-to-day control passes
to the new organisation. This is consistent with the government's stated
objective of removing the direct control of housing away from local authorities. A major incentive is that any management functions undertaken
by TMOs are not subject to compulsory competitive tendering.

A TMO is a legally recognised, democratic organisation made up of
tenants and residents, which takes responsibility for delivering some or all
of the housing management services to a group of properties. It negotiates
a management agreement with the landlord setting out respective responsibilities. Under the Right to Manage TMOs use a modular management agreement published by the DoE, which includes a budget negotiated
with the landlord for carrying out the management functions. Most TMOs
are run by a board of elected members. In some TMO boards, especially
in the Estate Management Board Model (EMB), there are also landlord
representatives, but always in a minority. The majority of the TMOs (about
200 in total in 1995) operate within council stock, with relatively few
existing in housing associations.

Tenant Management Organisation (TMO) is an umbrella term covering
estate management boards (EMB's) and tenant management cooperatives
(TMCs). The main difference between them is that TMCs are more independent of the landlord, while EMBs reflect more of a partnership, generally including councillors on the board, and with lower expectations of

RIGHT TO MANAGE

Key Stages with Maximum Timescales

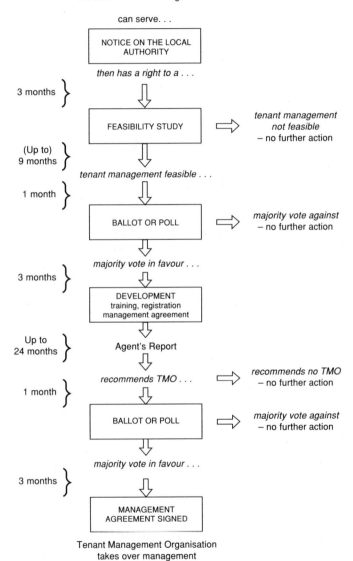

A tenants' organisation which meets the conditions in the Regulations

can serve. . .

NOTICE ON THE LOCAL AUTHORITY

then has a right to a . . .

3 months

FEASIBILITY STUDY → tenant management not feasible – no further action

(Up to) 9 months

tenant management feasible . . .

1 month

BALLOT OR POLL → majority vote against – no further action

majority vote in favour . . .

3 months

DEVELOPMENT training, registration management agreement

Up to 24 months

Agent's Report

recommends TMO . . . → recommends no TMO – no further action

1 month

BALLOT OR POLL → majority vote against – no further action

majority vote in favour . . .

3 months

MANAGEMENT AGREEMENT SIGNED

Tenant Management Organisation takes over management

Figure 5.2   Right to manage: key stages

Source: PEPtalk, issue 37, April 1994.

tenant involvement and responsibility. Prior to the Right to Manage, most EMBs used staff seconded from the landlord, thus reducing the employment responsibilities falling on the Board. However, against considerable opposition from tenant support groups and existing TMOs, the Right to Manage specified that staff must be directly employed by the TMO, significantly reducing the difference between the two models. Under either model, the tenants can choose, in negotiation with their landlord, which of the management functions to take on.

TMOs can be formed in any social housing, but the Right to Manage only applies to local authority stock. Once the process has been triggered there is then a very structured route to take the tenants' organisation into becoming a TMO (see Figure 5.2). Tenants' organisations can receive a grant from the DoE and their local authority (Tenant Participation, section 16, Grants) and appoint a development agency to assist with all aspects of setting up the new organisation. This will include training and testing the tenants to check their competence to run a TMO.

How important is the Right to Manage? Some people argue that it has made the process of setting up a TMO unnecessarily confrontational (Anonymous, 1995a). Experience suggests that even with the support of the landlord, it is an enormous task to establish a TMO, taking at least two years. If the landlord's cooperation is lacking, the task can become insurmountable, with the legal rights insufficiently strong to enable tenants to enforce their position. The DoE has apparently been disappointed at the relatively small number of groups pursuing the Right to Manage. In the first year (April 1994–April 1995) only 32 Right to Manage notices had been served, a decrease on previous years in the number of tenants' groups seeking tenant management (Crossley, 1995). Perhaps it is not such an attractive option as the government had hoped. Many groups are content with the services provided by their landlord, and have little motivation to set up a TMO. Others may have the motivation, but do not have the support to struggle through the complicated application forms for funds, endless meetings and bureaucracy. By making it impossible to second workers from the council, the Right to Manage may have made the prospect of setting up a TMO all the more daunting for tenants' groups. At the same time, it may also have made local authorities suspicious, viewing TMOs as a means to break up housing departments.

Although the Right to Manage does not apply to Housing Associations, they do have access to similar tenant participation promotion and advice grants (under section 87 of the Housing Act 1985) from the Housing Corporation. In 1994/95, £6.4m was available under section 16, and £2.4m under section 87 (*Hansard*, 16 March 94). Consideration has been given as to whether section 16 grants should be extended to fund general tenant participation activity, not only that leading to the establishment of a TMO (Anonymous, 1995b). This is particularly important for housing associations in relation to the Housing Corporation's commitment to building communities, particularly via 'Housing Plus' initiatives. Without the appropriate support, tenants will not get involved, and estates will remain collections of dwellings rather than active communities.

Where TMOs are established, evidence suggests that they are very effective (DoE, 1995d). They are generally able to provide a better, more locally accountable service, saving on management and maintenance costs, using the savings on improvements that wouldn't have been funded by their landlords. However, they currently comprise only a tiny proportion of social housing stock, representing less than one per cent of council stock (*Hansard*, 8 Feb. 94)

Compulsory Competitive Tendering (CCT) of Housing Management and Tenant Participation

CCT has opened up further possibilities for tenant participation in local authority stock. The legislation (see Chapter 7) places a legal obligation on local authorities to consult tenants at all the main stages of the CCT process: contract packaging, specifying the service, selecting the contractor and monitoring the contract (see Chapter 7). Although tenants do not make the final decision on which contractor's bid to accept, they have been placed in a position of influence not previously enjoyed. This has had the effect of requiring local authorities actively to promote tenant participation in order to fulfil the legal requirements of consultation. There is evidence that the DoE will enforce this consultation requirement. In 1994 Harrow LDC's attempt at voluntary tendering was ruled unlawful, partly on the grounds of inadequate tenant consultation. (Morris, 1994c).

CCT has also ensured that for the first time there will be a clear definition of the landlord service and targets for performance standards. The advantage for tenants is that it will be easier to monitor whether an adequate service is being provided, and to lobby where it falls short. However, it has the disadvantage of reducing flexibility within rigid contract specifications, potentially limiting housing managers' ability to respond to pressures for change. Many tenants' groups are opposed to CCT of housing management, arguing that it will lead to unaccountable contractors running housing management and that the process is wasteful of time and resources. This has been borne out in the substantial costs incurred by local authorities in tendering their services, often meeting little or no competition. The result is that tenants have to meet these costs out of their rent. However, only time will tell whether CCT has a beneficial effect on tenant participation.

Equal Opportunities and Tenant Participation

The absence of adequate equal opportunity policies has been identified as one potential problem in tenant participation initiatives. Tenant groups are sometimes unrepresentative of the communities they purport to serve. While there are reasons why this might occur, it does not have to be so. Imbalances often occur because tenants are prevented from engaging with the process of participation by a range of personal and occupational factors. It may be that the demands placed upon tenant volunteers are too great, particularly for those with caring responsibilities. Meetings may be timed inappropriately, language may be a barrier, as might cultural issues. For interested individuals in full-time employment, the personal cost of involvement may be too great. The resolution to each of these barriers may lie with housing organisations recognising the need to provide supportive networks for effective, representative tenant participation to develop.

Tenants need training, resources and workers provided in a way which acknowledges the particular needs and profiles of different groups. It is important to recognise that not all tenants' associations will be homogeneous, and that needs will differ according to locality, environment and tenant profile. Nor is it always the case that tenants groups will naturally arrive at decisions which reflect equal opportunity considerations. In these cases, housing organisations need to have provided clear indications of their expectations and must carefully monitor their tenant organisations for equal opportunities policies and practices. To ensure that such objectives have both substance and consistency, legislation such as the Right to Manage must make provision for effective equal opportunities. Tenants groups should not be blamed for problems which in reality are caused by their housing organisations lacking serious commitment to representative tenant participation.

Tenants are no more prone to discrimination than officers or elected members. However, the checks and balances on TMOs are, as with any other social landlord, vitally important. The onus is therefore on tenants' groups to develop and implement equal opportunities policies and on landlords to promote and ensure equal opportunities by both training and enforcement.

Case Studies of Successful Tenant Participation Initiatives

Hornsey Lane Estate, Islington, London

Background to Hornsey Lane Estate

Hornsey Lane Estate is an inter-war council estate in Islington, North London. There are 173 units, in 9 blocks of three and five storeys. In the mid-1970s it was the type of estate where tenants could not get milk delivered, or property insured. By the early 1990s, visitors remarked on how proud tenants must be to live there. What has caused this dramatic change?

The most important factor has been the commitment by a group of determined tenants to improve their estate. Their hours of voluntary work have not been wasted, partly because they have been working in an environment that has become increasingly supportive to tenant participation. Initially, in the mid-1970s they had to fight very hard to get their voice heard. The chair of the tenants association had to stand on the table in a housing committee meeting to get her point across to Islington council. Councillors were invited on to the estate to see the conditions that tenants were putting up with. It had an effect, and the council began to listen. In subsequent years although there have been many battles between the tenants and the council, there has generally been an underlying commitment from the council to support tenant involvement.

Forming the Tenants Association (TA)

In the mid-1970s the estate was neglected, vandalised, damp and overcrowded. A tenants' association was formed with assistance from two voluntary organisations, the North Islington Housing Rights Project and the Islington Bus Company. They lobbied the council and achieved a series of improvements, including accelerated transfers for large families; estate-based management and repairs contractor; a grant-funded community worker; a community flat; a grant for running costs; and a feasibility study for major rehabilitation, with tenant involvement.

Hornsey Lane Estate Rehabilitation Programme

Between 1981 and 1988, a £4.5m rehabilitation programme took place incorporating a rolling programme carried out block by block. This enabled the majority of tenants to stay on the estate by moving from their block into one previously completed. There was extensive tenant consultation during the feasibility study which identified the following areas to be tackled in the programme:

- Sub-standard room sizes and overcrowding were dealt with by reducing the number of bedrooms in each flat by one, by adding an extension to kitchens or by combining a ground and first-floor flat to make a single maisonette.
- Primitive kitchens and bathrooms were modernised. The lack of heating was dealt with by providing individually controlled gas central heating. Problems of condensation and poor insulation were improved, although not totally resolved by installing additional insulation and ventilation.
- Entry phones were installed at communal entrances, to reduce security problems. Ground-floor units were provided with individual gardens, and extensive landscaping was carried out to the communal areas to improve the external environment.

Tenant involvement in the rehabilitation programme was considerable. Although the rehabilitation would probably have been eventually undertaken, it would have been later without local intervention, and have been less responsive to tenants' needs. Nor would tenants have felt the same degree of ownership of the improvements or commitment to future maintenance. The process of tenant involvement also had the effect of highlighting the problems on inter-war estates to officers in the housing department. As a result, the London Borough of Islington (LBI) drew up a borough-wide programme of rehabilitation.

Hornsey Lane Estate Management Board

How the improvements made by the rehabilitation programme could be maintained was an obvious concern of the tenants' association. The building work was completed in 1988, coinciding with the 1988 Housing Act and the threat of Tenants' Choice. Neither LBI nor the tenants association wished to see Hornsey Lane Estate transferred to a private landlord. As a result, the tenants association reacted positively to an approach from LBI to the option of forming a Tenant Management Cooperative (TMC).

A feasibility study into the establishment of a TMC was carried out by SOLON Cooperative Housing Services. They found little support for the idea on the estate. However, in February 1989, a Priority Estates Project worker introduced tenants to the idea of an estate management board which proved more attractive to tenants for several reasons. One was the more explicit sharing of responsibility with the council, with councillors represented on the board. Another was that a lower proportion of tenants on the estate needed to be actively involved. Finally there was a belief that in an EMB the tenants could take on fewer management functions. Hornsey Lane Estate tenants were keen not to have responsibility for the sensitive areas of rent collection and allocations. The TMC model that tenants were familiar with included responsibility for these areas. The EMB model therefore appeared more attractive.

In April 1989 a steering group was formed. In October 1989 a ballot was held and 90 per cent of those voting (70 per cent turnout) were in favour of the steering group continuing discussions with the council. The steering group decided to take on day-to-day repairs, caretaking and cleaning and tenancy management (up to court action). They recommended direct employment of workers, which was unusual for an EMB model. This stemmed from a positive experience gained by the tenants' association in previously employing workers. The proposed EMB was put to a tenant ballot in February 1991. There was a 75 per cent turnout of which 77 per cent were in favour. The EMB commenced operation on 30 September 1991, two years from when the steering group had been formed.

Even with a supportive landlord, it took two years of hard work to get the EMB established. The demands on those tenants actively involved was enormous. Motivation stemmed from a combination of the wish to keep the improvements on the estate in good condition, a belief that they could do this better than the council, and a concern to avoid the threat of a private landlord taking over under Tenants' Choice. Housing officers' motivation was a combination of a genuine commitment to tenant participation and a wish to avoid private landlords taking over council estates.

The process of tenant participation has clearly changed the outcome for tenants. Tenant representatives are making decisions about the caretaking, cleaning, day-to-day repairs and tenancy management. Tenants and residents are receiving a better service than before the EMB was established. The estate is cleaner and repairs are carried out with greater speed and efficiency. Savings have been made from the management and maintenance allowance and used for improvements on the estate. There is an easily accessible, locally accountable office on the estate. The structures are there for all tenants to get involved in the EMB. However, the proportion who are actively involved remains small.

It has also had an effect on the housing department and housing officers. The housing department has had to adapt. The estate manager and caretaker who were working on Hornsey Lane Estate have had to be moved to other duties, since the EMB has chosen to employ their own workers. The neighbourhood office has had to learn to relate to a tenant-led organisation in their patch. This is not too problematic in Islington where there is a history of TMCs in council property.

Tenant involvement on Hornsey Lane Estate has been successful. It has been effective because of a partnership between a group of hardworking committed tenants and a council prepared to listen to tenants and to provide the support needed.

Kirklees Federation of Tenants and Residents Associations

Background to Kirklees Federation of Tenants and Residents Associations (KFTRA)

KFTRA operates in the Kirklees Metropolitan Council area which covers about 160 square miles of West Yorkshire, including both urban and rural areas. There is a population of about 376 000 people including a variety of different ethnic minority communities, particularly people of Asian and Afro-Caribbean origin. There are just under 32 000 council homes, reduced by about 6000 since 1981 due to Right to Buy. Only about 2 per cent of the housing stock is owned by housing associations.

KFTRA was started in 1987 by tenants and residents worried about the threat to council housing resulting from the 1988 Housing Act. Its aims are to:

- Unite tenants and residents in Kirklees
- Defend council housing against government attacks and private takeover
- Represent tenants' views to the Council
- Campaign to develop and extend tenants' rights
- Identify and bring forward issues of importance to tenants

- Strengthen the tenants' movement by getting resources to help set up new associations and support existing ones.

By 1995, KFTRA had about 112 Tenants and Residents Association members, covering approximately 85 per cent of the Council stock. KFTRA employed four full-time and two part-time paid staff, in addition to many volunteers, all answerable to the KFTRA management committee. KFTRA is partly funded from the Housing Revenue Account (£94 584) and partly from the General Fund (£23 000) (1994/95 figures). Kirklees council also has five community development workers, paid for out of the housing revenue account, who work closely with the KFTRA.

KFTRA is a democratic organisation with a strong representative structure. This consists of a management committee, which meets monthly and takes overall responsibility for the running of the association, and a series of subcommittees and working groups covering areas such as training, equal opportunities and dogs. A monthly newsletter is produced to keep members informed.

KFTRA has a strong commitment to equal opportunities and all member tenant and resident associations must accept its equal opportunities policy. Kirklees council has a monitoring role for all tenants and residents associations. If they do not meet the criteria laid down, the council will no longer recognise that association.

Commitment of Tenants and Residents

What makes Kirklees special? The most important factor has been the commitment of the tenants and residents, many of whom have been prepared to put in hours of voluntary time to build up the federation and to make it work effectively. For the officers it is practically a full-time job. The attitude of the council which has been prepared to be won over to tenant participation has also been vital: 'Tenant involvement in Kirklees . . . underpins everything we do. It is at the very heart of the Council's strategy for housing and has been for many years' (KMC/KFTRA, 1995, p. 3). There have been recent changes in the political composition of the council, but this has not seriously affected the work of KFTRA, since they have the support of the three main political parties.

Some of the prerequisites for successful tenant participation which exist in Kirklees are as follows:

1 Tenants' and residents' associations, and the federation have access to resources. The federation has a sizeable grant, and tenants' and residents' associations are eligible for start-up grants, annual grants and assistance in getting premises.
2 Tenants and residents have access to training through KFTRA. This includes everything from informal locally based sessions on working together in a committee, through to council-wide sessions on rent setting.

3 The council has provided KFTRA with a large enough grant for them
   to be able to employ their own workers. They can provide the administrative back-up for the KFTRA, to enable the tenants and residents to be effective.

The council is committed to providing its tenants with the necessary
information for them to be able to participate. 'When consulting tenants,
officers must make sure that tenants have all the relevant facts and background information. Tenants need to know clearly what it is they are
being asked about, why the Council is consulting them, what options are
available and the likely consequences of their choosing a particular option.'
(Kirklees Consultation Charter Procedure Manual, 1995, p. 13). However,
this hasn't always been successful and KFTRA has lobbied for more.

KFTRA and the council help to provide tenants with the motivation to
get involved. They make it relatively easy to establish a tenants and residents' association and then they provide a motivation for keeping it in
existence. Each estate is involved in drawing up an estate manifesto list-
ing the tenants' and residents' ideas on how to improve their estate and
the services they receive. Where possible these are incorporated into the
annual budget process.

Tenant representatives are involved in council-wide decisions, and can
be seen to be having an effect, and so the motivation is maintained.
Tenant representatives have been included on the panel for appointments
of housing officers, including the chief housing officer. Tenant representatives were involved in the process of selecting the building contractor
to do repairs. KFTRA has had an effective campaign to deal with dog
nuisance.

Kirklees council and KFTRA have worked out a structure for the involvement of tenants and residents. Kirklees is special partly because of
its strong commitment to tenants and residents' associations and the federation, and the lack of interest in tenant management organisations. It
seems that TMOs do not appear attractive when the landlord offers the
level of involvement in management offered by Kirklees. It is clear that
Kirklees council has provided many of the prerequisites to enable effective tenant participation to flourish.

KFTRA Achievements

What could go wrong? KFTRA has so much influence partly because they
have pushed for it and partly because the council is prepared to let them
have it. If the council decided to withhold grant and access to council
committees from the tenants and residents, KFTRA could not continue to
be as effective. The hope is that the tenants and residents have now made
themselves sufficiently useful in taking burdens off councillors and in setting popular local priorities, that the council will not want to withdraw
their support. The fact that KFTRA's status rests on this hope and on only

few legal rights is one of the main differences between their position and that of a TMO.

Summary

The promotion of tenant participation has, in recent years, become less of an option for social landlords and more of a requirement. The introduction of incremental legislation and Housing Corporation requirements have set the consumer centre-stage in terms of offering choice, consultation and accountability. For local authorities, the introduction of CCT imposes specific requirements for tenant involvement in evaluating contract specifications and bids. Housing associations have been left in little doubt that access to public subsidy, i.e. HAG, will be jeopardised unless they can demonstrate adequate mechanisms for consultation and participation. Even without such duress, many organisations have already found that properly structured and resourced tenants' and residents' groups can pay dividends in producing effective, efficient and sustainable services.

Yet despite the evidence supporting an active tenant role in housing management, the reality is that it remains largely underdeveloped, and often tenuous even where it is enthusiastically supported. There are several reasons for this:

1 Most housing organisations do not have a natural culture of consumer involvement. While housing has not enjoyed the status of more established professions, services have historically been distributed according to the perceptions and priorities of practitioners. For such a change to take effect, a major retraining of staff is required, and an evaluation of existing policies and practices to place participation as a core activity. Without such a development, even currently supported tenants' groups remain vulnerable to cuts in funding and support as resources get tighter.
2 Many tenants remain unwilling or unable to become involved in managing their housing. For some, this will reflect a genuine level of satisfaction with the efforts of their current landlords. For others, it more likely results from a combination of cynicism and mistrust, a lack of adequate training and support, or an inability to participate due to conflicting personal commitments.
3 There are clearly insufficient sanctions exercised against those organisations who continue to hold out against tenant involvement. Housing associations are even more at fault than local authorities in this respect. The expectations are explicit, but are not enforced.

Many senior staff and members of committees perceive an increased role for tenants as constituting a threat to the control of the organisation in delivering its objectives. In particular, concerns have been raised by some housing associations who fear that their access to private finance may be compromised by tenant representation on management boards. However, there is no evidence to support such conjecture. Indeed, the opposite is true, with numerous examples of properly trained and supported tenants' groups making a real contribution to the management of *their homes.*

The ultimate success of housing management is in reality reliant on the effective interaction between staff and tenants/residents. Professionals alone cannot deliver successful services in isolation from their consumers. There has been a growing recognition that successful housing environments can only be achieved by the forging of partnerships between a wide range of interested parties. It can easily be argued that no one is more interested than those whose homes are directly affected.

6 Community Care and Housing Management

> 'The purposes of community care services should be to help individuals achieve and sustain a fulfilling and rewarding life when this has become difficult as a result of mental disability.'
>
> (Murphy, 1991, p. 144)

In a social housing environment increasingly dominated by performance and control, community care has proved one of the most significant policy trends within recent years. Although not primarily a housing policy, it has had the effect of redefining the parameters of housing management almost by default. The process has involved the relocation of the treatment and support of frail and vulnerable individuals and households away from long-stay institutions, into domestic settings within the community. This has generated considerable resource implications for the health and caring professions as decentralisation often proves more resource intensive than delivering services centrally. The impact on housing professionals has also been significant, having been expected to shoulder additional responsibilities which have required new skills and extra resources. The locus of community care has shifted beyond developing specialist, sheltered accommodation, to a position in which many mental health sufferers are increasingly rehoused into general needs housing. In many cases the transition to community care, i.e. rehousing people with acute care needs into independent accommodation, has created few problems. It usually represents the culmination of a successful process of rehabilitation and reintegration into the community. However, a small but significant minority cope less well, often failed by the support systems designed to sustain them. In such cases, the result is often a breakdown in the relationship between the individual and the neighbouring community, frequently requiring urgent, coordinated action.

Where such problems are encountered, housing managers have often proved impotent in effecting sustainable solutions. This is usually due to a combination of insufficient training coupled with a degree of ambiguity about the nature of their contribution to community care. 'Many housing officers were caught in a dilemma over how to treat tenants with community care needs. On the one hand it was recognised that they had additional needs to most tenants. However, this conflicted with the objectives of normalisation...which stressed the need for all tenants to be treated the same' (Clapham and Franklin, 1994). Even where this is not the case, the difficulties in accommodating community care have been exacerbated by the increasing residualisation of social housing and decreasing resources with which to respond to housing need. Housing managers are therefore frequently squeezed between attempting to do the right thing by tenants whilst delivering efficient and cost-effective services, subjected to open market competition. The scale of disadvantage and deprivation on many large housing estates often severely hampers the maintenance of a reasonable balance between the rights of vulnerable individuals and those of their neighbours or landlords. Not surprisingly, many housing practitioners feel that they are often left holding the baby as a consequence of a policy with which they might be in complete sympathy, but over which they have little or no control or influence.

This chapter examines the implications of community care on the management of general needs housing, in particular the ways in which the expectations placed on housing staff has resulted in changes to their working practices and training needs. These changes have come at a time when local authorities and housing associations are rationalising services in response to the demands of competition. Trends have therefore been towards divorcing the delivery of bricks-and-mortar management from that of personal care. The effect has been to create a significant element of ambiguity around the expectations of housing staff in the community care process.

What is Community Care?

Community care has been largely conceived around the movement of care or treatment away from large-scale institutions, into dispersed residential environments, the object being that those in need of such treatment will achieve a level of 'normalisation' by being part of a community rather than being isolated. The success of such a strategy is predicated on several assumptions:

- the availability of resources to facilitate the decentralisation of services and accommodation
- the re-orientation of care services to provide the necessary care and support to dispersed locations
- the desire and ability of most or all individuals suffering mental illness to be 'normalised' and to live outside of an institution
- the desire and/or ability of *the community* to offer care to its members.

However, there has been widespread concern that the implementation of community care has not always delivered its policy objectives, leaving significant gaps through which considerable numbers of vulnerable households have fallen. This impression has been perpetuated in the public domain by a high level of negative media exposure which has focused on a small number of notable failures which have resulted in injury or death. However, even amongst the professionals most closely involved in implementing community care, there are acknowledged failings. Shortages of qualified care staff coupled with other priority demands have compromised the ability of health and social services professionals to respond adequately to community care needs. Considerable gaps also exist in the liaison and consultation between care services and housing managers. This has often resulted in estate officers having to cope with incidents which are more clearly related to personal support needs. The experience of many housing officers, wardens and caretakers is that they are the professionals simply unable to walk away from the issues arising from community care.

There are no accurate indications of how many people might fall within the remit of community care. Mental illness is particularly difficult to quantify, depending on the definition used and the transitional nature of some illnesses. Estimates on the range of serious mental illness ranges from 200 people in every 100 000, to an upper level of 3.2 million who suffer *severe* mental illness (Health Committee, 1994). Pressures to support frail and vulnerable people in their own homes will increase as the numbers of elderly increase significantly into the next century. Already social landlords are allocating a growing percentage of lettings to single vulnerable people. The trend is therefore for increasing levels of dependency to be supported within the community.

The official commitment to community care was introduced in the 1959 Mental Health Act, following the report of the Royal Commission on Mental Illness and Mental Deficiency which indicated 'a reorientation of the mental health services towards community care and away from hospital care except where the special facilities of the hospital are needed'. However, a series of false starts and political and professional ineptitude resulted in little substantive progress over the next thirty-five years. The 1975 White Paper, *Better Services for the Mentally Ill*, noted, somewhat pessimistically, that services were unlikely to be in good shape for the next quarter of a century: 'Financial resource constraints alone, quite apart from the physical and manpower constraints mean that it will inevitably be a very long time before a broadly comprehensive modern service can be achieved in every area of the country' (DHSS, 1975, p. 84). It proposed a comprehensive, integrated solution containing four facets:

- an expansion of local authority personal social services providing a range of facilities to enable mentally distressed people to live in the community
- specialist psychiatric services located in local settings to allow greater access to treatment facilities
- greater coordination and cooperation between the various professionals involved in community care
- an increased level of staffing to provide better individual treatment, earlier intervention and preventative work.

(DHSS, 1975, para. 2.22)

However, the White Paper proposals proved no more effective than that which had gone before. In December 1986, the Audit Commission published a report highly critical of the existing public sector framework of community care services. Entitled *Making A Reality Of Community Care,* it contained radical recommendations geared towards achieving value-for-money and developing a more effective framework for implementation. Major structural changes were proposed, including the recommendation that continued NHS responsibility for mental health services should be contingent on the purchase of local authority services on a contractual basis. This approach held considerable appeal to the government who subsequently commissioned Roy Griffiths to produce a report reviewing the funding of community care and to advise on how it might become more effective. The findings, published in *Community Care: Agenda For Action* (DHSS, 1988), were generally welcomed by professionals but less so by the government. One of his recommendations involved placing responsibility for identifying community care needs with local authority social service departments. To a government committed to reducing the role of local government, this was particularly unwelcome. However, this was partially redeemed by further recommendations that local authorities should plan, organise and purchase care services but not directly provide them. Griffiths believed that the introduction of competition would result in a greater diversity of services.

The contents of the Griffiths Report influenced the government to issue a White Paper in November 1989, entitled *Caring for People: Community Care in the Next Decade and Beyond.* (DoH, 1989) It accepted that local service assessment and delivery should reside with local authority social services departments, and that payments for personal benefits should be channelled through them. Under the new proposals, the responsibility for the assessment and organisation of care would fall to local authorities, but health authorities would have an influence over social care spending plans. Further to this, health authorities could no longer discharge patients without an individual care plan having been approved and agreed with the local authority. The White Paper also reiterated the overall commitment to the closure of large institutions. In June 1990, these measures were enacted within the NHS and Community Care Act.

The Housing/Care Interface

The Process of Implementing Community Care

The 1990 NHS and Community Care Act established the framework within which community care currently operates. It implemented a number of key changes intended to provide impetus into a community care programme which had until that point been largely ineffectual and poorly managed. The main points were as follows:

- Social services departments were given overall responsibility for community care
- Local authorities have to produce and publish community care plans
- Local authorities must assess people who they think may be in need of community care services
- Local authorities must arrange for the provision of care
- Local authorities must encourage and promote the development of private and voluntary agencies by purchasing care and/or services from them
- Local authorities must establish a complaints procedure.

The main objective of the Act was to ensure that community care was effectively implemented within an environment which sought to balance quality with value for money. Thus, local authorities have been expected to 'manage' demands for care by targeting resources at those most in need. To be eligible for services, individuals must first be properly assessed in order to ascertain the extent of their needs. This allows personalised care packages to be assembled while filtering out those in less need. A further key feature of the Act was the promotion of an independent care sector from which care managers would purchase services. This has reflected the government's commitment to a mixed economy of welfare in which better, more efficient services have expected to result from increased competition.

There is little doubt that since the 1990 Act was introduced, community care has received a new lease of life. However, significant gaps remain in the coherence of its objectives in delivering integrated packages of care and support to enable independent living. The development of strategic plans has often been dominated by the 'care' perspective with little opportunity for housing professionals to be involved. This was particularly true prior to 1990, when health authorities had the lead role, but even since this time the number of coordinated, tripartite partnerships established has been few and far between. An interdisciplinary project group reported in 1994 that 'while significant new approaches to achieve common policy aims were being explored, progress was impeded by a lack of shared vision, coordinated planning/commissioning or integrated systems among social services, housing, health and other agencies at a local and national level' (DoH, 1994).

There have also been serious concerns about the management of community care resources at an operational level. An Audit Commission report in 1994 identified four reasons for funding problems which in some areas threatened to completely disrupt the provision of key services. These included inadequate financial controls, the erosion of social service budgets for other purposes, excessive demand for resources, and changes to the government's funding formula. The effect of this was to create a major crisis for a number of county councils during 1994–5, which threatened to leave many vulnerable people without the services they needed. In

Nottinghamshire, cuts of £4–5 million were required to keep within budget, Surrey projected a £5 million overspend and Shropshire was over-committed by £1 million. These were not isolated examples, leading to situations in which support services were cut back to reflect available resources. Inevitably, the withdrawal of support for people already in the community has impacted directly on those practitioners, particularly housing staff left to cope with the manifestation of support gaps. Although the funding position subsequently improved, a further Audit Commission report in 1996 indicated that resources continued to dominate the community care agenda. In particular, local authorities have come under considerable pressure to cut costs in line with the independent sector. The effect has been to divert attention away from the collaborative approaches needed to successfully implement community care as greater emphasis is placed on the demands of resource management.

Normalisation

One of the major principles on which community care has been based is that of normalisation. This does not refer to the process of making people 'normal', in a way which might meet popular perceptions. Nor can it be assumed that individuals placed within the community are necessarily *cured* of any mental illness or disability. Normalisation refers to the process by which people with learning difficulties or mental illness can be effectively supported within the community to live as independently as possible. It is therefore, in part, a process of developing personal skills, self-belief and support networks which will provide the foundation for independence. However, equally important is the need for a programme of community education which will overcome stereotypical images, and evolve an environment in which *community care* can take place.

   One of the key features of normalisation is that it has resulted increasingly in the use of ordinary homes as the location of support and care. This has entailed the decentralisation of services away from large institutions usually on the basis of no additional cost. In contrast, the experience of housing decentralisation during the 1980s was that effective implementation was resource-intensive. The cost of providing a localised service to a level equal with that of a central location is undoubtedly more expensive, requiring additional staff, systems and premises to be effective. In restricting community care funding, the process has appeared to be geared more towards closing institutions than adequately reproviding for their residents. A limited amount of new sheltered accommodation for the frailer and more seriously ill has been developed, usually managed by either health authorities or in the private sector. However, such resources have usually only been provided where independent living is not an option. Many who have housing, either in their own right, or as part of a household, have opted to remain in this accommodation, either through choice or the lack of viable alternatives. The result has been that care and support has increasingly been informally provided by family and friends. Such a responsibility often proves onerous and demanding, with little recognition of the emotional and resource-intensive costs to the carers. However, many vulnerable people lack any such support, becoming totally dependent on professional services for their survival. In these cases, the formal care packages developed on their behalf constitute a lifeline to enable them to live independently, with front-line staff, including housing officers, playing a key role in the implementation process.

This process has not been without its problems. A number of issues have emerged which have generally fallen into two categories:

1 the professional and organisational implications of working with health and social services departments on strategic and implementational issues
2 the needs of individuals and communities resulting from the day-to-day implementation of community care.

In both areas, housing officers have experienced difficulties with the lack of effective coordination and inadequate resources to fulfil properly the tasks expected of them. Housing may indeed be the foundation on which community care is based: however it has often been the poor relation in contributing to the process of policy development and implementation strategies.

Professional Relationships

Community care by its very nature is a collaborative process relying on the coordinated approach of a trinity of key service disciplines: housing, health and social services. Housing is the key to the successful implementation of a community-based approach to care, without which there can be no possibility of independent living: 'it is beyond belief that it could be considered feasible to deliver a care package to someone who is sleeping in a shop doorway' (Health Committee, 1993, p. xxiv). The physical environment is often as important in support packages as the personal support offered by care agencies, and inadequate housing has often constituted a barrier to effectively achieving community care.

Those living in either owner-occupied accommodation or the private rented sector receive little housing support, although grants may be available to improve and adapt the fabric of a building in certain circumstances. Many single vulnerable individuals have therefore been left to fend for themselves in poor quality hotels or houses in multiple occupation (HMOs) which are frequently overcrowded, insanitary and often constitute fire hazards. In contrast, the social housing sector has offered a more structured approach to housing management, providing a service which has balanced the management of bricks and mortar with tenants' personal requirements. The social rented sector has increasingly acted as a safety net for the more vulnerable and disadvantaged in society for whom there is no adequate alternative. While Conservative governments have considered such support to be responsible for perpetuating social dependancy, there can be little doubt that community care could not be implemented without it.

In view of the importance of housing in the care equation, it is perhaps surprising that housing practitioners have been allowed little influence in strategic and operational planning for community care. This in part has been influenced by professional jealousies: 'This lack of government interest in encouraging links between housing and health services is reinforced by entrenched professional and administrative interests . . .which see no vested interest in developing closer working relationships' (Conway, 1995, p. 147), and also by traditional animosity: 'Housing professionals and social workers have often expressed antipathy towards each other' (Means and Smith, 1994, p. 190). Although the housing/social services interface has improved at a strategic planning level, operational relationships often remain difficult. However, even the limited dialogue developed between housing and social services, which may both be part of the same corporate structure or directorate, has rarely been mirrored with health authorities. This may be in part due to health authorities' increasing preoccupation with the massive internal changes they have been required to implement. It may also relate to the nature of the relationship enjoyed between the carer and patient within a traditional hospital setting which health workers are often reluctant to compromise. The result has been that 'housing agencies have had to force their way into the debate and devise working relationships with health and care providers on the ground' (Conway, 1995, p. 145).

Housing Managers or Care Workers?

The location of care within a community setting has changed the emphasis of the traditional professional/client relationship. The trend for mental health to be supported within general needs housing rather than supported or sheltered accommodation has focused more on mainstream housing staff and less on specialist care/support staff. This has had the effect of extending the additional need for management support across the whole stock rather than within a relatively few, highly resourced projects. This strategy has also assumed a much higher level of community participation within the 'caring' process. However, this may often only be given involuntarily by a body of social housing tenants characterised by high levels of multiple deprivation and vulnerability. Many households have their own problems to cope with, raising doubts about the capacity of many communities to offer the necessary level of support to sustain vulnerable people.

The shortcomings in care and community involvement in providing support inevitably impacts on housing managers. The long tradition of local authorities in housing the more dependent and demanding in society has recently fallen to housing associations as the main providers of social housing.

While having a proven track record in special-needs housing, they are less experienced in managing challenging behaviour within the general needs stock. However, their obligation to rehouse local authority nominees has resulted increasingly in housing departments taking the opportunity to offload the most 'difficult households or individuals. Thus, potential difficulties in housing the mentally ill are often exacerbated by inappropriate nominations, as problem tenants are transferred from one landlord to another. This creates difficult choices about the most appropriate allocation to be made under such circumstances. In many cases, the only housing developed for single people has been either for the elderly or in the form of special-needs hostels with intensive support. Few facilities exist for the growing number of vulnerable individuals falling outside these categories.

While 'vulnerability' may often be imperceptible providing an adequate regime of care and support is offered, when such mechanisms break down, the picture may change rapidly. This may be compounded by a relatively small number of highly visible individuals whose vulnerability may be displayed more publicly, in the form of erratic behaviour, violence, personal neglect and cliques of friends and hangers-on who have little concern for others. In such circumstances the dilemma is whether to house potentially disruptive nominees within the general needs stock, creating the likelihood of complaints and dissatisfaction amongst existing tenants. The alternative is to create special-needs 'ghettos' which in effect become dumping grounds for the ill and vulnerable. Both prospects may be equally unpalatable, although the latter solution has the potential benefit of localising the problem. This, however may be a double-edged sword, on the one hand limiting the number of households disrupted, while on the other escalating the problem to unmanageable proportions.

Such dilemmas might be avoided if the decisions were based on calculated risks, made with an appropriate level of intelligence about the individuals to be housed. However, often applications or nominations for housing are accompanied by incomplete and inadequate medical information and/ or assessment for independent living. Frequently the reason is linked to the issue of confidentiality, which lies at the very heart of the relationship between care workers and their clients. The reluctance to release crucial information to housing staff can pose significant difficulties in professional liaison. While housing practitioners may share the commitment to confidentiality, they are often more pragmatic in sharing information, particularly where the potential exists for violence or self-neglect.

Research into community care and housing management in Oxford (Gregory and Brownill, 1994) indicated that housing officers were often forced to work in ignorance because of insufficient information about their tenants. While a policy of confidentiality is wholly justifiable, it creates the potential for individuals to be placed in danger because of incomplete data: 'we can only respect an organisation that refuses to tell us things which we need to know, but there is that . . .genuine dilemma there and the fact that there is this whole issue about whether other people are in physical danger and neighbours as well as staff and other workers' (quoted in Gregory and Brownill). Such information can be particularly crucial in conducting home visits, where staff may be advised not to visit alone.

The issues surrounding confidentiality illustrate a further example of where professional perspectives are often quite different. Housing managers are expected to safeguard the interests of many households, offering the same standard of support and protection to all. In contrast, health care professionals and social workers work largely in a one-to-one client relationship. In considering when it may be appropriate to share information it is important to be clear about the purpose for so doing: whether it is merited on the grounds of ensuring the security and protection of a vulnerable individual, or constitutes an infringement in their rights and independence. Often vulnerable tenants are most at risk, suffering abuse, taunts and harassment from neighbours, local children and unscrupulous gangs or tricksters. Tenants suffering mental illness are more likely to be complained about than others in the community and may be less able to put their side of the story. It is therefore vital that allocations are sensitive, informed by the needs of both the individual and the surrounding community. If they are not, problems will inevitably arise which may threaten the whole community care process. This has been highlighted by the introduction of probationary tenancies, which offer groups of residents the potential to conspire to have a new tenant evicted because they appear to be 'odd'.

In balancing the interests of the community against those who are ill and vulnerable, to what extent should the support needs of mentally ill tenants rest with housing staff? Where are the legitimate boundaries between housing management and care agencies? In practice such parameters are fluid, dictated by local circumstances, personalities and available resources. Government policy has sought to separate the task of managing housing from that of supporting its residents. This is reflected in the scope of 'defined activities' for CCT, the establishment of the concept of a 'Social Housing Product' (see Chapter 11), and the Ealing judgement (see Chapter 2). Although housing managers primarily have responsibility for property management, this cannot easily be separated from the needs of tenants. They can rarely walk away from problems simply because they fall outside their normal brief. Reductions in resources and the redeployment of staff within health and social services has increasingly impacted on housing staff who have often been required to act in the absence of adequate care, increasing the expectations on already pressurised workloads. 'As ordinary homes are increasingly a resource for community care, housing managers should be prepared to take on increased responsibility for helping vulnerable people to maintain their tenancies' (Ghosh, 1994). Unfortunately, increased responsibility of this nature is often assumed informally, with local authorities or housing associations declining to formally recognise the extent to which additional demands have fallen on individual officers.

As a result, front-line staff may find themselves providing support with inadequate training, insufficient resources and a lack of supportive backup.

It is possible that this position may get even worse. Concerns about the motivation behind housing associations' growing involvement in the area of special needs have increased in recent years. Many ambitious associations seeking new areas for expansion, perceive community care as an attractive proposition, potentially generating additional funding which may offset losses within general needs programmes. However, 'the issue is whether they have the professional experience for it or whether its just a convenient way of continuing their expansion' (quoted in Cullen, 1995). If the motivation is primarily expansionary, the potential for disaster is enormous. For those choosing to specialise in providing care, there are major implications for training, service delivery, diversity of professional interests and organisational image. The interests of consumers and staff alike can be served only by organisations responding to the cultural changes necessary to implement community care effectively.

Community Care and CCT

In parallel with the structural difficulties involved in implementing community care, the application of Compulsory Competitive Tendering (CCT) to housing management has been an added complication. It has split local authority housing departments, dismantled service delivery mechanisms and located the delivery of services within a more commercial environment (see Chapter 7). The effect of competition has been to drive down costs for providing housing management as in-house contractors have reorganised to beat external bids for contracts. Despite protestations to the contrary, price has become a driving force in dictating the standards of housing management in the majority of local authorities. These changes have provoked concern that the pressures inherent within CCT may be incompatible with the effective implementation of community care.

The client/contractor split in housing mirrors that of the purchaser/provider relationship within social service departments and health authorities. In each case, the effect has been to fragment service organisations by separating the specification of need from the delivery of services. In the case of housing, this has been predicated on the assumption that housing management is a bricks-and-mortar function rather than one involving any significant levels of personal support. As a result, government guidelines have no meaningful attempt 'to address how either the social and welfare dimension of housing management or the extra requirements of those with community care needs can be catered for within the CCT process' (Clapham and Franklin, 1994, p. 2). The absence of such guidelines will result inevitably in inconsistent approaches and variable service standards between authorities. Users of these services may therefore once again find themselves disadvantaged as the result of location rather than the urgency of their need. Perhaps even more significant is the implication that the specification of community care functions within CCT contracts will not necessarily receive government backing and may be considered anti-competitive.

Dictated by market forces, the commercial effects on housing management will be a major influence on the implementation of community care: 'concern was voiced . . .that commitment to, and the cost of providing, housing management for people with community care needs might not be compatible with the pressure to keep the cost of housing management services low' (DoH, 1994, p. 17). Although efforts have been made by many authorities to safeguard service quality in the face of pressures for cost savings, they might prove limited in the long term. Some in-house teams may have submitted unrealistically low tenders in their eagerness to win contracts, resulting in contracts limping along, with the contractor trying to meet the specification wherever possible. In such situations, it is unlikely that a potentially demoralised workforce would be prepared or able to offer the level of sensitivity needed to support vulnerable tenants in their homes. This may be further undermined by government guidance issued following the first round of CCT indicating that quality assurance mechanisms such as method statements should only be used sparingly. It was the view of the Secretary of State that 'most quality and environmental standards, together with equal opportunities issues, can be explicitly stated in the specification for the service or work in question' (DoE, 1996). Such an assertion may be both unrealistic and disingenuous, placing the promotion of competition above the maintenance of standards. It is in the very nature of community care that individuals will require different care packages which may fluctuate over time. It is therefore impossible to predict the demands on officer time and the nature of the involvement required. Should additional demands emerge after a contract has been specified, how will they be accommodated?

The competitive threat also has other knock-on effects which may undermine an already tentative relationship between housing, social service departments and health authorities. A major failing in community care strategies to date has been inadequate liaison between statutory organisations, particularly housing and health. This is unlikely to be eased by an environment which values performance and output over all else. Failure to meet targets or remain competitive could be disastrous for an in-house contractor. Such a prospect is likely to result in information which might be considered commercially sensitive, being kept within an organisation rather than shared. The effect may be to drive a wedge between departments rather than to encourage dialogue: 'collaboration . . . requires trust and a non-competitive environment' (Conway, 1995). There is also the danger that contractors will become obsessed with process and costs rather than retain a commitment to corporate policies such as community care: 'the contracting process often focuses organisational attention inwards . . . rather than outwards' (Goss and Kent, 1995, p. 18).

Nor do the pressures resulting from competition encourage open partnership on anything other than commercial terms. Organisations whose futures hang in the balance will do nothing to jeopardise their viability. Collaboration involves the sharing of knowledge, often requiring the ceding of power in the belief that the resulting partnership will provide a whole greater than the sum of its parts. While CCT may not prevent this happening completely, it will undoubtedly erect barriers.

Competition will inevitably keep costs low, and organisations may therefore be less prepared to invest in the breadth of training which would adequately equip housing officers to cope with community care. It is unlikely that contractors would be prepared to spend money training staff in areas of work not specified in the contract. Even where community care forms a part of the specification, it is difficult to see how it could demand the quality of training required in this area. Housing officers will therefore often be faced with complex situations with vulnerable individuals who may be a danger either to themselves or others, for which they have had little or no training. This is not a problem for housing staff alone. Virtually no formal programmes exist which coherently integrate the housing/social work/health perspectives, although social services and health have collaborated to some degree. Professional staff therefore continue to plough a narrow, functional furrow rather than taking a broader, interdisciplinary perspective. As a result, the gap between housing professionals and their counterparts appears unlikely to be bridged in the near future.

The Training/Skills Gap

The absence of a structured approach to training has been a major failure in the implementation of community care planning. Competition alone cannot explain such a gap; even prior to CCT there was little coordinated recognition by housing organisations of the demands of community care. Officers have often been expected to provide a service with little explicit direction by way of either written policy, practice/guidance notes or resources. All too frequently, individual officers provide practical support while senior management argue with social workers or health authority employees about where responsibility should lie for such actions. This partly emanates from the poorly developed relationships between these professional disciplines which are often distant and hostile. This predictably leads to a corresponding lack of understanding about the abilities and limitations of each other, resulting in services at the point of delivery which may be inadequate or even dangerous.

The successful implementation of community care resides in the effective coordination of a series of inputs from a variety of agencies and practitioners. However, support networks are only as strong as their weakest link, and failure by any one of the agencies involved may lead to a breakdown in care packages. Where gaps appear, housing officers are often forced to fill them, in effect providing substantial support and assistance to a small but demanding client group. This has not only been time and resource intensive, but has required a range of skills and expertise not previously expected of housing officers. As a result, a skills gap has developed out of the hiatus which effectively exists between the reality of many housing managers' daily workload and the training and support offered them.

However, the picture is not universally bleak. A number of housing associations active in care-related housing management have employed specialist staff. In an NFHA survey of nearly one hundred London associations, almost half indicated that they employed specialist staff to provide support, ranging from resettlement workers to community support workers. A similar number indicated that formal or *ad hoc* special-needs training was offered to staff. This covered topics such as mental health issues, HIV/AIDS, alcohol abuse, and neighbour disputes. Significantly, training appeared geared towards addressing the problems, rather than equipping housing officers to engage with existing structures of support. 'This raises the question of whether housing associations are taking on board the provision of support services themselves, rather than ensuring their tenants are receiving statutory services' (NFHA, 1995d). If this were the case, it would indicate that existing care services were perceived as inadequate in meeting the needs of tenants with mental health problems.

However, while some associations have taken action to respond to community care, the London experience is not necessarily universal. Research in Oxford indicated the position to be variable, with many housing practitioners considering themselves inadequately trained for the range of tasks expected of them (Gregory *et al.*, 1995). Even where training has been provided, it has focused specifically on one perspective, i.e. housing, social work or health. This has highlighted professional divisions rather than building links between them:

'strategic discussions between housing managers and social service managers ... will only take root within their organisations if field staff are encouraged and supported to work together. A training strategy needs to be developed to ensure staff in housing departments and housing associations understand the community care reforms and their resources and priority implications for social services. Equally, social services staff need to be made more aware of the resource constraints and priority implications of housing agencies.'

(Means and Smith, 1994, p. 194)

The fact that joint training has not received its due priority reveals a structural weakness in the implementation of community care. Without greater understanding and coordination between those involved, the whole process remains vulnerable to under-performance and short-termism. Yet the factors largely responsible for this situation appear not to have been addressed. The barriers which have characterised inter-agency relationships remain as formidable as ever: 'professional and agency defensiveness continues to prejudice joint training and, in the community care field, joint working and training are usually confined to health and social care agencies; housing staff are rarely involved' (Arnold et al., 1993, p. 27). This picture relates not only to training, but also to strategic planning and operational matters, significantly handicapping the development of support networks in the community. A further hurdle to the development of adequate training is the increased pressure on resources. This is particularly true within local authorities where in-house contractors have generally reduced training budgets in an attempt to be competitive. The attractions for such a strategy are obvious, but may prove problematic in the medium and long term. 'Although it may be tempting to economise on training budgets, more resources rather than less should be invested here. The alternative is to leave staff ill-equipped to carry out their work, which will have a detrimental impact on tenants and the service provided, causing unnecessary stress to staff' (Gregory et al., 1995).

Accommodating Community Care

There has been broad agreement that housing professionals should be involved in the community care process: 'housing has a major role to play in community care and is often the key to independent living' (DoH, 1994). Despite existing shortcomings, there is evidence that progress has been made in community care since the 1990 Act: 'in most authorities visited there were examples of good joint working between health/social services and/or social services/housing' (DoH, 1994). However, in many local authority areas the housing perspective continues to be substantively omitted from community care planning. Only in authorities where a deliberate effort had been made to revise the joint planning mechanisms and integrate housing into the process, has it worked well. Health authorities in particular appear content to view housing as a practical detail, rather than a strategic consideration. There is therefore an urgent need to develop new planning mechanisms where absent, and consolidate and extend joint working where it currently exists. Yet even at an operational level there is little indication that relationships fare any better than occurs in the strategic process. Front-line practitioners within housing, health and social services often have little understanding of the others' perspective, preferring to work in isolation.

However, only by ensuring that housing expertise is properly represented within the strategic planning process can problems be avoided at the point of delivery. Community care plans are of little value if they are based on erroneous assumptions about the availability of accommodation. Equally, housing departments should, in pursuing their enabling function, ensure that housing strategy statements and Housing Investment Programme

(HIP) bids adequately reflect the housing dimension of community care. While housing staff have often been distanced from community care mechanisms, many have made little attempt to recognise the potential for joint working. Professional rivalries, as described earlier, have often obscured the true potential of interdisciplinary cooperation at all levels within organisations. However, improved liaison between housing, health and social services at a strategic level might potentially percolate down to operational staff. This would be further enhanced if supported by a parallel programme of joint training.

Support for improving the mechanisms of collaborative working have come from a number of quarters: 'further work is required to secure that early progress to address more fully the range of other agencies who need to be in the picture . . . in particular Housing Authorities and providers' (DoH, 1995). In a draft code of guidance issued in 1995, the Department of Health and DoE indicated that 'effective joint planning in housing and community care will be based upon:

- a partnership between local agencies who have the responsibility for services, i.e. Social Services Departments, Housing Authorities, Health Authorities and the Probation Service. Involving local purchasers, such as GP fundholders will also be important.
- good communication and involvement, with providers as appropriate so that their knowledge and expertise is used to inform the strategy, for example, in detailed planning once projects have been commissioned.
- participation by users of community care services, and by carers.
- developing mechanisms that enable the delivery of a co-ordinated package of housing, health and social services to address individuals' needs.'

(DoH/DoE, 1995)

Considerable improvements need to be made in each of these areas if joint planning is to become an effective tool for implementing community care. However, once attained, effective partnership can generate significant benefits across a range of strategic and operational areas: 'joint planning offers the only possibility of drawing in additional resources from both established and previously untapped sources' (Watson and Conway, 1995). In addition, joint working can produce significant benefits for the recipients of services at the point of delivery. Care packages can be tailored to meet individual needs in the context of specific environments. Indeed, the environment itself can be more appropriately selected when effective liaison exists between all agencies involved in the process. For this to happen would require improved communication and the sharing of crucial information which would ensure the development of viable care packages, including housing. This might involve joint assessments in which a more coordinated, inter-agency approach is applied to the assessment of housing needs. 'Arrangements for assessment are fundamental to community care. It is essential that individuals' requirements for social, health and housing services are identified' (DoH, 1994).

In many authorities, assessments for housing and care are undertaken independently, often resulting in contradictory conclusions or unrealistic packages being produced. The main vehicle for coordination is often via a special housing panel whose remit is to consider cases where needs may be multi-faceted. However, while they may bring interdisciplinary expertise to bear on particular decisions, they do little to achieve effective joint working. Usually operating at a senior level, they rarely bridge the gap which may exist between front-line staff. Cases referred to special panels are often the subject of disputes between departments, and what amounts to a process of arbitration usually fails to assuage professional rivalry and resentment. This can only be achieved by the establishment of formal joint assessment procedures which include joint training for all relevant practitioners.

One potential benefit from joint assessment is the increased availability of coordinated information about housing need which can more accurately inform housing strategies. This is important for local authorities, as their stock is either static or diminishing, placing an onus on them to use existing dwellings in the most effective manner. This may include special approaches to the allocation of housing which reflect community care objectives. An example might be the redesignation of low-support sheltered accommodation for the elderly to cater for younger single people in need of support. It may also involve adapting and upgrading dwellings to meet specific needs, such as disability and/or the provision of communal or medical facilities. Housing associations can also use such information to develop good practice when building new special and general needs housing. Although increasingly the need generated by community care is for non-adapted general needs housing, property type and location can be critical to a potential occupant. Clearly a dwelling's internal layout, size and floor level will each have a bearing on its future resident. Location is also extremely important, with some areas proving unsuitable for the most vulnerable individuals.

Dealing with Equality

Community care has been founded on the concept of 'normalisation' which may be difficult to realise in practice. The process centres on individuals and groups for whom discrimination and disadvantage are often a fact of life. Problems experienced by drug and alcohol abusers and ex-offenders frequently impair their ability to adequately cope within the community. This may be further exacerbated for minority ethnic households who have traditionally suffered additional stigmatisation and marginalisation. There is little evidence of the community care needs of minority ethnic needs being effectively catered for. 'Progress in identifying and meeting the housing and community care needs of black and minority ethnic people was often ad hoc, unco-ordinated and hard to sustain' (DoH, 1994). The most obvious reason is racism. However, black people are also more likely to receive less sensitive treatment due to cultural misunderstandings, manifesting in a tendency towards the prescription of drugs rather than counselling. They are also disproportionately likely to suffer mental illness, which frequently goes undiagnosed and untreated. As a result, many end up in prisons or other custodial institutions for behaviour which is a manifestation of their illness.

One of the dangers in community care is that standards of mental health may be judged against criteria relating to 'normal' behaviour, i.e. the majority, indigenous population. In reality this often reflects a level of behaviour that society would like to see as a norm, i.e. controlled and unthreatening. However, within an increasingly diverse and multi-racial society it is unrealistic to expect such homogeneity. If community care is to be successful, it must recognise the diversity of needs and behavioural expectations which exist, creating a service based on the twin pillars of ease of access and flexibility of treatment for differing needs.

Minority groups within the community may experience greater difficulty in obtaining appropriate services in areas where their numbers are relatively small. It is usually difficult to justify specialist provision for a few in the face of overwhelming demand from the majority. For others whose first language is not English, the problem of independent living is exacerbated by the language barrier. The inability to communicate effectively will often mean that such individuals may not receive the services they need, when they need them. They may therefore be perceived as aloof or introverted by their neighbours, whose ignorance of the tenant(s) next door may lead to suspicion and resentment. This may be exacerbated by religious or cultural behaviour which can further separate an individual from their immediate community. Vulnerability is also likely to attract greater risk than is the case with households who are able-bodied and healthy. Frail and/or disabled individuals, living alone, are often easy prey to harassment, bullying and violence. They are usually less able to respond or defend themselves, leaving the way clear for exploitation by the unscrupulous. Without adequate support, such situations can easily escalate, resulting in tenants becoming prisoners in their own homes. Tenants whose behaviour is erratic, possibly through mental illness, are also more likely to be the subject of complaint, while being less able to respond in their own defence.

It is clearly optimistic to believe that 'the community' will offer a duty of care envisaged in community care to all individuals equally. Race, gender, age and disability will all influence the degree of empathy between carers and the cared for. In reality, much of this 'care' is little more than location and treatment in the community rather than any real semblance of independent living. This is often clearly illustrated in the 'nimby' (not in my back yard) syndrome exhibited by communities when faced with the prospect of mentally ill neighbours. The usual reaction is one of immediate rejection based either on the fear that house prices will be adversely affected or that they or their children are in imminent danger. This is caused in part by blatant prejudice and in part by ignorance. The debate amongst housing/health/planning professionals is whether it is better to inform potential neighbours about the nature of an individual's illness before moving them into the community, or to respect confidentiality at all times. Proponents of the former option suggest that some level of preparation may allay fears and galvanise supportive intent. Opponents retort that 'normal' people do not have to get the permission of neighbours before moving into a new home; why should it be necessary simply because someone is ill? Clearly, the rights of the mentally ill must be upheld, particularly when they are not in a position to do so themselves. However, a pragmatic view might be that any arrangement which improves the possibility that community care will work effectively may be justified.

This dilemma encapsulates the tension between community care and equal opportunities. The effectiveness of the normalisation strategy hinges on the ability of individuals to lead a life of their own choosing, free of victimisation and discrimination. However, communities rarely allow even fit and healthy households to achieve such an objective. Discrimination on the grounds of race, gender, disability, sexual orientation, etc. are well-documented phenomena; mental illness adds yet another level on to multiple discrimination. Support networks therefore often experience considerable pressures in preventing such problems threatening independent living. To succeed, a range of management responses is required, including sensitive allocations which ensure that vulnerable people are not rehoused in blocks or on estates where nuisance and harassment is rife. Speedy responses to evidence of victimisation or abuse are also needed, whether through legal action or other forms of intervention. Most importantly, effective liaison with the community and other agencies such as the police, social services, health authorities, probation service, etc. is vital to ensure the best possible support is available when required.

Summary

Community care is undoubtedly one of the most significant social policies to affect social housing managers within recent years. More radical organisational change may have resulted from decentralisation and/or CCT, but neither have universal application to social landlords. Mental health sufferers are not confined to inner cities, nor to areas of poor housing with high levels of housing need. While the problem may be exacerbated by these factors, the impact is as likely to be experienced in rural Devon as in urban London.

It has come to the fore as housing managers have grappled with the effects of an established process of residualisation (see Chapter 4). The profile of new tenants moving into social housing indicates greater levels of economic dependency and deprivation, while at the same time resources have declined, due to reducing subsidy levels and constraints on the ability to raise finance. The 'community' into which many vulnerable people are being placed is often therefore in no position to offer the level of support and sustenance which community care might envisage. In many cases, discharge into independent housing merely constitutes a localisation of treatment rather than a programme of developing an improved quality of life. While there may be limited dissent amongst the non-incarcerated that the large Victorian mental institutions offered little in the way of true rehabilitation or dignity, they did offer security. Many ill and disabled people who live independently have found themselves to be the butt of harassment, abuse and violence from the communities in which they live.

There are no statistics which definitively measure whether community care is working. As a process to empty mental hospitals it appears to have been successful. However, what is less clear is whether the resulting outcomes have improved lifestyles or created additional problems for those who have been relocated. In the majority of cases, community care may have proved a positive experience, opening up new horizons and providing additional opportunities. However, for a significant number, the outcome has been less satisfactory. They have been unable to adapt to their new environment either because of the pressures of independent living or because of shortcomings in their own behaviour. In such cases, housing officers are often drawn into providing services which go far beyond their role as housing managers.

There appears to be a growing acceptance amongst many housing organisations that they cannot rely on formal care packages delivering the necessary levels of support. Rather than seeking to further develop relationships with social services and health, many housing associations have employed specialist care staff responsible for community care issues within the organisation. Although the provision of specialist accommodation has traditionally been an area in which associations have had substantial experience, the increasing use of general needs accommodation for the mentally ill has created the need for a new style of service. 'The challenge will be to ensure that these tenants receive adequate care and support services. Housing managers may need to redefine their activities so that they are delivering this support. On the other hand, they may take the view that these services are the responsibility of other partners. Either way, landlords will not be able to duck the responsibility of ensuring that vulnerable tenants receive the support they require' (NFHA, 1995d).

If the quality of services required to sustain independence is to be achieved, community care has to be collaborative. However, while joint working between the three main 'players', social services, health and housing, has improved, this has not been widespread. Nor has housing featured highly in the strategic planning process which drives the overall implementation programme. Serious gaps continue to exist at both senior management level and amongst front-line staff, threatening to undermine the credibility of community care. Fault does not lie in any single area; political, professional and organisational frictions all combine to erect barriers to effective partnership. Attempts to overcome these have not been helped by the increasing pressures of competition across the public sector. The effect has been to produce an environment in which mistrust, confidentiality and performance is more apparent than partnership and collaboration.

Those suffering most from the lack of coordination are the community and the front-line staff whose job is to provide day-to-day services. While social workers and health professionals can withdraw from providing support, either in response to a client's wishes or as resources contract, this is rarely an option for housing staff responsible for managing stock. They may be left isolated, attempting to resolve or contain highly volatile situations, often with little training or support. In many cases, they may be acting intuitively rather than with any certainty that what they are doing is correct. This has been exacerbated by the lack of joint training which might clarify professional boundaries and disseminate information about the different professional constraints and objectives which dictate practice.

There is an undoubted dilemma inherent in community care which is difficult to resolve. Most social landlords and their staff are committed to delivering high-quality services to their consumers, particularly those most in need. Few housing officers would be happy to draw an arbitrary boundary around their involvement with mentally ill tenants simply because they were acting outside of a contract specification or job description. However, the practical pressures all point to this happening. Employees of contractors will be expected to resolve tenant problems in the least expensive way, thus keeping within the contract price. Housing association staff are facing similar pressures, with the rationalisation of costs resulting in larger patch sizes and broader responsibilities. The result is that staff are often caught between their conscience and the demands of the job. This will be perpetuated as long as community care continues to be implemented as it is currently. If housing is not fully integrated into the planning and operational mechanisms of community care, the danger is that the community will not become a safe place to live and that community care will become discredited and despised.

While much of this chapter has highlighted the negative aspects of community care, there are also many examples of good practice and innovation. It would therefore be wrong to consider the policy a failure, because substantial benefits have accrued to the many individuals benefiting from newly found independence. However, the success stories tend to be *ad hoc* and dispersed, often relying on the enthusiasm and expertise of one or more individuals. There is much to be improved if such benefits are to become the norm rather than isolated examples. In the meantime the signs look ominous, with few indications that the hurdles to community care can be overcome any more effectively in the future than has been achieved in the past.

7 Privatising Housing Management

'Competitive tendering for the local authority housing management function will clarify and define the whole business of housing management. Tasks and activities will have to be specified – and who does them, how often and to what standard of performance . . . Above all, competitive tendering will ensure that services are provided by those best able to provide them. This can only be in the interests of tenants, chargepayers and taxpayers alike.'

(Sir George Young, 1993)

The Framework for Compulsory Competitive Tendering (CCT)

Perhaps the greatest impact on social housing has resulted from the trend towards the privatisation, or rather *commercialisation*, of the management function. This has been one in a raft of policies (see Chapter 1) designed to shift the locus of control for social housing away from local authorities. The main, but not exclusive vehicle for implementing such change is CCT, the effects of which have been felt from April 1996, as authorities have systematically tendered their landlord functions. This chapter details the policy and statutory framework within which CCT operates, and the main issues inherent in its implementation. Also examined are different organisational approaches to CCT, including illustrative case studies of specific local authority experiences.

For most local authorities, the imposition of CCT has proved a major diversion, eclipsing virtually every other operational issue. Already it has impacted on all aspects of housing departments' work imposing major structural changes and the reappraisal of all working practices. At this stage it is possible only to speculate on the potential long-term impact on both the providers and consumers of services. Although the first round of tendering has seen the majority of contracts won by in-house teams, future service delivery will undoubtedly change as a result. This will largely follow from the reorientation of cultural attitudes and working practices which have accompanied the tendering process.

Privatisation is not a new concept for social housing. One of the first actions of the Thatcher government elected in 1979 was to introduce the Right to Buy which offered the opportunity for council tenants to become owner occupiers. Its success was such that by 1987, proceeds from housing privatisation, principally council house sales, had outstripped all other government privatisation programmes added together (Forrest and Murie, 1988). The result was the removal of over a million and a half dwellings from the public sector, relocated into private ownership. However, despite the dramatic effects of such an initiative, 'Far from the Right to Buy representing the thick end of the privatisation wedge, in retrospect it may be seen as the precursor to the complete dismantling of the council house sector and the removal of housing provision from the control of locally elected bodies' (Forrest and Murie, 1988, p. 5). Additional measures were introduced in the Housing Act 1988 to encourage council tenants to opt for an alternative landlord, under both the provisions of Tenants' Choice and proposals for Housing Action Trusts (see Chapter 8). At the same time, local authorities were being increasingly required to compete for capital resources as greater proportions of the government's Housing Investment Programme (HIP) was hived off into special initiatives such as Estate Action, and area improvement programmes. The culmination of this privatisation trend has seen the imposition of open market principles into the management of council housing via Compulsory Competitive Tendering (CCT). This has paved the way for a realignment of the traditional values of public housing management towards a contractual model, at the same time interpreting social housing management within an increasingly narrow perspective (see Chapter 2).

CCT has been considered by many to be the most fundamental and far-reaching change to housing management since public housing was substantively established in the 1920s and 30s. The implications may be so widespread that the whole face of social housing may be altered. Although the measures currently relate exclusively to local authorities, housing associations have and will be inexorably implicated by the process as potential contractors or the beneficiaries of housing stock transfers pursued to avoid CCT. At the time of writing the full effects can only be the subject of speculation, with much depending on future changes in government. However, irrespective of the actual outcomes of the contract tendering process, CCT represents a wind of change unlikely to be completely reversed irrespective of political control. It has already prompted the widespread re-evaluation of key operational areas. These include organisational culture, employment and staff development policies, style and content of services, the role of consumers, and the orientation of the housing profession itself.

A Policy Framework for CCT

The framework for CCT was introduced by the Thatcher government soon after its election in 1979. Initially, proposals related to those blue-collar services which had an equivalent counterpart in the commercial sector such as refuse collection, cleansing and catering and grounds and vehicle maintenance. They were founded on the strongly held belief within government circles that providing such services within the relatively closed world of local government was compromised due to a lack of real competition. The perceived effect was that inefficient, or at the very least *uncompetitive* services cost more, undermining the government's efforts to reduce the level of the Public Sector Borrowing Requirement (PSBR). This was linked to the tangential, but highly significant issue, that those local authorities with the most developed manual services were also most likely to be inner-city, labour-controlled councils, often openly opposed to government policies.

It has been widely speculated that the drive for housing management CCT came directly from the prime minister (perhaps emanating from his previous experience as a local authority chair of housing) rather than from the DoE. At the Conservative Party local government conference on 2 March 1991, John Major indicated 'If a council's housing management is not delivering results, then it is high time to bring in a new management team. The job of councils is to choose the best way of providing what people want; it is not to protect their own staff if they are not performing up to the mark.' References had already been made, however, in the 1987 White Paper, *Housing: The Government's Proposals*, which indicated:

'In some areas the system has provided good quality housing and management. But in many big cities local authority housing operations are so large that they inevitably risk becoming distant and bureaucratic. Insensitive design and bad management have alienated tenants and left housing badly maintained. . . . Exposing councils to healthy competition should also contribute to a better general standard of services even for tenants who do not transfer [to other landlords].'

The policy rationale behind CCT has therefore been to locate housing management services within the framework of competition, designed to deliver value for money and greater sensitivity and responsiveness for consumers. Its success in achieving these objectives remains to be evaluated over time. However, whatever the commercial success of housing management CCT, the requirement to compete in the open market and the process of tendering will generate considerable spin-off effects.

In a speech to the ADC/AMA conference on CCT in December 1992, Sir George Young introduced the government's proposals for housing management CCT in the following manner:

'This Government shares with all of you the aim of good management of social rented housing. And I suspect all of us recognise that in some areas housing management at present remains inadequate and ineffective. And in all areas – good and bad – there is always scope for improvement. Tenants have a right to expect good management. In the Citizen's Charter we are committed to quality in housing management, as in other areas of the public services. Good management must be cost-effective, but above all responsive. That requires diverse and flexible systems which allow – and indeed in some cases require – local authorities to delegate management tasks to others where they think, or it can be shown, that they will be better undertaken.'

He went on to outline the government's commitment to promote 'three routes to the delegation of housing management', which were:

- a general power for local authorities to delegate the management of their housing stock (or in most cases parts of it) to a third party
- delegation to tenant management organisations
- compulsory competitive tendering.

CCT was therefore introduced as a policy built on three pillars: delegation, competition and tenant involvement, outlining a timetable which envisaged the first contracts being let at the beginning of 1996/7. This accelerated the CCT debate which had already commenced in June 1992 following the issue of a DoE consultation document, *Competing for Quality in Housing*, which stated: 'Recent government reforms have been designed to increase the efficiency with which councils manage their housing, to improve the service they give to their tenants and to ensure that tenants get full value for the rent they pay' (DoE, 1992b, p. 2).

The rationale for CCT was justified as offering 'the prospect of breaking down entrenched monopolies and generating large gains in efficiency through competition', pointing to significant cost savings, ranging from 6 to 15 per cent, achieved in other services already subject to CCT. Eight pilot authorities were established in 1992 (Table 7.1), each of which was designated to examine the practical operation of a specific aspect of CCT and feed the results back to the DoE. However, the arrangement was purely voluntary, and the government offered no additional funding to reflect the increased workload. Most participants felt that the potential benefits of being involved at the outset, thus having the opportunity to shape CCT legislation, was worth the cost, which would in any event have been incurred at some future date.

A further consultation paper, *Compulsory Competitive Tendering of Housing Management* (DoE, 1993c), was issued in 1993. It indicated the government's intention to introduce specific provisions for comprehensive tenant consultation before management agreements are entered into: 'there is no question of authorities being able to enter into management agreement without tenant consultation'. This would also be extended to the subsequent monitoring of the contractor's performance. Also contained within the paper were proposals for the scope of defined activity, a categorisation which would ultimately determine which functions had to be the subject of competition. The scope of the 'definition' centred largely on those functions accounted for within the HRA, representing the landlord role.

An important principle established by the paper was the expectation that the process of CCT would result in the splitting of housing depart-

Table 7.1   Pilot authorities for CCT

Rochdale	– tenant consultation before a management agreement
Westminster	– monitoring management agreements
Derby	– the scope of the defined activity and the client/contractor split
Brent	– the development of contract specifications
East Staffs	– the need for management and the cultural change because of CCT
Newham	– the interface with capital programmes
Mansfield	– the effect on warden services
Mid Suffolk	– the potential effect of CCT on small housing authorities

ments to facilitate the separation of the client and contractor functions. The divisions would relate to the strategic and policy functions, known as the *client-side*, and day-to-day management, termed the *contractor-side*. Only the functions carried out by the *contractor* had to be tendered, and these were covered by a list of *defined activities* (see Table 7.3). The result would be one of three possible outcomes: that the landlord functions would continue to be carried out in-house if the contract was won competitively; it would be contracted out if an external bid was cheaper/ better; or it could be contracted out voluntarily. The client, or strategic and enabling role was excluded from the scope of defined activities and therefore not expected to be tendered. Also excluded from the scope of defined activity were tenant consultation, providing tenant information, and dealing with complaints and enquiries. In addition, local authorities were specifically prevented from delegating their statutory responsibilities, i.e. the provision of housing benefit, Right to Buy, Rent to Mortgage adjudications and homelessness determinations. However, certain aspects of the *administration* of these functions might be contracted out.

Competing for Quality in Housing (DoE, 1992b) also proposed placing authorities into a series of bands which would determine the timescale by which they would be required to go to tender. This phasing was in recognition of the fact that 'not all authorities would be as well prepared for subjecting their housing management to CCT and that a market would need time to develop' (DoE, 1993c). The initial proposal was for authorities to be placed into three bands based on: size, number of contracts to be let, readiness, and the existing tenant consultation mechanisms in place. However, both the timing and banding subsequently changed due to the emergence of several significant factors which would affect the ability of some authorities to adequately prepare for CCT. These factors included:

- Consultation with tenants
- Local government reorganisation
- Large Scale Voluntary Transfers.

The number of bands increased to five, a response to the relative lack of readiness of many smaller authorities to go to tender within the original timescale. In addition, the government was concerned that to flood the nascent market with many similar types of contracts would overload the resources of potential bidders, thus stifling competition. The result was that these authorities were placed into two bands, thus spreading the process of tendering over two years. However, so as not to suggest that this was an option for delay, 60 per cent of the overall value of the tender would be invited during the first year. This facility would, however, only apply to authorities with 15 000 dwellings or above. The twenty-eight largest authorities, with more than 30 000 dwellings, will also spread contracts, over three years – 40 per cent in the first year and 30 per cent in each subsequent year.

Anti-Competitiveness

In pursuing CCT, the government has been acutely aware of the potential problems involved in creating the level of contractor interest to stimulate competition. The main source of these problems would most likely derive from two factors:

1 the lack of appropriate private sector organisations interested in competing for local authority contracts; and/or
2 the creation of barriers by authorities, thus discouraging competition.

Prior to the introduction of CCT, the private sector had no experience or direct equivalent of the type of housing management service provided in the past by local authorities. While the private residential sector had developed expertise in the *contractual* management of housing, the only approximation to local authority's expertise in *welfare* management has been provided by housing associations.

While for some authorities the decision was taken to bring in external contractors, most have expected to retain the management of their stock in-house. It is therefore reasonable to expect that such authorities will attempt to give every possible advantage to the in-house team when drawing up specifications and tender lists. It is with this in mind, that the government has offered guidance on what might be considered to be *anti-competitive*, and therefore unreasonable behaviour on the part of local authorities in the tendering process. 'The Local Govt Acts do not set limits for contract sizes under CCT. To avoid claims of anti-competitiveness a contract specification must enable the market to respond and produce a reasonable show of competition. Contracts must not be packaged in such a way as to restrict, distort or prevent competition' (DoE, 1993c, pt IV), with the Secretary of State having the power to intervene where appropriate. Subsequent guidance was not totally prescriptive about what maximum size of contract is likely to be considered uncompetitive, indicating that this would depend on the 'make-up of individual contracts and the particular authority's circumstances' (DoE, 1993c). This allowed the benefits of the economies of scale to be retained in appropriate circumstances.

The government's expectation was that in deciding the division of contracts, 'the implications of good housing management should be taken into account' (DOE, 1993c), which would provide a balance between effectiveness and accessibility to tenants as well as delivering competition. In deciding the appropriateness of contracts, the consultation paper offered guidance in terms of relevant criteria:

- a responsive service to tenants
- reflected 'natural' local areas with some recognisable identity
- allowed cost-effective service delivery
- attracted a good show of genuine competition.

The normal expectation would be for contracts covering a range of housing management functions within large authorities to be limited to 5000 dwellings. This might be varied for smaller authorities where a holding of 7500 dwellings might form the basis of a single contract. Detailed guidance (DoE Circular 10/93) was also provided as to the style and content of contracts and the expectations placed on authorities during the process of tendering if they were to avoid anti-competitive behaviour (see Table 7.2).

The Statutory Framework for CCT

CCT is a measure originally enacted by Part III of the Local Government Planning and Land Act 1980, extended subsequently by both the Local Government Acts 1988 and 1992, and the Urban Development and Housing Act 1993. In additional to these major pieces of legislation, there have been a number of further orders and regulations which have implemented detailed operational aspects of the process.

The Local Government Act 1988 – Part I contains the core legislation for CCT, providing powers for the Government to specify:

- 'defined activities' – the housing management functions which a local authority are required to put to open competition (see Table 7.3)
- the conditions governing the CCT process
- the setting of financial objectives and the form of trading accounts to be adopted by any Direct Service Organisation (DSO) operating a contract having successfully bid under CCT.

The Act defined a number of activities to which the CCT provisions would directly relate, including refuse collection, grounds maintenance and catering. More importantly, it gave the Secretary of State power to extend CCT to other service heads by order. This power was exercised in 1989 to include the management of sports and leisure facilities and subsequently turned towards white-collar housing management functions. Also

Table 7.2   Government requirements relating to anti-competitive behaviour

- pre-tender questionnaires to contractors wishing to be included on a list of approved contractors should not be unnecessarily detailed.
- work should be packaged in such a way as to make it attractive to potential contractors.
- authorities should avoid packaging together unrelated areas of work *if* such a package would deter contractors working in only one of the fields concerned. Authorities wishing to package unrelated areas should be able to demonstrate that they would create sufficient competition and produce value for money by so doing.
- contracts should be either for the duration of a specific task (e.g. a construction period) or for a maximum of five years.
- authorities should not specify that the staff employed by a contractor should possess relevant professional qualifications unless these are essential to guarantee proper performance of the work.
- authorities should not require contractors to provide detailed documentation with their tenders unless this is essential for the proper evaluation of the tender. In other circumstances contractors should only be asked to provide general descriptions of the methods of work to be employed or evidence to support proposed resource levels.
- contract requirement should not be unreasonably onerous – authorities should consider using, where available, standard forms of contract.
- an authority may stipulate that a contractor has a presence in a particular neighbourhood or district, where this is crucial to the achievement of the contract. However, it is likely to be anti-competitive to require that all staff other than those in direct contact with service customers should be located in this way.
- contractors should be able to compete for other commercial work within an authority of the same nature as that undertaken for the authority providing that this would not produce a conflict of interest.
- tenderers should not be specifically required to have BS 5750 certification and should be allowed to prove the quality of their systems of management and production.
- 'The Secretary of State accepts that it is for local authorities to decide on the appropriate balance between price and quality in evaluating tenders, in accordance with fair and even-handed procedures. This may, in some cases, lead to a decision to reject a lower bid in favour of the DSO. Where this is the case, an authority would nevertheless be expected to have specific and well founded reasons for such a decision.'
- authorities may require that contractors use an authority-owned asset such as an office or building, providing it can be shown that this is 'essential to ensure the efficient and effective delivery of the service to the standards sought'. This does not, however, extend to the use of IT systems which the authority continues to own, but should be given the opportunity to do so. However, if the contractor chooses to use their own systems, the authority should be able to specify the data to be collected and held, form and frequency of reports, and arrangements for security and confidentiality.

Source: DoE Circular 10/93.

Table 7.3 Defined activity for housing management CCT

Rents and Service Charge Collection

- notifying rent and service charges to tenants and leaseholders
- monitoring rent and service charges paid by current and former tenants and leaseholders collecting rents, service charges and contributions to tenant insurance schemes ensuring payment of rents and service charges (excluding service charge loans) including the arrears of current and former tenants. Leaseholders negotiating, monitoring and ensuring compliance with payment agreements for rent and service charge arrears recovering rent and service chase arrears.

Letting of Property

- contacting nominated applicants for dwellings, offering allocated properties and arranging tenancy agreements
- processing applications for transfers and exchanges, including management transfers, interviewing tenants and making recommendations in connection with such applications
- accompanying applicants on viewing visits and undertaking home visits to tenants
- terminating tenancies, inspecting properties and resolving outstanding tenancy issues
- processing applications and letting garages, parking spaces and stores relating to the qualifying properties.

Tenancies

- issuing tenancy agreements and leases ensuring compliance with agreements and leases, taking action to stop or prevent breaches of agreements and issuing warnings responding to disturbances, harassment and domestic disputes involving tenants, including attendance at scene where required, liaising with tenants, residents and specialist agencies to deal with conflicts or make recommendations.

Vacant Properties

- arranging the vacating of properties and taking possession
- inspecting vacant properties and arranging clearance, repairs, cleaning, decoration, security and maintenance
- preventing vandalism and illegal occupation
- obtaining possession of properties occupied by illegal occupants.

Repairs and Maintenance

- receiving requests for responsive repairs, assessing and transmitting requests to contractors

140

Table 7.3 cont.

- monitoring and ensuring progress with responsive repairs monitoring performance of contractors, carrying out post-repair inspections and reporting compliance by contractors
- reporting contractor performance, carrying out stock inspections and condition surveys
- receiving and assessing claims under right to repair and right to compensation for improvement schemes and recommending action, including arranging the payment of compensation.

Caretaking and Cleaning

- operating concierge schemes monitoring condition of common areas and grounds of multi-occupant dwelling blocks ordering repairs, maintenance, cleaning, rubbish removal and disinfestation services of common areas in multi-occupancy buildings, reporting contractor performance.

Source: Association of Metropolitan Authorities, 1994.

included was the concept of anti-competitive behaviour, which required authorities to act in a manner which would not have the effect of 'restricting, distorting or preventing competition' (DoE, 1994).

In addition, other legislated features of CCT include:

- Housing management will not be treated as a defined activity where the estimated gross cost of the activity in the immediately preceding year does not exceed £500 000. The effect of this is to remove a substantial number of smaller district councils from the process of competition.
- A maximum of 95 per cent of contractor activities to be exposed to competition at any time, leaving a competition-free element of 5 per cent throughout the life of the contract. This is intended to allow local authorities flexibility to package contracts in such a manner as to enable comprehensive housing services to be maintained.
- Authorities which had already carried out voluntary tendering prior to 1 September 1994, in which at least three private sector bidders were involved and which resulted in the awarding of the contract in-house, would not be required to repeat the process.
- Direct Service Organisations (DSO) are required to ensure that all activities break even after allowing for a 6 per cent return on capital employed.

What Does CCT Involve?

Introducing CCT into housing management would, in the view of the then Secretary of State for the Environment, Michael Howard, provide increased choice for council tenants, including those who 'cannot shop around for themselves', delivering diversity, value for money and efficiency in addition to offering choice. However, competition is not new to local authorities. The process of bidding for capital and revenue resources has become increasingly competitive over the last decade. The top slicing of the social housing budget for specific projects such as Estate Action, area improvement and homelessness initiatives is an example of this. Similarly, the introduction of initiatives such as City Challenge and the Single Regeneration Budget (SRB) have included competition as a core determinant of their distribution. The allocation of these funds has been largely based on performance-related criteria, linked to value for money, partnership with the private sector and the delivery of value-added outcomes.

A Question of Quality

However, existing measures have proved insufficient to convince the government that local authority housing departments have achieved acceptable standards. Ministers have continued to believe that despite many authorities adopting a more performance related culture, 'there is still scope for greater efficiency and cost savings in many authorities. The quality of housing management in some authorities is still depressingly poor' (DoE, 1992b, p. 2). In this context, quality was linked directly to cost savings, indicating an interpretation of value for money which emphasised efficiency over effectiveness. Undoubtedly, achieving greater economy would clearly be beneficial if authorities were able to offer equivalent levels of service at reduced costs, thus stretching resources further. However, in the continued push towards leaner, more cost-efficient services, economy has tended to become the main determinant of service quality, threatening to bring greater standardisation and reduced choice.

It is likely that non-essential services may be scaled down or scrapped altogether, adopting less sensitive and flexible approaches in dealing with rent arrears or complicated cases of neighbour dispute or racial harassment. More complex cases will involve more officer time in tackling them, and within commercial environments time is money. Many authorities have already introduced staff time-sheets as a means of monitoring activities. However, accurately apportioning time between activities can be extremely difficult for staff engaged in complex interactions of responsibilities involving repairs and maintenance, void work, community development, tenant liaison, neighbour disputes, racial harassment, etc. This diversity, considered by many to be at the root of successful housing management may suffer in a more cost-dominated approach to specifying housing management services. Already the 'defined activities' have adopted a narrow interpretation of housing management. It is therefore feasible that CCT will become the vehicle for implementing the transition to a contractual model of housing management, with a resulting loss of breadth and responsibility for housing managers.

However, many authorities have addressed the quantitative bias by introducing a set of weightings for quality-related criteria which form an integral part of the tender evaluation process. They relate to issues 'common to most councils ... such as service delivery structures, customer care, tenant and member involvement, health and safety, equal opportunities, internal systems and track record' (Ledgerwood, 1995). Authorities are not bound to accept the lowest tender if by so doing service standards would suffer. However, where the lowest cost is not accepted, particularly where an in-house bid is favoured, the decision-making process must be seen to be justifiable and transparent. Thus any criteria and formulae used to determine the award of contracts other than price, must be clearly articulated within the tender documents. Attempts to safeguard against tenderers sacrificing quality in favour of economy has seen the development of *quality plans* and *method statements*, both of which may be required as part of the tender submission. They are designed to indicate how quality is to be maintained, and the approaches to be undertaken for the specific tasks contained within the specification. The client's priorities are reflected in the scores awarded to each of the contract requirements, the outcomes of which will achieve the desired balance between economy and quality. For an authority emphasising equal opportunities, the weighting for systems and processes achieving this policy will be relatively high. 'The evaluation framework is a means of expressing the council's values . . . the wrong [one] could lock the council into a contract where it has to settle for second best' (ibid, 1995).

Even staunch opponents of CCT have acknowledged that despite concerns, unarguable benefits have resulted in preparing for competition. The requirement to review policies and procedures, produce formal policy manuals, and promote greater tenant involvement, has been long overdue for many authorities. A further spin-off has been a greater sensitivity to the needs of tenants and consumers of other local authority services, increasingly referred to as 'customers'. Sir George Young indicated to an ADC/AMA conference in 1993 that, 'This Government shares with all of you the aim of good management of social rented housing . . . tenants have a right to expect good management . . . In the Citizen's Charter we are committed to quality in housing management . . . [which should be] cost-effective, but above all responsive.' While such sentiments might attract support from all quarters, concerns have been voiced that CCT will not achieve them in practice. Margaret Moran, Chair of the AMA Housing Committee, speculated that rather than achieving improvements in efficiency and effectiveness, CCT might have the opposite effect. Her fears were for increased bureaucracy and costs; less flexibility and responsiveness; the diversion of resources into writing contract specifications rather than service delivery; and that services may be more fragmented and harder to integrate effectively (AMA, 1994).

Concern also exists about the potential costs of CCT. Research undertaken by the Centre for Public Services (1995) has indicated that every £1 million saved by local authorities through CCT, costs the government £2 million through unemployment costs, increased benefits and the loss of national insurance, income tax and indirect taxes. Whilst the study related to blue-collar services, it suggests that similar consequences might result from the tendering-out of white-collar services.

Despite expectations that competition will reduce the costs of service provision, it will have quite the opposite effect for the client-side whose task it is to police contracts and ensure that specifications are properly complied with. Additional staff, enhanced systems and sophisticated monitoring procedures will all result in increased costs falling to the Housing Revenue Account (HRA). The test will be the extent to which contractor savings outstrip additional expenditure elsewhere. Initial trends indicate that many local authorities are spending huge sums of money in getting out to tender, but attract little or no competition. For larger authorities, this is likely to approach £250 000, with six-figure sums being the average. The result is a disrupted workforce and increases in rents as tenants pay the costs of the process, with perhaps little or no appreciable differences in services. Far from achieving savings in the short-term the process results in increased rents with little return.

CCT – an Agent for Change

Irrespective of the outcome of contract tendering, CCT will have significant implications for the future of social housing management. Key changes to the service will result simply from being exposed to the process and its regulation. It is arguable that even if CCT were to be scrapped at some future date, the effects on organisational cultures, ethos and structure are unlikely to be completely reversed. Depending on tender outcomes, housing managers could change every five years, or more frequently, depending on the length of contracts. Such a prospect will inevitably affect organisational culture, ethos and employment practices. Management planning will become geared towards short-term goals rather than long-term development.

One certain result of CCT will be the evolution of new organisational cultures. The resulting change may only become apparent over time, and the end result may not be what was originally intended. While change is an explicit expectation of CCT, it is primarily related to process. If, however, the result is to distort core values and objectives of an organisation, this may be to the detriment of organisational effectiveness and, ultimately, consumers. In such circumstances, the danger is that competition becomes the objective rather than a means of improving service delivery.

For in-house contractors the practicalities of steering an ostensibly public organisation through the stormy waters of competition are considerable. They are faced with delivering the services which they had previously been responsible for as social landlords, within the ethos of the private sector, i.e. profitability. Staff who have been recruited, trained and socialised into a public sector organisation may find the realities of the new world involves major reorientation. Some may find the process uncomfortable, while others consider it unacceptable. The degree of change is often most pronounced for those responsible for managing the contractors. They will often find the learning curve to be steep, with the likelihood that many will be found wanting. Managers are not simply required to acquire new knowledge or develop different skills. Organisations generally achieve success on the back of vision, intuitive ability and business acumen, qualities which one would not previously have found in abundance in the public sector.

Competition has also resulted in relationships altering within organisations. The most obvious example is the client/contractor split, which has placed erstwhile colleagues on opposite sides of the desk. In addition, corporate relationships have also changed with what previously constituted central services, i.e. accounting, legal services and planning, all of which have also been placed on a competitive footing. For service departments such as housing, this has generated significant benefits, in that traditionally they have often received poor service at a high cost from these departments. However, strategically, such a move further weakens the effectiveness of corporate management.

Developing a Housing Market

Prior to CCT there has been no clearly defined 'market' in social housing management. The organisations most similar to local authorities in terms of style, motivation and experience of social housing management are housing associations. The government anticipated that they would be the most likely challengers for CCT contracts. Sir George Young considered them to be 'natural agencies who have reservoirs of relevant skills' and the government clearly expected that 'Housing associations will be well equipped to bid to manage certain parts of authorities' stock' (DoE, 1992b, p. 6). Yet evidence already exists to indicate that this is less realistic than the government believed. Early experience of the tendering process has shown associations to be unable or unwilling to submit tenders, often proving expensive where they have bid. Housing associations have traditionally been more expensive in their management costs than local authorities. Unless they can rectify such a disparity, in-house teams or private companies would appear to be more geared towards achieving further success in future bidding rounds.

Other evidence also indicates that housing associations are generally unprepared to actively participate in CCT. In a DoE report, *Managing Social Housing* (DoE, 1993a), the perceptions of both local authority and housing association staff indicated a lack of commitment towards the implementation of CCT. Nearly all of those interviewed in a series of case studies perceived CCT 'only in terms of commercial companies coming in and running housing services' (DoE, 1993a, p. 154). While this may be predictable amongst local authority staff with most to lose, the report also found similar views amongst many housing association staff: 'Some staff were not convinced of the merits of taking over local authority stock. A few stated that they did not want to risk the relationship they had with the local authority or authorities in their area. . . . Some were generally hesitant about taking on local authority stock by whatever means . . . because of the arduous management problems which were felt to exist within some of that stock' (ibid, p. 155). However, a number of the larger, more ambitious associations are seriously addressing these issues. Motivated primarily by the objective to mount more competitive CCT bids in the future, there may also be an element of fear that at some point it may be extended to them. However, the effect is that associations are beginning to resemble local authorities in a number of significant areas, with larger patch sizes an inevitable consequence of keener costings.

There are housing association practitioners who believe themselves to have a positive and proactive role to play in CCT. This may emanate from a genuine belief that they are able to offer a better service to tenants, and/or driven by concerns for their future in the light of falling Housing Association Grant (HAG) rates and reductions in the level of the Approved Development Programme (ADP). In most cases, associations are unlikely to play an active part in bidding for contracts unless invited to do so by local authorities (Morris, 1994b). However, this may change should the financial regime become even more stringent. If associations are to compete, not only against local authorities, but also against the private sector, they will need to move further towards a private sector ethos than has been the case to date. They must also to be prepared to invest considerable resources in the time and expense required to compete seriously. Should this happen, it would most likely signal the death knell to the voluntary sector ethos which has motivated the movement to date.

Structural Changes

In addition to the cultural and philosophical changes indicated above, CCT has heralded a new era of structural change within social housing management organisations. Such change has been fundamental to the government's proposals for reform in the public sector. In his 1992 speech to the ADC/AMA, Sir George Young indicated 'They [housing managers] will need to change the ways in which they work and there will need to be a substantial cultural and structural change throughout many housing departments.'

The Client/Contractor Split

Perhaps the most obvious change for most local authorities has been the restructuring of what had previously been integrated housing departments into separate client and contractor divisions. The defined activities (Table 7.3) required to be tendered cover the landlord functions normally undertaken by estate management staff.

The process of achieving such a split has frequently proved difficult. Major problems often exist relating to the physical location of staff coupled with the need to develop new systems and create new structures. In addition, potential mismatches may also exist between existing incumbents of jobs and the skills and qualities which might be most needed within the new organisation. The transition has also been made more fraught by the 'down-sizing' of staffing complements in the attempt to curb costs. This has proved particularly painful amongst senior management, where second tiers consisting of four or five assistant directors may contract to only two: one client and one contractor.

The split between what constitutes a defined activity and what becomes a client responsibility is not always operationally straightforward. The choice between a 'soft' or 'hard' split is often influenced by political as well as operational issues. For local authorities which had previously been significantly decentralised, the transition would be much easier than those remaining largely centralised. In the latter case, CCT has often involved dismantling centralised teams and reshaping jobs and procedures into a more appropriate structure. This process has been complicated by the implicit requirement that costs for the newly created in-house contractor should be kept as low as possible. The temptation has therefore been to retain as many existing staff as possible on the client side which remains fully funded by the HRA.

Despite the government's expectation of a 'hard' client/contractor split (i.e. the physical separation of the two functions), not all local authorities have pursued this option. Some have chosen the 'soft' split option, i.e. to retain existing structures, but to account for activities separately. In this model, a number of staff may be engaged in both client and contractor functions as part of the same job. The advantage of this approach is that it reduces the disruption caused by major reorganisation, avoiding what many people have found to be artificial boundaries. However, disadvantages may result from a reduction in focus on the disciplines required of a successful contractor, and the problems which would ensue if the in-house team failed to win the contract.

Breaking Up the Comprehensive Housing Service

A further casualty of CCT may prove to be the comprehensive nature of many housing services. The government has perceived no obvious conflict between exposing housing management to competition while supporting the retention of comprehensive housing services (see Chapter 8). They have argued that an appropriate level of management responsibility and control over the delivery of the functions undertaken should not be diminished by the contracting-out of all or part of the housing function.

However, through measures such as the ring-fencing of the HRA, the scope of the defined activities, 'comprehensiveness' has been redefined within the much reduced, contractual model of housing management. Although some flexibility has been allowed in the inclusion of non-defined functions within contracts, this will be closely monitored and controlled 'provided that the resulting combination is not anti-competitive, i.e. does not result in a package of work which deters prospective contractors from bidding' (DoE, 1993c, s26).

An implication of defining comprehensiveness in relation to landlord functions alone, is to potentially limit the range of skills and functions which will consequently be required. In many local authorities it has often been the existence of a critical mass which has proved the catalyst for expanding horizons and developing partnerships. The compartmentalisation of expertise within a more constrained framework threatens to undermine such creativity in two ways:

1 by potentially removing the knowledge and skills exercised by the contractor side to an outside organisation
2 by restricting functions to those directly related to stock management.

'The question that must be asked in the light of CCT is "if the direct knowledge and involvement of parts of that service are lost, if they are exercised second hand through contractors, or if the flexibility of provision is constrained by formulaic standards and performance measures and measured by profit, or the fear of loss, can such a range of innovative and integrated provision survive, let alone develop and adjust over time to meet new or changed circumstances?"'(Pankhurst, 1993). There is a danger that by containing the housing management function within tightly drawn boundaries, local authority housing departments will, by default, become devoid of certain *contractor* skills and expertise. Accusations that the public sector is poorly equipped to compete with the private sector may therefore become a self-fulfilling prophesy.

CCT and Employment

Change of Employment Conditions – TUPE

An inherent consequence of competition is that there will be winners and losers. In the relatively new market for white-collar housing management, those standing to lose the most are the established contractors, i.e. local authorities. Although relatively few contracts were awarded to private companies or housing associations in the first round of tendering, there were some council 'casualties'. However, the loss of a contract does not automatically spell unemployment for those housing officers previously employed to manage those dwellings. The EC regulation on the Transfer of Undertakings (TUPE) offers short-term job protection to all housing department staff affected by an unsuccessful in-house bid. It inhibits unfair competition by preventing competitors undercutting costs by reducing staffing levels and conditions of service. The result is that in winning a contract, an external organisation is required to employ the existing workforce on protected conditions for up to a year.

  However, those successful organisations taking on local authority staff have indicated the intention to make reductions in personnel over the life of the contract. It is likely therefore that any protection offered by TUPE will be short-term at best. In other service areas, there is evidence that wages and job opportunities have been adversely affected by the process of privatisation. 'Even where contracts have been won in-house, councils have frequently been forced by competition to reduce staff, reduce their hours, and remove fringe benefits such as pensions and holidays. The tendering process has changed the culture of local authorities. No longer are jobs for life, with guaranteed pensions and security' (Wolmar, 1992). There are already indications that where in-house teams have restructured to take account of the tendering process, conditions of employment have worsened and jobs have been lost. The fact that many authorities have subsequently won contracts with considerably lower bids than their competitors, indicates the potential effect of competition to cut deep into established workforces.

Even prior to CCT, the trend has been for senior local authority staff to be appointed on fixed term contracts, with no guarantee of renewal on their expiry. This uncertainty is often compensated for by higher salaries and incentivised pay. For staff employed on the contractor side of the local authority, this trend may inevitably filter down to cover all staff. It would be commercially untenable to employ staff on permanent contracts when the organisation's own contract is only guaranteed for a fixed period. However, rather than salaries increasing generally to reflect this increased uncertainty, it is likely that for many jobs, wage levels may decrease to reflect market levels.

CCT and Equal Opportunities

One result of the growing influence of commercial employment practice is that many local authorities will find it harder to retain their position as high-quality employers. Many have taken their responsibilities under equal-opportunity legislation seriously, offering high standards of health and safety, equality of access into employment and support for training and education for their staff. However, the requirements to avoid anti-competitive conditions within contracts, will result in such policies inevitably falling foul of the drive for economy and efficiency.

Removing the contractor function may also in some cases restrict local authorities' ability to develop initiatives designed to generate local employment. Many inner-city authorities have, to date, been the largest single employer in their area. They have endeavoured, in their strategic role, to create additional opportunities within deprived areas where levels of unemployment have been extremely high. By targeting resources at disadvantaged groups within the community, such opportunities have often contributed to the wider regeneration of run-down areas. Whilst CCT may not completely impede such initiatives, it will undoubtedly reduce local authorities' ability to deliver opportunities directly. They must work instead in partnership with other public and private organisations which may not wholeheartedly subscribe to the same objectives. While some commercial organisations may be keen to participate in training and employment initiatives, they can only promote community development within the constraints of their own profit-motivated environment.

CCT may therefore have an adverse effect on equal opportunities in employment. Practice in the private sector has been towards increasing levels of fixed term contracts and part-time working. It is generally staff on lower salaries who are worst served by these practices, often tending to be women and/or from the black and minority ethnic communities. Authorities may put mechanisms in place within the client evaluation of tenders to try and limit the impact of this phenomenon. However, there must be some doubt whether such regulation can be truly effective within a market-led system.

The ability to deliver equal opportunities in service delivery is also questionable. Quality plans and method statements may go some way to ensure that quality is maintained or even improved. However, reflecting the inequalities of deprivation and marginalisation within a contract specification is far from straightforward. In many of the most difficult areas to manage, issues may relate not only to housing, but also to unemployment, social mix, poverty and isolation. These are issues of a strategic nature which can only be successfully confronted by a coordinated approach. This becomes much harder to achieve when service delivery is fragmented between a number of contractors and disciplines. The same is true in terms of Care in the Community, which also presents a range of problems which do not easily lend themselves to resolution through CCT. These are discussed in greater detail in Chapter 6.

Despite attempts at damage limitation, CCT will not easily coalesce with the aims of equal opportunities. While the spirit of equality may be potentially compatible with a performance culture, there is little evidence from the private sector that it has been seriously embraced to date. Even in the lead-in to CCT, many authorities have already reduced training budgets, limited personal development to job-specific training, and become highly introspective in the fear of commercial confidentiality. The indications have therefore not been positive.

CCT and Tenant Involvement

CCT potentially represents a major opportunity for empowering tenants to shape local housing management standards. Provisions within the legislation promote the role of tenants in influencing, although not having the final decision over, the content of specifications and the successful contractor. This development undoubtedly affords a more significant role for tenants than has previously existed in most local authorities. However, doubts remain whether the deal offered to tenants by CCT is really as good as it may first appear. 'There is no evidence that tenants actually want CCT. The results of tenant satisfaction surveys up and down the country have revealed that most tenants are satisfied with the standard of service they receive' (IoH, 1991, p. 3). The experience of the government in its abortive attempt to impose HATs, demonstrated that the majority of local authority tenants are generally supportive of their landlords. Whilst many would wish to see improvement in service, they are against the compulsion attached to tendering. Rather than perceiving CCT as an initiative designed to improve the lot of tenants, many believe that 'Competition clearly remains much closer to the heart of the CCT ethos than consultation' (Hood, 1993).

While some tenants will achieve real influence through CCT, the overall impact will inevitably remain somewhat variable. In many authorities there is little or no history of an organised tenants' movement and therefore no structure on which to build to facilitate this new role. In such situations, it is not merely a case of training tenants to be able to participate, but of identifying representatives from scratch. The requirements that contracts will be awarded only after full and meaningful consultation with tenants will therefore ring rather hollow in some instances.

Tenants may also lose out in terms of value for money. The results of the first round of CCT during 1996 resulted in the vast majority of contracts being awarded in-house, often against little or no competition. The costs of the tendering process have to be directly borne by the HRA, generally out of tenants' rent. The result has therefore been that tenants have directly funded a process which has produced little improvement to services and which they may not have supported.

Alternative Routes to Contracting

A number of authorities have reacted against the prospect of CCT. For some, it has been sufficient to tip the balance in favour of a total transfer of their stock through large-scale voluntary transfer (see Chapter 8). A few others have developed tenant management organisations to control specific estates. In either of these scenarios, the outcome has been sufficient to exempt the resulting organisation from having to tender.

A third way of avoiding CCT has been by pre-empting the requirements, opting instead to tender contracts voluntarily, known as Voluntary Competitive Tendering (VCT). This route has generally been taken by two types of authority: those wishing to let contracts externally while seeking to retain greater control of the tendering process; and those already nominated as pilot authorities (see earlier explanation).

A list of those management contracts let prior to the first round of CCT is contained in Table 7.4. In a number of these situations, authorities were obviously keen to externalise housing management, allowing no in-house bid. In the two pilot authorities, Newham and Westminster (see case studies), the contracts were comfortably won in-house. However, Westminster subsequently awarded one contract to manage 1200 dwellings to Johnson Fry Property (JFP), a private company submitting a loss-leading bid in an attempt to undercut the in-house team and win the contract. JFP gained the contract despite being below the quality levels required by the council, and having submitted a higher bid than the in-house team. Although opposed by both officers and tenants, the award was justified 'in the interests of increasing choice' (*HA Weekly*, 2 June 95, p. 5).

The mechanisms for competitive tendering therefore do offer scope for manipulation and interpretation. In the effort to ensure a balance between economy and quality, sufficient flexibility has been allowed to enable authorities to produce the result they wish to see. This may explain why authorities of opposite political control can find comfort in the same policy.

Table 7.4 Housing management contracts

Authority	Contractor	No. of houses	Value (£m)	Length	Start date
Bexley*	Orbit HA London & Quadrant HA	4 000	0.80	4 years	April 1994
Brent*	CSL	4 300	0.77	4 years	April 1994
Dartford	Hyde HA	1 470		2 years	April 1994
East Herts*	Network HA	5 500		5 years	April 1995
	Wherry HA	3 500			April 1995
Harrow*+	Jephson Homes HA	3 500		5 years	na
	Chiltern Hundreds HA	2 700		5 years	na
	Housing 21	550		5 years	na
Newham	In-house	7 800	3.00	3 years	April 1994
Rutland*	CSL	3 500	0.51	5 years	April 1993
South Oxfordshire	PSEC	5 500		5 years	April 1995
Wandsworth (Tooting)	In-house	4 500		3 years	Aug 1993
(Ethelberg estate)	In-house			3 years	Aug 1993
(Park Court)	In-house			3 years	Aug 1993
(Harwood Court)	In-house			3 years	Aug 1993
(Wendelsworth)	Scotts	350		3 years	Aug 1993
Westminster	In-house	1 794	0.27	3 years	Sept 1994
	In-house	1 151	0.25	3 years	Sept 1994

* No in-house bid
+ DOE refused to approve contract and ordered retender.

Source: Centre for Public Services (1995).

On the face of it, Newham, a staunchly labour London borough, would not be expected to accept or embrace CCT, while Westminster, a flagship of Conservatism, has been a pioneer of contracting and privatisation. Yet both authorities became 'bedfellows', as pilot centres in the lead-in to CCT. How such differences are reconciled is examined in the following case study.

Case Study

This case study illustrates the diversity of issues affecting organisations in pursuing their duties. It examines the context and approach of two politically opposed local authorities, both of which chose to participate in the implementation of CCT as pilot authorities. Their motivation was significantly different, yet the outcomes were largely similar.

London Borough of Newham

Newham is an inner-city, Labour-controlled authority in East London. It owns and manages in excess of 27 000 dwellings, via a comprehensive housing department which has active strategies for both public and private sectors.

The council's approach is to oppose the principle of CCT and ensure that 'as much as possible of the work undertaken by the Council is done by the in-house workforce to ensure quality and level of service' (Majority Group Manifesto). In August 1992, the council were approached by the DoE, inviting them to be one of the six pilot authorities for CCT, concentrating on two issues: CCT and the capital programme; and the social/welfare issues involved in housing management. The council agreed following consultation with trade unions, tenants organisations and councillors.

In deciding to participate as a pilot authority, officers and members balanced the criteria for and against the proposal. They considered that the *advantages* of participation were:

1 The authority might gain access to additional resources for their work relating to the capital programme. These could extend to both set-up costs and extra capital approvals.
2 Participation would enable Newham to influence the final regulations and to ensure that they were sensitive to the complexities of housing management.
3 By going to competition early, it is likely that the competition would be underdeveloped with little effective opposition from the private sector.
4 It would allow the authority to disseminate information from Newham's experience, thus benefiting other authorities.
5 It would enhance Newham's reputation across a broad spectrum,

including within government circles. It might also enable the recruitment of good staff who may perceive the authority as pioneering.

The *disadvantages* were:

1 The risk involved in tendering earlier. As one of a few authorities tendering contracts they might become the focus of the limited competition.
2 Newham might be seen as an authority favouring CCT and thus seeking to cooperate with external contractors. As a result, they might attract more competition than under normal conditions.
3 Being a pilot authority might be seen by other Labour authorities as helping the government prepare for a process which they, including Newham, disapprove of in principle.
4 The pilot might enable the government to identify potential loopholes and close them.

On balance, members considered the potential advantages outweighed the disadvantages. The approach was based on pragmatism in the light of the almost certain imposition of CCT at a later stage. The potential for gaining capital, both politically and in terms of resources, proved an attractive proposition. However, sensitive political issues might have militated against the pilot status had the make-up of the council, or the approach of tenants or trade unions been different.

In the event, Newham tendered a contract covering 7000 dwellings, to a value of £3 million, in April 1994. There were no competitive bids against the in-house team which duly won the contract for a three-year term. The gamble to become a pilot authority was therefore vindicated.

In winning the contract, the in-house team restructured their staffing, losing posts in becoming as lean and competitive as possible. In the event, on price consideration alone this proved unnecessary, but this could not have been known at the outset. However, those drawing up the in-house bid would point to future benefits, making the structure more competitive when the contract becomes due for renewal.

London Borough of Westminster

Westminster is a Conservative-controlled authority, situated in the centre of London, managing 25 000 dwellings. It has for a number of years been a flagship authority for the government, pioneering new methods of privatisation and being at the forefront of council house sales.

The council's approach to CCT has been to embrace the policy wholeheartedly. In practice, Westminster had pursued the practice of voluntary competitive tendering for manual work some years in advance of the CCT legislation. Had housing management CCT not been the subject of legislation, it is likely that they would have developed their own model. It is not therefore surprising that the authority should be approached by the DoE to become one of the other pilot schemes.

Since 1985, Westminster has progressively divided its stock into 17 estate bases, termed *villages*. The intention has been to locate housing management services as close to locally identifiable communities as possible. Two of these villages were selected for the pilot tender, one an estate of 1800 dwellings, the other a mix of smaller estates comprising 1200 dwellings.

In pursuing competition, the council sought not only to produce keen prices for service delivery, but also to offer residents as wide a range of choice as possible. For Westminster, the term *resident* is particularly relevant, as council estates are heavily pepper-potted with dwellings sold under the Right to Buy. The often higher expectations of leaseholders has created a culture of local responsiveness.

The two estates, Churchill Gardens and Paddington Green, were tendered in 1994, with a number of local housing associations and property management companies invited to submit tenders. In the event, the in-house team submitted the lowest bid in both cases, also scoring the highest marks in the quality assessment exercise.

In both case studies, the end result was identical although the factors influencing approach to the process were completely different. For Newham, the decision to become a pilot scheme to avoid competition clearly differed from Westminster's intention which was to generate competition. The fact that both found the competition weak indicates the current immaturity of the housing management market. This was also found to be the case by Wandsworth when they too went out to VCT at the start of 1994. It is likely, however, that the private sector companies who consider themselves to be serious competitors will use the experience gained in these early forays to gear themselves up for the real thing. This has been demonstrated by the recent loss-leading bid by JRP for a management contract in Westminster.

Initial Experiences

The first round of CCT was completed during the second half of 1995. The result was that 96 per cent of contracts were won by local authorities, with only 2.7 per cent going to private companies and 1.1 per cent to housing associations (Morris, 1996). While this proved a positive outcome for the public sector, it was tinged with some bitterness. Many contracts were awarded by default, without any external competition. The costs of the exercise were substantial, with Wakefield MDC spending £1 million and Rochdale MDC's costs amounting to £500 000 (Bright, 1995). There have also been other costs, most notably the morale of housing staff subjected to the tendering process. In a survey of local authority housing directors, *ROOF* (Dwelly and Blake, 1995) found that 65 per cent thought that CCT lowered staff morale, 35 per cent said it had made no difference. None believed that morale had improved. This was in some part due to the fact that many staff were forced to accept reductions in salary and conditions of service to bring them in line with the private sector. Of equal significance, less than half, 44 per cent, thought that CCT would bring an improved service to tenants, 10 per cent envisaged a worse service, 46 per cent thought it would have no change.

This picture appears to suggest either that local authorities have reacted rather better than expected to the prospect of competition, or that the private sector, including housing associations, severely underestimated the task facing them. In reality, both premises are probably true. It is possible that the political rhetoric promoted by Conservative governments about the inefficiency of the public sector may have lulled the competition into a false sense of security. It is equally feasible that tenants' strength of support for their local service providers was also underestimated. In either event, it is likely that private contractors and housing associations will have learned lessons from their first foray into the social housing management market. To some extent, they may be in a better position in the future as the onus rests on local authorities to maintain their performance in the light of reduced costs and staff unrest. The trump card often remains the goodwill of the tenants. While local authorities retain their tenants' support, they must remain favourites to retain contracts against hostile bids.

The apparent failure of the private sector to perform adequately brought reactions from disgruntled contractors and the government. Charges were levelled against a number of authorities on one of two counts: firstly that anti-competitive behaviour was widespread; and secondly that some authorities were cheating the system by claiming to spend less than £500 000 on housing management and thus becoming *de minimis*. As a result, the government announced in December 1995 that it was to investigate nineteen councils for alleged anti-competitive behaviour and a further eleven authorities to test their claims for *de minimis* exemption. The result, announced in April 1996, was that a new, tougher regime was to be introduced which emphasised price over quality, limiting the extent to which method statements might be used. In addition, despite finding that the authorities investigated for *de minimis* irregularities acted within the rules, following pressure from the private sector, the qualification threshold may be reduced from £500 000 to £250 000 and subsequently abolished altogether. Any initial feelgood factor generated by the first flush of success has therefore been dampened by these additional constraints. What has become clearer is that the objective behind CCT appears less about making councils competitive and more about transferring housing management to the private sector. The effect may be to persuade more local authorities to consider the option of transferring stock to a housing company as the best way of safeguarding services.

Summary

The effects of CCT will only really become apparent over the life of the initial contracts and perhaps even longer. Yet even in the early stages, fundamental changes to existing housing management practice were evident. Supporters of CCT state that competition will ensure quality at reduced cost, with increased choice for consumers. However, there are indications that such assertions may be questionable. The practice of organisations 'buying' contracts at a loss so as to undercut in-house teams must be a cause for concern about the long-term quality of services. In general, loss leaders are intended only to be short-term expedients, with financial benefits such as increased income and greater market share being generated over time. Such practices do not constitute legitimate competition, with in-house teams placed at a substantial disadvantage. In an authority tendering only one or two contracts, if the in-house team is beaten, it will inevitably mean its demise, effectively reducing competition and choice when the contract is next tendered.

Question marks also exist over the ability of CCT to generate cost savings. The substantial costs of tendering and the hidden costs of sustaining lower conditions of employment suggest that competition may be a false economy. Yet if CCT cannot guarantee savings, quality or increased choice, what are its merits? The process of preparing for CCT has generated some organisational benefits, improving internal systems by requiring the production of written policy and procedure guides and contract specifications. Staff are therefore more likely to be aware of the expectations placed on them and of desired outcomes. It has raised staff awareness to the needs and perspectives of consumers, underlining the importance of customer care. The commercial imperative has also had the effect of creating a more financially responsible approach to the delivery of services, promoting an awareness of private sector alternatives. This has included questioning whether in-house teams always provide increased quality over the competition. The recognition that competitive tendering can produce benefits when applied selectively and as part of a coordinated approach to council services is the point at which most practitioners would draw the line. Many fear that *compulsory* competition will ultimately diminish the quality of service delivery.

While these fears may well have substance, it could also be that the threats posed by CCT have been exaggerated. In the short term, there is unlikely to be much change in front-line staff. The protection offered by TUPE will safeguard employment whether within an in-house team or a successful external bidder. In addition, service standards will be determined by the authority's client side and enforced whoever wins the contract. Most tenants simply require the basic housing management functions to be performed well. Provided they are properly specified and the contractor is chosen carefully, it may matter little to tenants whether contracts are won in-house or externally, provided the service remains the same or even improves. Does CCT therefore present a greater threat to professional staff than to service consumers? Are protestations of diminishing services really more about dwindling empires and reduced job security? There is little doubt that the service offered by some authorities within recent years has been poor and change may be for the better. But will CCT deliver the benefits suggested by its proponents or is it simply another measure to further emasculate local authorities? Does the outcome of the tendering process really make a difference? In all probability it will, perhaps not in the short term, but over the life of two or three contracts. Inevitably the culture and working practices of the private sector will dominate approaches to service delivery. Whether they can deliver sufficient flexibility to cater for the needs of all council tenants remains to be seen.

8 The Changing Structures of Housing Organisations

'Social housing at below market rents does not have to be publicly owned. There is a long tradition of private trusts and charities providing housing in this country . . . We want to take this principle further, breaking away from the tradition of large monopoly local authority landlords by transferring existing council housing to new landlords.'

(DoE, 1995b, p. 28)

Across the social housing sector, many organisational structures have had to change to meet the new expectations of the public sector of the 1990s. Central government policy has been geared towards extending choice in rented housing through competition. This has involved introducing CCT for local authorities (see Chapter 7) and promoting a range of alternative landlords, thus breaking up a perceived local authority monopoly in the process. As a result, observers of the housing scene in the 1990s have become familiar with new types of social housing organisations which would not have existed a decade earlier. Housing companies, and Large Scale Voluntary Transfer housing associations (LSVTs) are poised to become the mainstream social landlords of the future, changing the traditional face which has centred on local authorities and housing associations. For existing landlord organisations, the immediate future promises considerable organisational and structural reappraisal as they realign themselves to meet the challenges of performance and competition.

However, the dynamic of change is not consistent across all housing organisations: 'Some are untouched by the new ideas. Some merely pay lip service to them' (Stewart, 1988, p. 21). For example, in many smaller rural districts (approximately 150 will avoid CCT through being *de minimis*) and non-developing housing associations, change has not been a major feature, and they remain locked into past methods and practices. Few operate in the same way, with major differences resulting from: locality; demography; spatial distribution; and political control. It is therefore often difficult and misleading to make generalised comparisons between either local authorities or housing associations. In many cases they not only operate on substantially different scales, but have markedly differing aims and objectives.

In the past, social landlords have been largely autonomous in determining the nature of their services. However, this is changing, with achievement becoming increasingly measured against externally specified performance targets. The Audit Commission's three 'E's have spawned a framework of scrutiny based on largely quantitative measures, geared mainly towards the attainment of economy and efficiency and, to a lesser extent, effectiveness. Comparisons against commercial practice have increasingly pushed housing managers towards adopting private sector management methods. Where success could not be guaranteed within existing structures, others have been developed to take their place, hence the emergence of LSVT associations and housing companies.

Policies such as customer care and consumer empowerment have also prompted organisational change. From a position in which local authority housing departments appeared inviolate, impenetrable and insensitive, many have more recently found themselves having to justify their existence in terms of quality, effectiveness and cost. The recognition that to achieve this has required a much improved interface with consumers, or 'customers', has meant that, like Jericho, at least some of the walls have come tumbling down. Local authorities and housing associations have adopted more outward-looking practices, often via programmes of localisation and decentralisation, resulting in greater access to services for tenants and, in some cases, a devolution of power to tenants and estate-based groups.

Relationships between paid officials and service users have also changed, with initiatives such as the Citizen's Charter building on a series of *rights* introduced throughout the 1980s. The traditional organisational bastion which had long served to keep tenants and other service users at bay has systematically been dismantled, replaced by an expectation of transparency of operations, customer care and consumer choice. This has been accompanied by a realignment of working values, in which the traditional perception of local government as a safe, secure and controlled environment has changed in the light of competition.

For housing associations, both the establishment of the HAG grant regime in 1974, and the extension of their role under the Housing Act 1988 have proved significant turning points. Not only has rapid expansion proved common amongst developing associations, but there has been a discernable shift in culture and ethos away from the traditional values of the voluntary sector, towards a position reflecting the status of *social businesses*. This has resulted in a flurry of organisational changes, most notably mergers and the development of group structures, examined later, designed to provide a platform for further expansion and safeguard associations' financial stability.

This chapter specifically examines the new housing organisations which have emerged since 1988 and their approach to the management of their housing stock. Where possible, comparisons are made between the performance and output of these organisations against the ones they have replaced. In many cases, it is simply too early to make meaningful judgements. Housing companies as potential major landlords are still new, having been introduced in the Housing Act 1996, and several of the Housing Action Trusts (HATs) are also relatively nascent. However, despite this, the impact of these organisations is indisputable. LSVTs have already occurred within fifty local authorities, accounting for over 200 000 dwellings; the six HATs will together account for over £1 billion of housing expenditure over the next ten to fifteen years, and housing companies have the potential to change the face of local authority housing completely. The development of these organisations in the future will therefore hold enormous significance for both prospective employees and service users alike.

The Current Position

Currently, social rented housing is dominated by local authorities and housing associations. Together, they manage over five million dwellings, representing almost a quarter of the country's housing stock. Both have long pedigrees, housing associations having roots in the nineteenth-century philanthropic movement, and council housing dating back to the beginning of the current century. Together, they employ over 100 000 staff and in 1991 expended £8.2 billion on revenue costs and almost £4.5 billion in capital expenditure. In commercial terms, many would be considered substantial businesses.

However, the concept of a *social business* is a relatively recent phenomena. In the past, both local authorities and housing associations operated within a largely non-competitive, public sector environment in which they were guaranteed large allocations of public finance. Their development has therefore been rooted within a very different regime from that in which they currently find themselves. Each, for different reasons, has had to adapt very quickly to new methods of operation, the development of new skills, and revised operational imperatives. Not unexpectedly, some organisations have reacted to this challenge better than others.

There has never been a uniform approach to structuring the delivery of housing services. Among local authorities in England, just over half (56 per cent) have a separate housing department, whilst the remainder combine housing with one or more other local authority departments, usually Environmental Health. In 1993, only 29 per cent of local authorities considered that they provided a comprehensive housing service within a single department: 'sixty per cent of authorities with less than 5001 units of stock had 30 per cent or more of their housing functions managed outside the housing department' (DoE, 1993a). Outside of towns and cities, many smaller district councils have tended to separate the component parts of the housing function, locating rent collection and arrears with the finance department and repairs and maintenance with the borough engineer or technical section.

For housing associations, structures have traditionally reflected the nature of the association and its objectives. Whilst local authorities have common denominators in statutory functions, this is not true of housing associations. They not only have a variety of constitutions, but also differing

legal entities, i.e. companies, charities or industrial and provident societies. Structures have generally been influenced by the nature of the client
group(s), the stock characteristics, and the geographical spread of management responsibilities. Associations operating within a more constrained
geographical area are more likely to be centralised, while the largest associations, working usually in more than one local authority area (over 3000
dwellings), generally work through local offices (DoE, 1993a).

Perhaps the most significant structural determinant within recent years
has been decentralisation. Its effect has often been to improve services
such as repairs, void control and rent collection, and to change the culture amongst staff, particularly those working in local offices, to become
more tenant centred. One implication of localisation is the increased physical
access to housing offices, placing management staff directly at the point
of delivery. Research carried out on behalf of the Department of the Environment in 1993 indicated that 'overall, the evidence from the experi-
mental and control estates in this study does support the hypothesis that
estate management tends to improve the standards of housing service and
the quality of life of the tenants' (DoE, 1993). Yet the implementation of
decentralisation has varied nationally, with a little over half of local authorities locating functions within local offices. It is more likely amongst
larger local authorities than smaller ones; almost all local authorities with
a stockholding of over 10 000 properties adopt some level of localisation.
In contrast, only a quarter of authorities with a stock of 5000 or less have
local offices (DoE, 1993).

Housing associations have been more likely to be decentralised than
local authorities, albeit to a lesser extent. For larger regional and national
associations, the delivery of services through local offices has been essential. Increasingly, associations are also finding that a local presence can
open up greater partnership opportunities with local authorities, many of
which show a preference for associations with local knowledge and expertise. However, not all attempts at decentralisation have worked, and in
some cases significant problems have emerged as a result of it. Many
authorities would, however, have found the transition to CCT much harder
without it. Localisation has been highly instrumental in encouraging
the disaggregation of revenue expenditure to local cost centres, which
has been a crucial factor in enabling the development and costing of
specifications.

The current picture is therefore one of diversity. A wide range of social
landlords have being forced to adapt to a competitive, performance-related
world and achieving differing levels of success. Those which are more
advanced have generally evolved a dynamic approach to change, built on
the clear identification of core values and objectives, coupled with a sensitivity to external influences. The less-well-placed organisations have largely
resisted change, adhering to established policies and practices without
question.

New Versus Old

The combination of financial constraints, increased competition and seemingly intractable problems has provided the catalyst for many local authorities to seek change. The result has been the development of radical alternatives in an attempt to break the mould and deliver a new style of service. Often, initiatives are partnerships between local authorities, housing associations and other interested parties. The result has been a variety of new housing management arrangements implemented on local authority estates. These have ranged from fixed term estate management contracts, to the permanent transfer of stock via LSVT or trickle transfer, i.e. the gradual transfer of dwellings to an approved landlord as they became vacant. The common denominator across each of the alternatives is that change has and will continue to result, affecting both landlord and service consumer.

Over time, comparisons will inevitably be made between the performance of these new managers and the more traditional approaches. However, assessments based on output alone would often be misleading. Local authority managers have often been disadvantaged in operating within the additional constraints of political involvement and the corporate influence. As such, they may find themselves outperformed on factors some of which are outside their control. They may well face competition from contractors geared specifically to succeed within the new performance culture. In contrast, within many existing local authorities and housing associations, the culture is determined as much by what has gone before as by the efforts of current staff. Thus, reaction to the threat of competition has been strongly informed and influenced by existing job incumbents, past practice and personal politics, all of which are likely to have been rooted in the public sector. Few restructuring exercises have purely reflected organisational needs, without intervention from elected members and trades union officials. The result is that structures and appointments within housing departments have often proved an imperfect compromise designed to satisfy as many parties as possible. Such attitudes may not be best geared to achieve success within an increasingly competitive environment.

Many local authorities remain firmly entrenched 'role cultures', i.e. hierarchical bureaucracies. Perceived as 'Greek temples' by Charles Handy (Handy, 1985), the result is a situation in which all of the power resides at the top of the organisation, whilst the staff employed to deal directly with the public generally receive the least training and lowest pay. In many private sector companies which have already won housing management contracts, the structure is more task-related. Staff directly involved in delivering services have much greater levels of autonomy and responsibility, with senior managers taking on more strategic, supportive and facilitating roles. Much of the strength of the organisation is therefore focused at the point of greatest impact, i.e. the point of service delivery.

For local authorities and existing housing associations structured along conventional lines, this new approach has emphasised the need to revise

their cultural orientation. CCT remains the obvious threat to service organisations as they currently exist, but not the only one. The creation of
other quasi-public landlords, e.g. LSVT, and support for housing companies has been in keeping with the government's goal of widening choice
and increasing competition. Already, the cosy relationships between some
local authorities and housing associations have been soured by the potential of the latter to submit a hostile CCT bid. At the same time, associations are being forced to look hard at their housing management in the
light of significantly higher costs than those of their local authority counterparts. These often result from higher staff/property ratios and increased
expenditure of maintenance.

The following sections detail the new landlord organisations, evaluate
the pressures for change and describe the mechanisms for achieving it.
Most of the new organisational types described have been developed as
expedients to overcome the effects of financial constraint, rather than evolving
naturally. Where change has occurred, the results have impacted on both
consumer and staff, although it is too early to assess accurately the outcomes. They have occurred at a time when the very nature of housing
management has been thrown into the melting-pot. It is therefore difficult
to assess whether the emerging organisations have initiated change to housing
management or have merely reacted to it.

Mergers, Takeovers and Group Structures

Housing Association Mergers

As with much else in social housing policy, organisational structures have
become primarily determined not by service considerations, but by financial
expediency. Many social housing organisations, particularly housing associations, have tailored operations on the need to secure financial stability
and achieve a competitive edge via efficiency and economies of scale.
Increased levels of risk generated by the dependence on private finance
has forced many associations to reassess their ability to meet their constitutional objectives. The ability to provide affordable rents to households
on low incomes is often dependent on favourable private finance deals
negotiated on the back of a strong balance sheet and healthy surpluses.
This has increasingly favoured larger associations with substantial stock
holdings of pre-1988 HAG-funded properties, developed or acquired with
high levels of public subsidy and minimal private loans.

Small, newly formed or specialist housing associations without an adequate asset base to satisfy financial institutions are severely disadvantaged. With no prospect of development, many small associations have
felt obliged to seek an accommodation with a larger, more financially
secure association. The effect has been to reduce the number of highly
specialised and community-based associations, which have previously rep-

resented one of the strengths of the voluntary sector. The trend has therefore been towards a relatively small number of very large housing associations dominating the provision of social housing on a national scale. A document leaked from the Housing Corporation indicated the possibility of a move towards a 'super league' of fewer than a hundred HAG-funded associations all of which would have the resources and expertise to develop within an increasingly risk-based environment. While such a scenario has not materialised, funding practice has been rationalised with many associations experiencing much reduced levels of HAG allocation, whilst others have lost funding altogether.

Since 1990, over two hundred housing associations have been deregistered through merging with another organisation. In many instances, the process has been harmonious, benefiting all parties involved; a small number have occurred at the behest of the Housing Corporation because of inadequate performance. Sensitivity remains, however, whether such alliances result in mergers or takeovers. The former is seen as a partnership in which two or more associations retain elements of their original entities, but enjoy the administrative, legal and financial benefits of the merger. In the latter scenario, the smaller or weaker association is usually swallowed up by a more robust and powerful counterpart, resulting in the virtual loss of any previous independent identity. While this may be preferable to the difficulties arising from financial insolvency, it has the effect of stifling the diversity offered by smaller, more vulnerable associations.

Generally, however, the benefit of partnership between associations has proved significant. The result is often an organisational whole which is greater than the sum of its parts, with particular benefits realised in the following areas:

1 *Greater financial security* – combining the assets of organisations not only creates a more robust balance sheet, but also enables much easier access to development funding.
2 *Economies of scale* – small, or even medium-size associations may not have the resources to employ specialist technical and financial staff. This becomes more cost-effective within larger organisations.
3 *Diverse experience and expertise* – the linkage between organisations with different type of expertise, e.g. special needs and general needs, can strengthen and diversify the activities of the alliance.

The mechanism used to cement an alliance may vary according to specific circumstances. In general, four main options have emerged within recent years:

1 *Mergers* – where two or more associations combine legally and constitutionally to form a new organisation. Each will play a part in influencing the characteristics of the new organisation which represents an integrated partnership. In such instances, it is usual for a

completely new name, identity and structure to emerge reflecting the nature and previous identity of the constituent parts. Established examples of such an arrangement are Focus HA and Touchstone HA.

2 *Takeovers* – in which one organisation assimilates the staff and assets of another, often following financial difficulties or administrative irregularities. In such circumstances the organisation being taken over ceases to exist in its own right, becoming wholly controlled or completely absorbed into the main association.

3 *Group structures* – in which a number of distinct organisations involved in different activities are drawn together under a 'parent' or controlling body. In this way, the group preserves the independent and distinctive identities of its constituent parts, while enjoying the benefits of the economies of scale.

One example is Moat Housing Group which operates with a central, cabinet-style controlling body which provides specialist services such as administration, legal and financial services, and development to the other parts of the group. The other constituent parts, Plume HA (an LSVT transfer), Moat Housing Society (general needs and shared ownership housing), and Bailey HA (charitable housing association and special needs), provide housing services direct to their various consumers. There is therefore a separation of certain key, strategic functions between the controlling part of the group and its subsidiaries. Major benefits of this approach include avoiding duplication of skills and expertise, and the economies of scale. However, centralising key management responsibilities might, in extreme cases, result in deskilling within the service organisations. Should such a trend prove widespread, it might eventually lead to housing managers being viewed as purely service deliverers, with business managers responsible for strategic planning and policy-making.

4 *Consortia* – a form of alliance in which the constituent parties choose not to integrate totally, but enter instead into discrete partnerships with each providing specific functions. These are discussed in further detail in Chapter 9.

Advantages and disadvantages exist for each of these arrangements. However, they each reflect the need for associations to meet the challenge of competition in response to changing opportunities such as Single Regeneration Budget (SRB).

Local Authority Mergers

Housing associations are not alone in being forced to re-evaluate their structures. Local authorities have also been inexorably drawn into the process of reassessing mechanisms and the costs involved in delivering services. This has been prompted by major financial constraints, including Council Tax capping, HRA ring-fencing, and increasing competition through CCT.

In addition, the changing expectations of consumers and the major review of local government has resulted in a trend towards merging local authority departments, particularly housing and social services. This has often occurred in such a way as to reflect organisational cost savings and to strengthen working relationships between different services. This has also occurred within existing authorities such as the London Boroughs of Sutton, Bromley and Islington, and St Helens DC. In the light of the impact of community care (see Chapter 5), and the resulting interactions between housing management staff and social workers, this may appear a logical development. However, concerns have been raised that such mergers may be motivated more by cost criteria, than by a commitment to the development of good joint practice.

Arguments for greater integration may more often be based on organisational considerations rather than being service related. Proponents of generic management argue that the integration of services breaks down artificial barriers, offering the potential for a seamless service to the public. While this may be true, there appears little evidence to date that the professional differences which exist between housing management staff and social workers have significantly reduced. Unless professional hearts and minds can be brought together, there is a danger that departmental mergers become little more than administrative expedients.

Housing Action Trusts (HATs)

'The Government sees the concept of HATs as a vital part of their overall housing policy, and as a means of single-mindedly attacking some of the most difficult areas of local authority housing.'

(DoE, 1987a)

Housing Action Trusts (HATs) were initially unveiled within the 1987 White Paper, *Housing: The Government's Proposals* (DoE, 1987a), and subsequently formalised within the Housing Act 1988. They were designed as vehicles to tackle the worst council housing estates, while at the same time extending the available mechanisms to remove housing stock from local authority control. The remit of the new bodies was to take responsibility for identified areas of local authority housing and facilitate its renewal before passing it on to a diverse range of potential landlords. 'Housing Action Trusts . . . will provide scope for tenants in these areas to have a diversity of landlord and ownership. And as well as improving housing conditions, they will act as enablers and facilitators for provision of other community needs such as shops, workshops and advice centres, and for encouraging local enterprise' (DoE, 1987a, p. 16).

The original HAT proposals were unveiled on 11 July 1988, containing a list of eighteen council estates located within six local authority areas (Lambeth, Leeds, Sandwell, Sunderland, Southwark and Tower Hamlets).

In introducing these proposals, the government believed that tenants would leap at the opportunity to move from the control of a discredited local authority landlord, while at the same time receiving assurances of significant cash investment in their homes. However, this expectation proved unfounded as tenants in all six of the nominated areas mounted concerted campaigns to remove their estates from the HAT list. Highly sceptical of the government's motives and trustworthiness, worried about ultimately finding themselves controlled by a private sector landlord, and insufficiently disillusioned with their local authority landlords, tenants of all the proposed HAT estates succeeded in having them withdrawn. Even written assurances that local authorities would be allowed additional resources to buy back estates once the HATs were wound up was insufficient to change tenants' minds. In Sunderland and Southwark there were substantial 'No' votes during 1990, and proposals were subsequently withdrawn in Lambeth, Leeds, Sandwell and Tower Hamlets. However, this was not the end of the HAT programme. Two other local authorities had, for particular local factors, commenced negotiations with the government during the course of 1989 and 1990, to set up a different style of HAT in their authorities. These were Waltham Forest in London and Kingston-upon-Hull.

HATs – Mark II

It was not merely a quirk of fate that the original HAT proposals had failed and were replaced by two successful alternatives. It was not just that the government had chosen the wrong local authority estates and tenants to confront; the new HATs were substantially different in a number of key areas:

- Unlike the initially identified HAT estates there was no compulsion – in both Hull and Waltham Forest, the local authorities approached the DoE with the support of tenants.
- The management boards were more accountable, with greater representation of both elected members and tenants.
- Each local authority was guaranteed the option of being able to re-purchase the dwellings if tenants so wished.
- The consultation and negotiation processes were driven largely by the local authorities and tenants. In Waltham Forest, the tenants drew up a Tenants Expectations Document (TED) presenting the DoE with the tenants' demands, which were largely met.

The government made substantial concessions in agreeing the Hull and Waltham Forest proposals. In their eagerness to rescue something from the debacle of the HAT programme, they had agreed to substantial expenditure on schemes which would not have been countenanced three years earlier. Far from HATs tackling Britain's worst estates, in Hull 'you could be forgiven for thinking you weren't on a council estate at all' (Dwelly, 1991). In reality, the estate designated by Hull as a potential HAT comprised 2019 unimproved houses which would more appropriately have been dealt with through Estate Action funding for repair and improvements rather than the more far-reaching functions of a HAT. However, there were strong pressures on the DoE to approve both Waltham Forest and Hull, which was duly given, subject to a tenants' ballot. In Hull, a favourable ballot was conducted in March 1991, and Waltham Forest followed six months later.

What is a HAT?

HATs are *quangos*, i.e. non-departmental government bodies, under the control of central government. Tenants transferring to a HAT retain their existing tenancy rights as secure tenants with the Right to Buy. There are currently six throughout the country, the first of which, Hull, is due to complete its programme of work in 1998 and thereafter wind itself up. The others are due to continue into the new millennium (see Table 8.1). Income is received mainly as grant-in-aid from the DoE and supplemented by rental income, including that from any commercial property, EC subsidies, private sector investment, and disposals. The grant forms a major element of this funding, and without which, rents would become unaffordable and redevelopment proposals unviable.

The focus of HATs is broader than just housing management. Under the terms of the 1988 Housing Act, they are charged to achieve four main objectives:

- to improve the housing stock, by repair or redevelopment
- to manage the housing stock effectively
- to encourage diversity of tenure and ownership of the properties
- to improve the social, economic and environmental conditions of the area.

As such they are expected to adopt a more holistic approach to the regeneration of housing estates, including community development, training and employment. The philosophy of each HAT is to facilitate and empower tenants so that at the end of its life, the resulting community is strong, sustainable and has the ability to exercise control over its housing. To this end, the relationship between HAT staff and tenants tends to be more open and collaborative.

The HAT Programme

The experiences of Hull and Waltham Forest prompted renewed interest amongst other authorities who felt more comfortable with the new-style HAT. Further HATs were designated in Liverpool (February 1993), Tower

Table 8.1   The HAT programme

Name of HAT	No. of dwellings	Projected winding-up	Projected grant-in-aid (£m)
North Hull	2084	1998	115 190
Waltham Forest	2422	2004	177 027
Liverpool	5337	2003	112 414
Tower Hamlets	1629	2004	55 300
Castle Vale	4886	2004	77 664
Stonebridge	2042	2005	29 850

Source: DoE.

Hamlets (June 1993) Castle Vale in Birmingham (June 1993) and Stonebridge in the London Borough of Brent (July 1994), producing a national position as shown in Table 8.1.

The characteristics of each HAT are markedly different. As already mentioned, Hull centres on an estate of traditionally built houses, whilst Waltham Forest consists of four, system-built high-density estates. Liverpool, the largest HAT, is also the most dispersed, covering 39 separate sites including 67 tower blocks and 158 low-rise dwellings. Castle Vale is the only HAT to be contained within a single boundary, covering an area of 500 acres (200ha), including over 100 acres (40ha) of open space. The housing is a mix of high-rise blocks, sheltered housing, two-storey blocks, houses and bungalows of which over 1400 are owner occupied. Stonebridge and Tower Hamlets HATs are based on high-density, inner-city estates, with all the hallmarks of poor design and construction from 1970s-built housing.

The Cost of HATs – A Value Added Alternative?

'What does a HAT bring which cannot be provided by the local authority? It is a new body with new ideas and highly focused management. It involves the local authority, without being hampered by the complexity of the latter's problems; its tenants play an ever greater role in its decision making. It has an open mind to involving other partners particularly private business and local community organisations.'

(E. Chumrow, Chair, WFHAT)

One of the criterion against which HATs inevitably will be measured is the extent to which they improve services over those provided by the previous council landlords. Local authority housing managers will, however, justifiably protest that they might also have significantly improved services had they access to the generous level of funds enjoyed by the HATs. A purely output-related comparison would therefore be flawed. A more meaningful method would be one which accounted for any additional value added to performance from a holistic approach to communities and their environment. These might occur where:

1 the potential range or quality of services offered by the HAT model exceeds that which might reasonably be offered by their local authority counterparts
2 additional community-related benefits accrue as a result of the housing management services provided (see also Housing Plus, Chapter 9)
3 consumers believe they are receiving a more responsive and value for money service.

A tenant satisfaction survey carried out by Waltham Forest HAT (WFHAT) in June 1994 indicated that following the HAT taking control, 72 per cent of tenants believed that the housing service had improved, 18 per cent believed it had remained static, only 3 per cent considered it had got worse, and 7 per cent had no opinion. Accolades have also been forthcoming from external sources. Both Hull and Waltham Forest have been awarded the Charter Mark (see Chapter 3), with Waltham Forest also gaining a Tenant Participation Advisory Service (TPAS) award, in 1995, for their work in achieving tenant empowerment.

In terms of value for money, HAT managers are convinced that they are providing a more cost-effective service than the council were able to offer. This relates both to levels of performance and the overall cost of the service. Since their establishment, HATs have sought to achieve competitive prices by market testing for all services. This has ensured that if services remain in-house, they do so by offering both quality and value.

However, the cost of the six HATs remains substantial, amounting to approximately £90 million per annum, perhaps for the next decade. Can this level of expenditure be warranted at a time when the public sector has been forced to accept severe constraints on their spending? The answer is unavailable at this stage of the HAT programme. Whilst aspects such as estate management can be costed on a year-to-year basis, objectives such as community development and tenant empowerment are longer-term commitments. It is difficult to make direct comparisons between the services provided by the HATs and their local authority counterparts. HATs are an expensive option if taken to be a housing management service alone, but become much better value when considered as urban regeneration projects. Already, the achievements of the HATs are being used as a potential model for future Single Regeneration Budget (SRB) programmes.

Case Study:

Name: Waltham Forest HAT (WFHAT)
Location: NE London
Type of organisation: Housing Action Trust

Number of dwellings: 2422
Number of staff: 111 full-time equivalents

Background:

Waltham Forest HAT has a stock profile rather different from its counterpart in Hull. A stock condition survey carried out in 1985 indicated serious structural and fabric problems on four system-built estates constructed in the late 1960s and early 1970s. These estates comprised 13 twenty-one-storey tower blocks and 28 eight-storey large panel construction blocks. In addition, the estates were amongst the least desirable in the borough, with high levels of tenant dissatisfaction.

The local authority, having established an Estate Improvement team to evaluate options for addressing the problems of these estates, came to the view that any solution would have to include demolition and related new build. Following consultation with tenants, a number of innovative mechanisms to raise the necessary funding were proposed, none of which proved acceptable to the DoE. This prompted a campaign by tenants' groups which placed significant pressure on the Secretary of State to agree to a solution. The result in November 1989 was the offer of a HAT.

A joint steering group of tenants, the council and the DoE, was convened to agree a Tenants' Expectations Document (TED). This set out the policies to be pursued by the HAT if it were to proceed following a tenants' ballot. The costs of the exercise were borne jointly by the DoE and the council. A feasibility study supporting the viability of a HAT was published in September 1990, and consultants were appointed by the tenants as independent advisors.

The ballot took place between 13 and 31 July 1991, with 81 per cent of tenants voting in favour of a HAT on a turnout of 75 per cent of those eligible. The Designation Order formally setting up WFHAT took effect on 9 December 1991, with the transfer of the estates from the council occurring on 6 April 1992.

The managing board of the HAT, appointed by the Secretary of State, comprised a Chair, five non-resident members, four estate residents and a local councillor. Following transfer, WFHAT contracted with Waltham Forest Council to manage the estates as an interim measure whilst the HAT recruited its staffing complement and set up appropriate systems. The proposed life of the HAT was set at 13 years, with an anticipated winding-up date in 2004. During that time, the purpose of the HAT is to meet the objective of the Mission Statement which is: 'Working with tenants to develop homes, people and communities which will bring about long-lasting improvement in the quality of life' (Annual Report, 1993/4, p. 3). To achieve this, Waltham Forest is the only HAT embarking on a programme of complete demolition and rebuilding of its housing stock.

Each of the four WFHAT estates has its own local office, from which the majority of its housing services are provided. Although this is similar to the arrangement under the council, the range of services and approach is different. 'The theme of "empowerment" runs through the WFHAT programmes and strongly influences the redevelopment process as well as housing management and community development' (WFHAT Corporate Plan). The delivery of estate management services has only been determined after detailed consultation with the HAT's tenants over the contract specification for housing management; tenancy agreement; and lettings and allocations policies. The HAT has employed its own estate management staff during 1993/4, since which time the improvements have been made to estate security resulting in reduced levels of crime. Inroads have also been made into the huge backlog of outstanding repairs and maintenance issues inherited when the HAT took control of the estates. Perhaps the greatest change relates to staff attitudes, indicated in recent tenant surveys to have improved significantly.

As part of this holistic approach to community empowerment, WFHAT established a Careers Advice and Placement Project (CAPP) which had 1400 HAT residents registered for training or employment. Two training centres have also been set up, one relating to business and computing skills, the other to construction skills. In addition, initiatives have been developed to encourage local firms to tender for contracts with the HAT, support the setting up of new tenant-led businesses, and generally encourage the regeneration of the local economy. One notable achievement has been the successful bid for the estate cleaning service on one of the estates by a newly formed tenant company.

Large Scale Voluntary Transfer (LSVT)

Large Scale Voluntary Transfer housing associations have also emerged as an increasingly important feature of social housing since 1988, becoming the main vehicle for transferring stock away from local authority control. They owe their existence to the increasing constraints imposed on local authorities during the 1980s, which had the effect of centralising power in Westminster, rather than at a local level. By the end of the decade, local authorities faced an environment in which their ability to control their own housing stock was seriously undermined. Large numbers of dwellings had already been lost through the Right to Buy, particularly in the affluent south east, and Tenants' Choice offered a further threat. The final straw saw the ring-fencing of the HRA, which, in effect, removed local discretion over rent-setting policies. Revenue controls were accompanied by strict capital controls, development finance being routed away from HIP (Housing Investment Programme), into the coffers of the Housing Corporation. The result was an environment in which local authorities were faced with the threats outlined in Table 8.2. These were further compounded by the imminent imposition of CCT which promised to make even further inroads into democratic control. For many ruling groups, the

Table 8.2   Factors leading to LSVT

– the prospect of continuing and uncontrolled loss of rented stock through Right to Buy;
– very little prospect of being able to build council housing to replace lost stock;
– in some parts of the country at least, the prospect of a continuing fall in the number of lettings available for new tenants;
– continuing demands for council housing from applicants on the waiting and transfer lists, and from homeless households to whom local authorities had a statutory duty to make available temporary and permanent accommodation;
– the prospects of higher rents for council tenants to enhance or even to maintain the housing service;
– the prospect of council tenants increasingly subsidising other council tenants through rent rebates;
– mechanisms by which tenants could choose to transfer to another landlord – a prospect which might become more attractive as council rents rose and/or services were constrained;
– less concretely though no less significantly, a philosophical slant from central government in which local authorities were encouraged to switch from a service-providing role to a strategic and enabling role.

Source: DoE (1992d).

future appeared to offer little other than the prospect of presiding over deteriorating services.

The prospect of breaking free of these threats and constraints, whilst safeguarding the quality of services, was therefore tempting. The impetus towards LSVT originated at a local level, rather than by any coordinated central government policy. It was facilitated by the powers vested in local authorities for disposing of their housing stock under the 1985 Housing Act (ss32–34 and 43). 'Interestingly, the statutory powers for disposal in the 1985 Act were not introduced with voluntary transfer in mind, and those provisions of the Act which were oriented to voluntary transfer can best be seen as a response to local government initiatives already under way' (Mullins, Niner and Risborough, 1993). Much of the impetus and driving force has emanated from officers rather than members, although member support is vital for a transfer to proceed. Where transfers have proceeded officers have in practice gained the most. Not only are the financial shackles and the threat of CCT removed, but political control is also lost, resulting in a greater degree of autonomy.

The Framework for Transfer

By March 1996, 50 local authorities had succeeded in transferring their stock (Table 8.3). A further 27 had their proposals overturned by the tenants. The vast majority of successes and failures alike have been Conservative-controlled, southern shire districts. The exceptions have been Ryedale and

Table 8.3   Successful voluntary transfers, 1988–95

Local authority year of transfer	No. of homes transferred	% of tenants in favour	Total transfer price	Price paid per dwelling
1988				
Chiltern	4 650	85	£32.9m	£6 926
Sevenoaks	6 526	85	£65.5m	£10 037
Newbury	7 053	82	£47.0m	£6 664
1990				
Swale	7 352	54	£55.2m	£7 501
Broadland	3 721	53	£25.1m	£6 739
North Bedfordshire	7 472	72	£64.3m	£8 605
Medina	2 825	69	£27.9m	£9 858
Rochester	8 029	60	£77.0m	£9 590
South Wight	2 119	91	£22.8m	£10 776
Mid Sussex	4 426	77	£44.2m	£9 984
East Dorset	2 245	84	£21.6m	£9 620
1991				
Tonbridge & Malling	6 382	71	£54.4m	£8 524
Ryedale	3 353	82	£28.3m	£8 436
South Bucks	3 319	75	£34.0m	£10 244
Christchurch	1 621	54	£15.4m	£9 144
Suffolk Coastal	5 272	57	£34.0m	£6 508
1992				
Tunbridge Wells	5 519	60	£58.1m	£10 221
Bromley	12 393	55	£117.6m	£9 489
1993				
Surrey Heath	2 885	71	£28.7m	£9 962
Breckland	6 781	62	£60.2m	£8 879
East Cambridgeshire	4 266	70	£31.5m	£7 384
Hambleton	4 269	66	£33.5m	£7 873
West Dorset	5 279	65	£40.3m	£7 629
1994				
Havant	3 561	51	£35.2m	£9 893
Epsom & Ewell	1 740	53	£20.3m	£11 665
Hart	2 408	76	£23.1m	£9 593
South Shropshire	1 500	70	£14.1m	£9 400
Leominster	1 832	87	£15.5m	£8 460
South Ribble	3 445	78	£32.3m	£9 097
Hertsmere	8 284	78/76	£56.4m	£8 688
Cherwell	1 046	35	£10.7m	£10 250
Basingstoke & Deane	9 870	52/53	£52.0m	£11 724
Penwith	3 354	65	£30.5m	£9 093
Maldon	2 006	82	£21.6m	£10 870
Malvern Hills	4 817	83	£47.0m	£9 746
Mid Bedfordshire	2 971	73	£24.1m	£8 100
North Dorset	2 881	55	£25.3m	£8 775
1995				
Thanet	2 658	51	£21.5m	£8 087

Table 8.3 cont.

Local authority year of transfer	No. of homes transferred	% of tenants in favour	Total transfer price	Price paid per dwelling
Vale of the White Horse	5 028	67	£57.7m	£11 543
Wychavon	4 020	81	£42.9m	£10 678
Windsor and Maidenhead	3 236	60	£32.3m	£9 950
	2 981	54	£31.6m	£10 600
Kennet	4 915	87	£63.7m	£12 960
Rushmoor	5 102	69	£65.1	£12 759
N. Wilts	6 100	82	£54.8m	£8 984
Spelthorne	4 100	73	£50.09m	£12 217
East Hants	4 076	71	£53.1m	£13 027
Hastings	4 558	69	£44.6m	£9 784
Manchester	1 413	90	–	–
Wyre	3 000	73	£20m	£6 666
Eastleigh	4 400	76	£47.8m	£10 863
Total/average	223 059	69	£1 549.7m	£9 156

Source: DoE.

Hambleton in Yorkshire, Broadland and Breckland in Norfolk, and the London Borough of Bromley. The number of dwellings involved has varied from 1500 in South Shropshire, to 12 393 in Bromley. However, DoE guidelines issued in 1993/4 limited transfers to a maximum of 4000 dwellings, or 5000 if the housing stock is to be split between two or more associations. In addition to size restrictions, a 20 per cent levy has also been introduced on any proceeds from the sale. This is to offset the additional cost to the Treasury of funding claims for housing benefit which would have increasingly been met from the HRA.

The receiving association acquires the transferred stock at a 'tenanted market value', at a price determined by the DoE. This valuation is based on an assumption that the dwellings will continue to be let at *social housing* rents, and will take account of the maintenance expenditure required. The average price per dwelling received by local authorities following transfers to date is £9156, generating a total transfer sum of £1549.7 million.

The Route to Transfer

The road to transfer is often long and difficult, with the outcome depending on a protracted period of complex negotiation, and the ultimate support of a majority of those tenants affected by the proposals. 'A typical transfer process can take two years, cost almost £2 million in consultants' fees and transaction costs, and involve enormous amounts of (largely unpaid) staff overtime' (Mullins *et al.*, 1993).

Authorities pursuing the transfer option do so in the expectation of a more stable environment in which to manage their stock, rather than

Table 8.4   Advantages of voluntary transfer

- New lettings would not be subject to the Right to Buy
- The valuation and transfer would enable the capital to be raised to deal with major defects or disrepair
- Escape direct government financial controls
- No future threat of stock loss through 'Tenants Choice'
- Rent increases not controlled by new subsidy regime, or required to contribute towards the cost of rent rebates
- Possibility of operating more effectively than assumed by valuation methodology
- If transfer price exceeds outstanding debt, capital resources are then available to:
  - Repay other authority debt and strengthen revenue
  - Make additional new housing investment
- Single purpose housing body; no 'central' overheads

Source: Institute of Housing (1990).

being subjected to the continued uncertainty experienced by local government. An additional gain, depending on the terms of transfer, is that the capital receipt generated for the local authority may be ploughed back into new housing provision through local authority HAG. The seventeen LSVT associations formed by March 1992 had built over 2200 new dwellings in 1991/2, mostly financed by receipts generated by the transfer (Audit Commission, 1993b). Other perceived advantages are contained in Table 8.4. However, some of these projected advantages have looked increasingly illusory, as proposals in the DoE White Paper, *Our Future Homes* (DoE, 1995b), implemented in the Housing Act 1996 have extended sales to sitting tenants of charitable housing associations, and the possibility of greater funding competition via the extension of HAG to the private sector.

Even without the White Paper, the apparent advantages of transfer should not completely eclipse the potentially negative effects of such a move. In particular, the momentum for transfer can often result in the terms being geared exclusively towards safeguarding the interests of existing tenants in the attempt to win their support. This raises concerns that in gaining support for transfer, the future strategic function of the social housing stock may be compromised: 'Authorities must therefore, in evaluating the transfer option, consider the consequences for future customers, as well as for existing tenants and services' (IoH, 1990). There is also evidence (Joseph Rowntree Foundation, 1995 DoE, 1992d) that tenants have not always received sufficient information to enable them to make reasoned judgements in relation to their potential options. Some observers are concerned that in such circumstances, local authorities 'are placing more importance on getting the proposals through than genuine consultation' (Bickler and Hood, 1991). However, this appears to have improved in a number of recent transfers where tenants have had access to independent advice.

Table 8.5   Disadvantages of voluntary transfer

- New lettings would be assured tenancies subject to the 'Tenants' Guarantee', but with fewer rights than secure tenants in some respects
- Rents required to increase by 1–2 per cent in real terms per year
- Immediate substantial rent increases on relets
- Once and for all irreversible choice
- Upheaval of major institutional changes
- Loss of direct local authority control
- Impact on remaining local authority services
- Proposal may be rejected by tenants, leaving abortive costs to be met
- May be subject to Housing Corporation regulation
- Subject to fluctuations in the financial markets
- THE UNKNOWN

Source: Institute of Housing (1990)

The critical nature of this consultation for tenants is highlighted by the irreversibility of the move away from council control and the subsequent loss of democratic accountability. As mentioned elsewhere, the *democratic deficit* is a feature of housing associations. Other potential disadvantages are identified in Table 8.5.

Changing Cultures

Perhaps the most potentially problematic of these issues is that of the unknown. LSVT remains a relatively recent phenomenon, and its medium and long-term effects are still to unfold. One can speculate that service decisions are more likely to be dominated by financial considerations than might have been the case under local authority ownership. More crucially, the majority of LSVT associations have been conceived and born into an immediate culture of competition and risk, whilst carrying with them many of the same staff trained and socialised in a different style and ethos. The Chief Executive of West Kent Housing Association admitted in 1990, two years after transfer, that 'we underestimated the requirement for fundamental and radical change in moving from a council housing department to a private sector housing association. There are cultural and real differences between the two types of organisations, and not all senior staff adapt easily or quickly' (Hutchins, 1990). There appears little doubt that LSVT organisations do undergo a marked change of direction after gaining independence from the local authority. 'What was surprising was the extent of agreement about the ethos and approach of the new LSVT organisations and how different they were from the old authorities. Staff talked about the new housing associations as businesses' (Jackson, 1993).

Measuring Achievements

In general, the progress of LSVT associations has been good. In a five-year review of performance (DoE, 1995a), the DoE found that the perceptions of tenants, local authorities and the Housing Corporation had all remained favourable. In a number of cases, performance in areas such as repairs and void control had improved, and for existing tenants, rents were maintained at relatively low levels for a fixed period. In addition, nearly all of the associations had managed to undertake a development programme, which would not have been possible had they remained under the control of the local authority. However, there were also negative aspects. While existing tenants enjoyed low rents, new tenants were faced with much higher charges and were more inclined to be dissatisfied with the services received in terms of value for money. There were also concerns about the potential level of rent rises for existing tenants once the period of rent freeze was over. The financial stability of associations also varied. Those transferring earlier tended to be better resourced by avoiding the levy charged by the Treasury to offset housing benefit. In addition, some associations fared worse by misreading the financial markets in terms of interest-rate trends, or being over-optimistic in projecting future sales. There have also been some difficult times for staff as the organisations have followed a steep learning curve in their new environment.

The impact of LSVT associations is not limited solely to the staff and tenants of the transferred organisation. While they may have been relatively small as local authorities, the resulting housing association is relatively large. The presence of fifty medium-sized new housing associations has added an extra competitive edge to an already stretched ADP. Particularly affected are the smaller local housing associations who are finding life tough maintaining existing relationships with local authorities and competing for opportunities in their traditional areas. Already LSVT associations have been involved in bidding to take over the management of some local authority stock, although none have yet succeeded. There is little doubt that the ethos of the LSVT associations differs from many traditional associations in their approach to development and growth. Located more at the entrepreneurial end of the welfare/commerce continuum, they may well survive better than many other associations if and when the fight for HAG with the private sector begins.

Housing Companies

Recent proposals for the development of housing companies are, in common with many of the organisational hybrids detailed previously, a reaction to the constraints imposed by the prevailing financial climate. The idea is not a new one, achieving popularity during the late 1980s as a potential vehicle for local authorities to pursue 'leaseback' arrangements, i.e. to raise money by selling housing to a 'friendly' organisation, i.e. the housing company. In the event, the government plugged the loophole in March 1989, when the Secretary of State, Nicholas Ridley, removed the benefits of leaseback, reacting against a number of overt abuses by London Boroughs.

The issue was again revived in 1993, following a Joseph Rowntree Foundation report which indicated that by transferring council housing to local housing companies an additional £16 billion could be released for investment in social housing in England (Wilcox, 1993). The transfer to a private company could place any expenditure incurred by the new landlords outside of the Public Sector Borrowing Requirement (PSBR) and therefore central government capital constraints. Proponents also argue that such a policy would, as with LSVT, generate massive capital receipts which local authorities could subsequently use to improve and repair existing dwellings and build new ones. However, a disadvantage relates to the government requirement that housing companies must be clearly located within the private sector. Thus, transferring stock to a private company with only a minority council or tenant representation, would inevitably result in a loss of democratic control and accountability.

The Chartered Institute of Housing developed a housing company model to overcome such concerns. In *Challenging the Conventions* (CIH, 1995a), they promote the establishment of 'local public housing corporations' which would be wholly owned by local authorities, but legally separate bodies managed at *arm's length* as non-profit-making companies. Thus, although elected members would have control over the company's objectives, they would have no operational involvement. However, despite lobbying, this model has not been supported within government circles. To be successful, these proposals depend on the Treasury altering its accounting mechanism from PSBR to the General Government Financial Deficit (GGFD) system, as used in other European states. To date, little enthusiasm has been shown for such a change, even by the Labour Party. The uncertainty surrounding these prerequisites has clearly complicated the development of housing companies.

However, the government indicated support for housing companies within the 1995 White Paper, *Our Future Homes*, (DoE, 1995b) and introduced enabling legislation in the Housing Act 1996, in which they endorsed the earlier, Joseph Rowntree model of private ownership, i.e. removed from direct local authority control. Qualified support also exists within the main opposition parties, i.e. Labour and the Liberal Democrats. Equally important, housing companies also appear to have received enthusiastic support from potential private sector funders without whom the idea could not work.

In terms of housing management, housing companies represent a mixture of positive and negative opportunity. On the plus side, transferring to the private sector offers greater freedom in which to operate flexibly and proactively. This has become particularly important within recent years with the advent of major funding packages such as the Single Regenera-tion Budget (SRB), where the remit is much broader than housing man-agement. A more generic, non-housing specific structure offers greater opportunity to implement programmes which may include an element of housing, but also encompass community development and economic regeneration.

Against this must be set the potential loss of democratic accountability. Proponents would, however, point out that this is no worse a position than exists with housing associations, and might in some instances actu-ally prove more representative. A second concern is the implication for affordability of developing with loans from the private sector, mirroring the dilemma faced by many of the newer LSVT associations. This, how-ever, must be weighed against the inadequacy of the social new-build programmes achieved under more traditional funding mechanisms. Finally, housing companies are largely unknown quantities. Even if the model of non-profit-making public housing corporations were adopted, the culture and ethos would inevitably differ from that of the transferring local auth-ority. This phenomenon has already been experienced with the LSVT associations. Employment terms and conditions in the private sector differ from those in the public sector, as do mechanisms for accountability. This may be less of an issue under the local housing corporation model, which remains largely democratically controlled. This would not be the case where elected members and tenants are in a minority on the board of directors. While the proponents of housing companies propose strict regu-latory measures, these are likely to relate to financial management, pro-bity and control rather than qualitative measures. This may be effective where companies are committed to social housing. However, over time, a more diverse range of private companies may develop an interest in man-aging social housing which may test regulatory frameworks to their limits.

As a vehicle for privatisation, housing companies may go the way of Tenants' Choice and the initial HAT proposals. Yet the cross-party support would appear to make this unlikely. There is, however, the danger that they will merely become a substitute for LSVT as a mechanism to remove better quality housing from local authorities. In a survey conducted by the CIH in December 1995, 60 per cent of housing directors favoured com-panies, almost all of which represented non-metropolitan authorities. There appears little enthusiasm for transfer within the inner-city urban authorities where social housing is often in urgent need of increased investment.

Summary

As elsewhere in this book, the theme of change dominates. For many traditional housing organisations which have become a familiar part of the scene, retaining the status quo is no longer an option. Many would argue that this is a good thing. It is natural for organisations to change, evolving over time to reflect shifting trends, attitudes and personalities. The better organisations learn through experience, are open to new ideas and do not seek to replicate past practices without question. The nature of current change has marked a movement away from many of the more negative aspects of social housing management: paternalism, bureaucracy, and mechanistic approaches to service delivery. In their place has emerged a growing appreciation of the importance of the consumer and of external influences.

However, amongst all of the positive reasons for change, there is also the cautionary voice which says 'if its not broke, don't fix it'. Whatever the anecdotal and media-generated assertions that social housing is un-competitive and inefficient, there remains little or no hard evidence to support this. As in the private sector, there are organisations which are well-run and others which are not. There are also many examples of local authorities successfully evolving to take account of the changing needs of their consumers. However, many of the organisational changes described in this chapter have come about in an attempt to preserve a standard of service rather than extend it. Thus, in the case of Liverpool, the Director of Housing considered the city's HAT to be 'purely a mechanism for bringing money into the city. I don't think anyone supports the actual concept of HATs' (*ROOF*, January/February 1993, p. 20).

Yet of all the structures described in this chapter, perhaps HATs have the greatest claim to have produced a genuine change to the process of housing management. They have approached the provision of housing as constituting only one part of people's lives, recognising that communities function best when they have access to employment, training and ad-equate facilities. They provide a project-based organisation devoted to serving their communities. Certainly they are privileged in the level of resources to which they have access, and the ability to focus on a relatively small number of dwellings. However, it is possible that some areas of depriva-tion, poor housing conditions and marginalised residents can only effec-tively be tackled in such a way.

Supporters of LSVT associations might justifiably point to the record of their achievements as also providing clear evidence of improved service. While this may be true, the question must be asked, could such improve-ments have also been achieved by the local authority had the myriad of resource constraints been removed? In practice, any improvements have been purchased at the cost of an expensive process of transfer and the loss of democratic accountability. In some cases, the price of change has been justified. The opportunities for improvement within the local auth-ority structure were too limiting.

At present, the future of housing companies is uncertain. They have the potential to change the face of social housing completely should they prove financially and politically viable. However, considerable doubts remain about their costing profiles and levels of accountability to their consumers. Their primary benefit would be to circumvent the restrictions of the PSBR and thus generate additional resources. This once again gives substance to the widely held belief that Britain's approach to housing is influenced overwhelmingly by financial policy rather than by any form of coherent housing policy.

Questions remain about whether or not local authorities and housing associations can successfully tackle the problems which they now face. However, the emergence of the new organisations outlined in this chapter may mean that they will not get the chance. Local authority housing directors and elected members might reasonably argue, *if only we too had the resources.* But perhaps the problem goes deeper than that. Maybe the need is for more task-oriented, dynamic structures which can coordinate and focus rather than be diverted by the strategic enormity faced by local authorities. This may be the vision of the future – but at what cost?

9 Managing in Partnership

'The future of local authorities will essentially be a strategic one identifying housing needs and demands, encouraging innovative methods of provision by other bodies to meet such needs, maximising the use of private finance, and encouraging the new interest in the revival of the independent rented sector. In order to fulfil this role they will have to work closely with housing associations; private landlords; developers; and building societies and other providers of finance.'

(DoE, 1987a, p. 14)

In examining social housing, certain key themes emerge which are central to an understanding of the dynamics of the process. Working in partnership is one such theme, having grown steadily in importance during the 1990s. The continued drive by central government to fragment public services has created the situation in which strategic planning, development, management and maintenance of social housing can rarely be accommodated within single organisations. There is therefore an increasing reliance on identifying compatible partners with whom to devise and deliver appropriate housing services. This is true not only of local authorities and housing associations, which continue to operate within tight public expenditure constraints, but also the private sector, particularly in the construction industry where companies have suffered the effects of a crippling recession. The challenge across both sectors has been to reassess the production of housing and its related services, and devise new, flexible approaches which reflect relative strengths and available resources. The catalysts for partnership have therefore been both carrot and stick, emanating from a combination of government regulation and financial necessity.

Since 1988, the partnership between local authorities and housing associations has been institutionalised in the enabler/provider split. The government's intentions for local housing authorities were laid out in the 1987 White Paper, *Housing: The Government's Proposals* (DoE, 1987a) (as quoted earlier). Rather than providing housing directly, councils are expected to adopt a strategic, enabling role within which they facilitate others, redefining the rationale and approach of many housing departments almost overnight. As examined in Chapter 3, the transition to enabling has not always been smooth, the adaption to a new approach proving less straightforward than anticipated by some local authorities. The skills and attitudes for achieving successful partnership are not necessarily the same as those previously fostered and valued within autonomous, developing organisations.

Housing associations are more dependent on partnership. Although more likely to have fostered such an approach prior to 1989, they have been forced to extend such arrangements. Bids for funding to the Housing Corporation's Approved Development Programme (ADP) only stand to be successful with the support of local authorities. This has given teeth to councils' enabling role and guaranteed a dialogue to establish common priorities. The reduction in Housing Association Grant (HAG) since 1989 has also compelled associations to work with the private sector to raise funding and to deliver a cost-effective product. The die has therefore been cast, with inter-agency and inter-sectoral partnership becoming an established factor in the process of providing social housing.

This chapter examines the scope of and implications for partnership in housing management, in particular, the means by which many organisations have adapted to their changing environment by establishing new models of collaboration and facilitation. Included are examples of inter and intra-sectoral partnerships which have in some way heralded new methods of working. Each illustrates a specific approach to partnership which has either built on or expanded the boundaries of inter-agency cooperation. Also examined are the implications of partnerships on practitioners and their approach to consumers. While the organisational rewards from successful partnerships can be substantial, there are inevitable consequences which percolate down to the 'coal face'. These may be overlooked when establishing partnership frameworks, potentially resulting in a less effective working arrangement or, in extreme circumstances, the collapse of the partnership.

The Nature of Partnership

There have been many pressures in recent years towards the promotion of partnership in the social housing sector. A significant number have been generated by the activities of central government having shifted the focus of social housing provision from a predominantly publicly-funded resource to that of a mixed-funded commodity. The reduction in the powers and functions of local authorities has forced them to look outside of their internal resources to achieve local strategy objectives. This has been achieved largely through a financial stranglehold imposed on authorities, restricting their local autonomy in raising capital and revenue finance. The consequence has been that local authorities committed to maintaining and expanding services have been forced to look to prospective partners with whom they might cultivate a productive relationship. The measure of enthusiasm and effectiveness with which different authorities have approached this task has varied greatly. Many non-metropolitan authorities have traditionally been quite prepared to see other organisations, particularly housing associations, taking the strain in providing services. In contrast, inner-city, often labour-controlled authorities have been less disposed towards delegating what they believed to be municipal responsibilities. Housing associations, in contrast, have often been more overtly receptive to the concept of partnership. Virtually all associations have been dependent to some extent on either local authorities and/or the Housing Corporation for funding and have therefore been used to working with and through other agencies.

The nature and styles of partnerships have proved many and varied, ranging from informal arrangements to contractual commitments; from peripheral collaborations to organisational integration. They each, however, have a common motivation, i.e. the desire, whether voluntarily or under duress, to work with another party or parties. Some organisations prove better equipped to achieve this than others, as do the individuals upon whom partnerships often depend. Generally, organisations do not initiate contact with one another: individual members of staff do. Often, the most successful partnerships are built on informal networking between development officers or allocations staff, during which common problems are shared and joint solutions devised.

To sustain partnership and ensure that it flourishes, arrangements must generally be built on a foundation of trust and shared values, or in their absence a watertight contractual arrangement in which the roles and responsibilities are clearly spelt out. For many practitioners, the requirement to extend trust occurs at a time when they fear for their jobs following the fallout from CCT and the retrenchment in HAG funding. However, generally, the growth in partnerships has created opportunities rather than additional threats, often leading to improved financial stability, and has extended the range of skills and created a more externally focused, innovative environment in which to work.

However, while partnership can bring with it enormous benefits, it also has certain implications. The more fundamental the relationship between the partners, the greater the implication for change for the organisation involved. There can be little doubt that the effort and energy required to coordinate the actions of a number of partners is greater than that of an individual organisation. Similarly, the impact of a highly integrated, coordinated and focused vehicle for partnership may be much greater than that of a loose confederation of organisations. However, the internal changes required of each of the partners will also be correspondingly greater. In other words, there is usually a price to be paid for partnership – it is rarely a neutral option.

Partnership: The Nuts and Bolts

What, then, is partnership, that it can be so complex whilst at the same time being so potentially fulfilling? 'In the most simple terms, partnership is an organisational framework for policy-making and implementation which attempts to mobilise a coalition of interests and actors around a common agenda' (Geddes, 1994). Clearly the most crucial element of this definition is that of commonality. Partnerships cannot hope to develop or thrive where there is little common ground between the parties. Darke (1995) goes further, suggesting that in addition to commonality, the development of a partnership is often contingent upon existing links or of a broker able to bring the parties together. This has perhaps become less true of the local authority/housing association relationship, where many of the more thrusting and entrepreneurial associations have taken it upon themselves to actively seek out partnership opportunities. The need for targeted networking may however be more evident in non-standard areas of housing provision, or where smaller organisations have insufficient resources to develop the sophisticated marketing techniques adopted by their larger counterparts. This may be particularly true in special-needs housing and developing linkages with the private sector.

The main benefit of partnership is generally centred on the notion of *sharing*, whether resources, information, expertise or risk. This has often allowed a more cost-effective use of resources than could be achieved by individual organisations bearing the full cost of service provision. The maximisation of resource potential has become particularly important in an environment of risk and commercialism in which organisations must remain financially viable in order to survive. The trend towards running housing associations and local authorities as *social businesses* has demanded the development of a range of financial and management skills previously lacking. However, this has proved a costly exercise, significantly disadvantaging smaller associations with limited budgets. The use of partnership arrangements has lessened this burden in a number of ways:

1 Organisations can share risk and combine individual resources to offer greater levels of financial security.
2 Financial skills do not come cheaply. Partnerships can offer a framework in which specialist financial and personnel skills can be employed to serve more than one organisation in a consortium arrangement.
3 Resources and opportunities may be unlocked which might not have been available to the individual partners.

However, any move towards integrating organisations also inevitably opens a pandora's box of issues around culture, ethos, structures and staffing levels within each of the parties involved. The development of close working arrangements often generates threats and insecurity amongst staff who potentially stand to lose, whether it be job security, influence or status. The process therefore often calls for skilful negotiation and conflict resolution to ensure a commonality of approach rather than internal divisiveness.

In examining partnerships between local authorities and housing associations, Darke suggests that there are a number of factors which appear to contribute to successful partnerships. These are contained in Table 9.1.

Achieving such a menu can be daunting when in reality many partnerships are created from a 'big-bang approach rather than evolving over time. This often denies the conditions necessary for mutual trust to be nurtured, thus providing the foundation for future achievements. It is perhaps

Table 9.1   Ingredients of success for partnership

- mutual trust between partners;
- as much equality as possible within the constraints of other (pre-existing) structures of accountability;
- early agreement on aims and approach;
- lack of ambiguity and clear recording of agreement about:
  - objectives and strategy
  - division of costs, risks and returns
  - division of responsibility and authority;
- agreement on phasing of action programmes;
- prior agreement on how conflicts are to be resolved;
- protection of third party interests and rights;
- adequate support and control facilities;
- absence of hidden agendas;
- new partners not introduced at later stages unless carefully integrated;
- some early (even if limited) successes in order to build confidence and morale.

Source: Darke (1995).

unlikely that all of these conditions will be achieved in practice. They do, however, highlight those areas in which partnerships tend to falter and stumble irrespective of common aims and objectives. The result is that the process has to be carefully managed by individuals committed to and skilled in the art of partnership working. Whilst the availability of such individuals in social housing circles has been patchy, the situation is changing as recognition of the importance of partnerships grows.

Local Authorities and Housing Associations

The Developing Relationship

The dominant form of social housing partnership to date has been that between local authorities and housing associations. Having developed over a long period, there are distinct phases which have marked the changing relationship. The most notable are the periods: 1974–88, during which the Housing Corporation and the HAG system of funding was established by the Housing Act 1974; and 1989 onwards, which marked the introduction of the enabler/provider regime in the Housing Act 1988.

Prior to 1989, associations largely played second fiddle to local authorities, complementing rather than supplementing mainstream activities such as general needs housing. The niche for housing associations often centred on provision for the elderly, single persons and special needs housing. However, 'relationships between housing associations and local authorities are very variable; some are formal and well-established and others weak and irregular' (ADC *et al.*, 1984). Some municipally-minded councils have viewed the work of associations as unwelcome, although to most they have posed no significant threat. Many local authorities have provided a relatively small amount of funding to enable associations to develop schemes that they had identified as priorities. In reciprocation, associations have been expected to offer councils nomination rights to at least 50 per cent of the resulting dwellings. In cases of special-needs housing, the majority of nominees have come through social services departments or health authorities.

Capital funding for these schemes has been set against housing departments' Housing Investment Programme (HIP) allocation, diverting resources from council house building when this was an option. In many cases revenue funding was also provided, usually by Social Services for staffing and other support services. For associations, the process was largely benign and non-threatening. The residual HAG regime was highly advantageous, providing all the development capital not covered by the borrowing capacity supported by the fair rents. In addition, associations were often prevented from competing, by local authorities imposing a strict zoning policy. This involved dividing boroughs into geographic areas, or zones, within which only specified associations were allowed to operate. The intention was to prevent associations bidding against each other when purchasing properties for rehabilitation.

This rather cosy relationship came to an abrupt end following the Housing Act 1988. The main changes have been examined earlier in this book. However, in terms of the relationship between local authorities and housing associations, the key features were:

1 Local authorities became dependent on housing associations for new housing development.
2 Housing associations became potential threats by virtue of the introduction of Tenants' Choice. This enabled council tenants to vote to transfer to an alternative, *approved* (i.e. registered by the Housing Corporation) landlord, most likely a housing association. Such a potentially competitive relationship has subsequently been extended to management contracts as the result of CCT.
3 Local authorities became enablers, with greater strategic influence over the ways that housing associations operate within their areas. This is true not only of schemes funded by local authority HAG, but also those funded by the Housing Corporation.

A substantially new relationship was imposed upon both local authorities and housing associations which many local authority elected members found a difficult pill to swallow. This was not only because their power had become further emasculated by central government, but because there was little that they could do to resist the changes. The more staunch municipalists, previously lukewarm to partnership, had to develop relationships with associations very quickly, accepting the role of developing social housing at arm's length. In many cases relationships have developed in a positive manner, but sensitive issues have had to be resolved. Local authorities' first consideration has been to remove any perceived threat from associations to their existing stock, via either CCT or Tenants' Choice. In a number of local authorities, particularly in London, this resulted in the establishment of non-aggression pacts, in which housing associations guarantee to work within defined parameters and not threaten local authority housing stock. Such agreements were generally not supported by the Housing Corporation who considered that they diminished the independent role of housing associations and potentially undermined government policy. In a number of situations, tacit arrangements were adopted without the formality of a signed agreement.

This idea was developed further by the CIH and promoted as a formal agreement between housing associations and local authorities, called a *Social Housing Contract*. Such a contract would include:

- an indication of the criteria adopted by the local authority to decide with which housing associations it is prepared to work
- a commitment by the authority to work with associations meeting this criteria, in terms of: funding, sale of land, efficient payment of housing benefit and other partnership arrangements
- a range of commitments by housing associations to cover such issues as: nomination rights, meeting agreed 'target rents', implementing equal opportunity policies, the promotion of tenant participation and other like matters
- an agreed form of monitoring to ensure compliance on both sides
- associations would be accorded a formal role in the development of the local housing strategy (Fraser, 1991).

It was further envisaged that the Housing Corporation would be a co-signatory to the contract, although not necessarily exerting control over the final terms and conditions. The number of formal agreements have been relatively few. In the majority of cases, the spirit of collaboration and partnership works sufficiently well to enable the respective parties to work together satisfactorily.

A similar position has also developed around the role of housing associations as potential competitors in the CCT process. The majority of associations have indicated that they would not expect to compete against in-house teams for management contracts unless invited to do so. This is despite the fact that the government clearly considers housing associations to be ideally placed to mount such competition. Associations have, however, been acutely aware that they are heavily dependent on the goodwill of local authority partners for access to mainstream funding sources, i.e. local authority and Housing Corporation HAG. In addition, housing departments can often unlock access to cheap land and other opportunities (see later references to Housing Associations as Managing Agents (HAMA)). The potential gains in winning one or two management contracts would be more than offset by other losses.

Not all associations have been prepared to conform to this pattern of behaviour. Ironically, the most predatory organisations tend to be those formed following an LSVT, staffed mainly by previous local authority employees. Their approach to partnership has in a number of cases been based more on an entrepreneurial opportunism than on any traditional sense of loyalty. They have no history of such relationships in the past and find themselves having to carve out new opportunities within an already highly competitive market.

Partners or Agents?

The quality of local authority/housing association partnership is often not as wholehearted as might be wished. Whilst it may be open and collaborative in many situations, local authorities can be dominant and domineering in others. They might argue that this is the only way in which they can discharge their responsibilities as enablers, i.e. ensure high standards of service without having direct control. Housing associations have therefore 'bought' their new role at the cost of a certain level of independence.

This has been particularly evident in negotiations over nomination agreements. These agreements have been the basis on which local authorities have safeguarded their interest in social housing developed with the aid of public subsidy. The allocation of HAG to any new scheme has traditionally been contingent on the local authorities entitlement to 50 per cent nomination rights to the resulting vacancies. This has been progressively strengthened by the Housing Associations Act 1985, which provided local authorities with the power to require associations to provide 'reasonable assistance' in meeting their responsibilities towards the homeless. It was further endorsed by Housing Corporation Circular 48/89 which exhorted associations to increase their contribution towards dealing with homelessness. Since 1988, many authorities have taken a markedly aggressive approach to this arrangement, demanding increased percentages of nominations (often up to 100 per cent) on both initial lettings and subsequent relets. This is particularly true for schemes to which local authorities have contributed by way of funding, disposal of land or a combination of the two.

In a number of cases, this 'partnership' has resulted in the type of estates which bear the hallmarks of residualisation and deprivation (see Chapter 4). Having accepted the opportunity to develop (or acquire) additional housing units, associations are often left thereafter with the task of managing a potent cocktail of potential social and environmental decay over which they may have had little control. In effect, 'By passing over 100 per cent nomination rights to local authorities, housing associations have ... become effectively agents, rather than partners, of local authorities' (Page, 1993, p. 51). This domination of lettings by local authorities has also had the effect of reducing associations' ability to use their own stock in the most flexible manner, taking account of the needs of existing tenants.

Tensions have therefore been evident in the post-1988 period. A number of development-hungry associations have accepted opportunities to increase their stock regardless of potential management problems which might follow. They have done so by acceding to all the demands of local authorities no matter how unreasonable they might be. Such a trend has caused concern to the Housing Corporation, who consider that, 'the independence of housing associations is crucial. They must be apolitical and free to respond and help people in housing need. The distinctive contribution of the movement, its ability to offer choice and create diversity, disappears if its members surrender their freedom of action or allow themselves to be assimilated to another body' (Housing Corporation, 1990). However, despite their protestations, the Corporation have continued to allocate funding based on the sort of quantitative criteria which has been partially responsible for driving associations into inadvisable arrangements.

Innovation and Good Practice

On balance, however, housing associations and local authorities have worked well together, developing structures, mechanisms and practices which have cemented their relationship. This relationship has not been limited to an interface with housing departments. Constructive dialogue has also taken place with planning departments and social services departments. The use of Planning Agreements under section 106 of the Town and Country Planning Act 1990 has provided the vehicle for local planning authorities to work with housing associations to provide affordable housing in areas where it is most needed. This has been achieved by the designation of land specifically for social housing, thus depressing its open market value to a more affordable level, creating a significant platform for partnership.

Housing associations have also, in the past, contracted services both to and from local authorities. These have included the coordination of emergency call systems for sheltered housing linked to a central console, operated by the local authority. The facility may also be extended to elderly and/or vulnerable individuals in their own homes, thus providing 24-hour cover. Such a strategic approach to service delivery has taken advantage of the economies of scale, ensuring a consistent level of provision across the board. The contracting of services in this way is likely to increase as CCT becomes established.

Other examples of good practice have been:

1. Common Waiting Lists

The development of common waiting lists or common housing registers has been relatively recent. The timing of the first, developed in The Wrekin in 1992 owes much to the impetus generated by the post-1989 arrangements of enablers and providers. Despite the fact that associations were programmed to provide virtually all new social housing in the 1990s, the most urgent demand for housing continued to be channelled through local authorities. As a result, many authorities have developed waiting lists for social housing using sophisticated methods to prioritise need.

In contrast, many housing associations have chosen not to maintain active waiting lists because of the relatively few dwellings becoming regularly available prior to 1989, and also because of the opportunities created by working through referral agencies, including local authorities. By offering nomination quotas to a range of specialist organisations, e.g. housing aid centres, special-needs hostels and other public agencies such as the probation service, associations could delegate much of the complex process of prioritising allocations. Such a system worked while associations represented a supplementary resource to local authorities, it has however proved ineffective under the current arrangements.

Despite the potential benefits which might be delivered by common registers, there are a number of complex issues to resolve. The scope for unified working currently extends only to defining need. Few associations would be prepared to enter into an arrangement in which their ultimate control over allocations was indefinitely compromised. Indeed such a move would also prove unpopular with the Housing Corporation. In addition, issues such as common application forms, compatible technology and common approach are not without their difficulties. Housing associations operating across a number of local authority areas may be required to operate several different systems. However, a common approach to recognising and prioritising need is essential if the housing resources within an area are to be used effectively to address housing need. The strategic position occupied by local authorities makes them uniquely suited to operate any joint waiting list, which although primarily aimed at local authorities and housing associations, could also include the private sector. The role for common registers becomes increasingly significant in the light of the Housing Act 1996. The requirement that permanent tenancies can only be offered to households via a formal waiting list places a responsibility on the administrators of the list to ensure that it is both accurate in its prioritisation and sensitive to changing needs. The use of common registers marks a further significant step forward towards an integrative style of working in which local authorities and housing associations collaborate closely.

2. Transfer of Stock

The practice of transferring stock from local authorities to housing associations has become a major plank of partnership over recent years. It has been pursued via a range of models, the most popular being Large Scale Voluntary Transfer (LSVT) (see Chapter 8). This results in the transfer of an authority's total stock to one or more housing associations, creating a dependency on them to provide the dwellings required to address housing need. In the majority of cases, this has caused few problems, but in certain instances tensions have developed.

The motivation for such transfers has been largely financial, but has usually resulted in improved services and increased development opportunities. Association(s) acquiring local authority stock often receive an immediate financial return via increased levels of local authority HAG from the capital receipt generated by the transfer. In addition, revenue-funded services may also benefit by no longer facing the restrictions previously imposed on the Housing Revenue Account. The process of LSVT can therefore be financially advantageous to both local authority and housing association(s).

For authorities failing to obtain the support of their tenants for a full-scale transfer, or choosing not to embark on the complex and costly process of LSVT, an alternative model is trickle transfer. In this model, dwellings are transferred only when vacant, thus avoiding the need to get the permission of the occupant. The process is much longer term and gradual than a full-scale transfer. This option has also proved appropriate for authorities wishing to dispose of a limited number of specific dwellings, because of either maintenance or management problems.

Stock transfers have also been used to support and bolster the development of emerging black housing associations which need a property portfolio in order to sustain a viable organisation. This has been an important facility as black associations have emerged late on to the development scene and are therefore disadvantaged in attempting to build a stockholding within the current funding regime. Because they have few properties, opportunities to obtain private finance are limited, having few or no assets to offer as collateral. Without the opportunity to directly control their own stock, black associations are severely restricted in their ability to develop the management skills necessary to operate independently. Stock transfers have been made by both local authorities and housing associations on the basis of either a management agreement or transfer of ownership. The Housing Corporation, as part of its strategy for Black and Ethnic Minority associations, set a total target of 3010 transfers to be achieved by the end of 1996.

A Case of Partnership: Housing Associations as Managing Agents (HAMA)

HAMA is a further example of partnership between local authorities and housing associations building on the relative strengths and resources of each party involved. It has been both innovative and effective, spanning tenures and developing a relatively untapped source of needs-based housing. HAMA is an umbrella term used to describe a variety of arrangements where housing associations take on the management of privately owned accommodation to provide housing for people in need. It was launched by the government in 1991 to bring back into use private dwellings which would otherwise have been left empty. The objectives of the scheme were twofold:

1 to generate additional privately rented housing units
2 to assist local authorities in providing cheaper and more suitable alternatives than bed and breakfast for homeless households.

Most HAMA schemes have until recently been established in partnership with local authorities to provide temporary accommodation for the statutory homeless. Housing associations act as managing agents and may provide incentives to landlords, such as rental guarantees and guaranteed vacant possession at the end of an agreement. As revenue support from local authorities has been harder to obtain, housing associations have had to look at different ways to make HAMA work. It has been extended to house a wider range of client groups such as single homeless people, waiting-list applicants and young people leaving care.

In Oxford, where HAMA was first piloted, the City Council has been faced with a level of housing need which belies its provincial nature. Homelessness has continued to rise, while local authority resources have been steadily decreasing. At the end of March 1993, 500 homeless households were accommodated in temporary accommodation, 202 of whom were in bed-and-breakfast hotels. The average waiting period for an offer was almost 2 years. This reflected the diminishing supply of rented accommodation, of both newly built housing and relets of council or housing association stock. There was a particular shortfall in the number of family units available for letting which at one stage dipped below the number of households accepted by the council as homeless.

Oxford boasts a private rented sector which is significantly higher than the national average. The consistent demands of an expanding student population has prompted a rapidly expanding number of houses in multiple occupation (HMOs). However, these are largely unsuitable for families, creating significant competition for such housing, producing average rents in 1994 in excess of £150 even in cheaper areas. Yet even these levels are often considerably lower than the average gross cost of providing B&B for a homeless family (£182 in 1994), making HAMA an attractive proposition. The position was further improved even by the effect of the housing subsidy regime. 'For a family household on full housing benefit and accommodated in B&B the average net cost after subsidy to the Council is about £95 per week. If the same family was accommodated in a privately rented house on an assured shorthold tenancy, the comparative cost of the accommodation charge net of subsidy is about £7, as the Council receives subsidy of 95% on a rent allowance of £140' (Walsh, 1994).

Oxford Social Lettings Agency (OSLA) was launched in December 1991, as a joint venture between Oxford Citizens Housing Association and Ealing

Family Housing Association, taking its first properties into management in February 1992. During the three and a half years it has been in operation, it has expanded its management portfolio to over 350 properties and extended its operation into neighbouring district council areas. The success of the HAMA initiative has to be judged in terms of the objectives achieved set against any viable alternatives. Although it has been less successful in tackling the problem of long-term void properties in the private sector, it has made a significant contribution in facilitating the phasing-out of bed and breakfast in many local authority areas. From the perspective of Oxford City Council, the objective was clear: 'With regard to the future, the Council wishes to eradicate the use of B&B as temporary accommodation for the homeless and sees OSLA as the principal means to achieve this' (Walsh, ibid). During the latter part of 1995, this objective was achieved, not solely due to HAMA, although it played an important part.

The HAMA process has also been an important part of the developing partnership between the City Council and the participating housing associations. The effectiveness of the scheme has provided all parties with an indicator of what might be achieved when a local authority pursues its enabling function with vision and innovation. Since the HAMA partnership was initiated in 1991, Oxford City Council has extended its support for local associations, including the part funding of a new development at Blackbird Leys, on the edge of Oxford, which will provide over 1000 new social housing units. In addition, the success of HAMA has more recently prompted the neighbouring authorities of South Oxfordshire DC, West Oxfordshire DC, Cherwell DC and the Vale of the White Horse DC to follow suit and negotiate agreements with OSLA.

The Consortium Approach

One way in which partnership has developed within recent years is via the vehicle of consortia. These have tended to be developed in one of three directions: special needs, finance or development. However, each of these is built on a similar premise that organisations working together are often able to achieve more than they might have achieved individually. The consortium therefore becomes a vehicle via which a group of organisations come together to achieve a common objective. Arrangements may be short or long term, and may comprise either similar organisations, e.g. housing associations, or extend partnership to an interdisciplinary or cross-sectoral level. The main types of consortium are:

1. Special-Needs Consortia

The more traditional model is that relating to special-needs housing, which has its roots in the community care initiatives of the 1980s. It has achieved particular prominence as community care programmes have gained a higher profile within recent years. In these circumstances, the role of the consortium is to harness the resources and expertise of a range of statutory and voluntary bodies within a single organisation dedicated to a specific objective, often centred on reprovision from existing mental health institutions. This approach to special-needs housing has been adopted widely throughout the country, and by the early 1990s there were in excess of fifty such initiatives.

Although each consortium is unique in terms of membership and objectives, they share a number of common features:

- consortia are voluntary agencies, usually a limited company with charitable status or an industrial and provident society
- consortia usually comprise a group of agencies, often including one or more housing associations, the local authority, the health authority and relevant voluntary organisations
- the main purpose is usually to provide supported housing, with the care and/or support usually being contracted from the health authority by the consortium
- consortia have mainly provided housing for people with learning difficulties or suffering from mental health problems, but this has expanded to include the elderly in recent years (NFHA/GLHA, 1991).

The main benefit of the consortium has been to bring together a range of interested agencies to work together in a coordinated approach to supported housing. This has proved particularly beneficial in establishing a dialogue between local authorities and health authorities, where cooperation in the provision of housing has not always been productive. In addition to expertise, the consortium can also take advantage of access to resources which might not be available if the component organisations had acted individually.

As with other examples of partnership discussed in this chapter, the reality of running a consortium is often quite different from the concept. While one of the major benefits is to create an integrated approach, in practice the statutory and voluntary sectors, and local authorities and health authorities, tend to have very different cultures, professional attitudes and approaches. This often results in tensions and conflict within the committee of the consortium which can delay progress and cause problems. However, much of this is ironed out over time as the constituent parties become accustomed to the role of the consortium and their part within it.

2. Financial Consortia

The more recent initiatives have been related to the process of development within a financial regime which has placed a heavy reliance on private funding. Associations remaining keen to develop have found that there has been an increasing emphasis on activity taking place on a large scale. This has been true both in terms of generating finance, particularly from financial institutions operating on the money markets, and in generating development sites which offer value for money via the economies of scale. An example of the former is The Housing Finance Corporation (THFC), which periodically approaches the money markets for capital sums which usually amount to £40–100 million.

THFC was initially formed in 1987 by the Housing Corporation and the National Federation of Housing Associations (NFHA), as a non-profit-making industrial and provident society in anticipation of the private finance implications of the Housing Act 1988. The demand by the majority of associations was for long-term, fixed charge finance which represented the greatest security. The pension funds and life assurance institutions offering such loan packages were generally unwilling to consider requests for sums below £100 million. For the majority of small or medium sized associations, such sums would be impossible to contemplate, but collectively their needs might easily stretch to these limits. The role of the THFC has therefore been to coordinate the requirements of a number associations, ranging from the very small with several hundred properties, to the largest with several thousand, raising sufficient capital finance to attract competitive interest rates and reduce administration costs. Between 1987 and 1996, THFC raised £875 million in over three hundred loans for over 120 housing associations. In the process, they have facilitated development finance for associations which otherwise would have been excluded from the most favourable arrangements. In addition, they have educated the private sector to recognise social housing as a secure investment opportunity which improved the relationship between lenders and borrowers.

3. Development Consortia

The other development-related issue which has resulted in a proliferation of consortia is that of site availability. Prior to 1989, housing associations were generally seen as landlords of small, well-designed and well-built housing developments. Much of their work involved the rehabilitation of older, street property and any new-build sites were usually purchased from local authorities or came through some other negotiated source. However, the post-1989 regime has operated against rehabilitation because of the risk of unforseen costs during works, which would have to be directly funded by associations. The costs of sustaining a new-build programme with increasing private finance has forced associations to look for savings wherever possible in order to develop within parameters which will allow for affordable rents to be charged. Such savings have generally been achieved in one of three ways: either space standards have suffered in the attempt to squeeze more dwellings on to development sites; cheaper, less commercially desirable sites have been chosen; and/or larger sites have been developed in pursuit of the economies of scale.

The result is that a number of development opportunities have come the way of associations which have involved extremely large sites. Because of the potential risks of developing such sites and the difficulty in gaining access to sufficient HAG to enable them to do so, there have been a number of instances where a group of associations have made joint bids to develop land. This usually involves one association taking the lead, with the others also being closely involved in negotiations. By entering into this type of arrangement, associations gain a number of advantages:

1   access to development opportunities which otherwise might be denied them
2   shared risks and expertise
3   economies of scale
4   more scope for Housing Plus initiatives (described later).

Examples of development consortia are Windsor Park in Newham (seven housing associations) and Blackbird Leys in Oxford (four associations). In neither instance could the development have been undertaken by one association and the collaboration was supported by the respective local authorities and the Housing Corporation. The consortium model has also been adopted for the transfer of existing dwellings from one landlord to another. One example of this is the Holly Street estate in Hackney which was transferred from the local authority to a consortium of housing associations. However, while development consortia have distinct advantages, there are also drawbacks:

1   The partnership is rarely equal, with the associations not leading negotiations potentially being committed to actions about which they are unhappy.
2   The larger the consortium, the more complex the necessary communication and liaison.
3   Arrangements are often largely development-led, with less consideration given to the subsequent management of the estate.

Many of the more recent large-scale consortium developments are having to untangle the consequence of these issues in their long-term management.

Consortia have become an increasingly important vehicle in the drive towards partnership. Although the examples given above relate to the public sector, there have been many examples involving the private sector. The effect has been to break the mould of the traditional models of housing or health, introducing new approaches and attitudes. This has been reflected in the number of recent initiatives which have placed housing within a broader framework of employment and economic regeneration, such as the Single Regeneration Budget (SRB) and Housing Plus. Both have extended the concept of partnership, promoting a holistic approach to the needs of households and their environment, attempting to deliver quality of life rather than simply quality of accommodation.

Housing Plus

Housing Plus is not new in concept although the term itself has only become widely used following a Housing Corporation conference in February 1995. It denotes an approach to housing management which emphasises that the production of bricks and mortar alone does not represent the complete picture. Housing Plus takes as its premise the belief that housing managers should look to a broader range of issues which reflect that the confines of a dwelling make up only one aspect of the domestic environment. Equally important are the needs experienced by communities for employment, training and a range of other types of support. This is in sharp contrast to the contractual model of housing management which has been forced upon local authorities. However, support for such initiatives has not been accompanied by additional funding despite the Housing Corporation having indicated that bids for ADP (Approved Development Programme) funds may receive additional priority if they contain a Housing Plus element. The expectation is that the infrastructure for Housing Plus will be provided by associations either from within their own resources or in the deals they are able to forge with private developers and/or local authorities.

One widely expressed concern is that Housing Plus may be little more than a smokescreen to devolve the costs of public facilities, through the Housing Corporation, to housing associations. Support for Housing Plus is therefore not universal, either in its potential implications for housing associations, or the general principle. A number of senior managers believe that it goes beyond what should reasonably be expected of housing management. They argue that there is a danger of distorting the role of housing managers to such an extent that their true focus becomes obscured, thus affecting performance.

This contrasts with the alternative view that housing associations can be more flexible and productive without abandoning existing objectives, by making development capital go further. Indeed, there are many initiatives which can be undertaken without resource implication, relating more to attitude and approach. There is certainly evidence that this can be achieved given the right approach and appropriate circumstances. Leading the way in this approach is a group of associations which have joined together to form *People For Action 2001* (PFA2001) with the aid of funding from the DoE. The mission statement of PFA2001 is 'To enable local people to improve their opportunities in life and add value to their communities. People for Action 2001 members will develop a broadly-based approach that helps tenants, residents and other local people to gain maximum benefit from the investment that the housing association makes in the area.' This reflects the Page view that 'housing associations should be building not just houses, but also stable communities' (Page, 1994, p. 6).

The schemes developed under the Housing Plus banner have been designed to use housing provided as a focus around which the residents can improve the quality of their lives and by so doing produce sustainable communities. Housing is therefore recognised as a key component of the social infrastructure, but one which *contributes* to rather than guarantees comfort and security. Member associations of PFA2001 have, to varying degrees, extended their services to support the generation of other essential elements of community development, i.e. employment, training and economic viability. In addition, Housing Plus has also been geared towards the empowerment and facilitation of tenants' and residents' groups by the provision of meeting-rooms, support workers and other related facilities.

As indicated earlier, many of these initiatives are not new. Indeed, they build on the approaches pioneered by the Priority Estates Project (PEP) in the early 1980s and many housing associations and local authorities since then. However, there are differences which make Housing Plus an important development from what has gone previously. Perhaps the most important is that developing associations may find Housing Plus initiatives an essential prerequisite for successfully bidding for HAG allocations. Whilst this will encourage a more innovative and consumer-oriented approach to providing housing, there may also be drawbacks. The lack of additional funding to promote Housing Plus means that associations must either stretch existing resources to cover the costs or subsidise capital costs from reserves, which inevitably favours larger associations with strong balance sheets. These may be regional or national associations, with less of a community base than some local associations. This may give rise to the possibility that Housing Plus might be used by some associations as a means of 'buying in' to additional HAG funding by offering up some additional community facilities. The implication is that such initiatives may have little long-term sustainability if they are not supported by the community and/or integrated into the management approach of the landlord.

However, partnership initiatives like Housing Plus have clearly become the way forward at a time when public resources have been stretched to their limit. For those housing associations committed to maintaining an active development programme, the ability to devise schemes demonstrating a 'value added' element is crucial. Such an approach also complements other policy initiatives geared towards blurring the divide between public and private sectors. The production and management of social housing has become less critically located within the sole domain of social housing organisations. The development of initiatives such as Estate Action, City Challenge, and more latterly the Single Regeneration Budget has placed the partnership between the public and private sectors at the very heart of their operation. This is to some extent clearly ideologically motivated by a preference for the competitive nature of the private sector. However, in many cases, it has had the effect of drawing together sectors which have in the past had little or no understanding of each other's respective roles and abilities.

Working with the Private Sector

One growth area of partnership has been that involving both public and private sectors. 'The promotion of partnerships between local authorities and the private sector is a major aim of Government policy' (Mason and Sopp, 1988). The ideological preference of the Conservative governments of the 1980s and 1990s for the private sector has been discussed elsewhere in this book. However, irrespective of the contentious nature of competition and the role of the market, the private sector has already demonstrated that it has much to offer social housing. Perhaps one of its most attractive attributes is the relative absence of government constraints on private companies' ability to access and spend capital and revenue finance. The restrictions which do exist usually relate to commercial viability.

The government's early initiatives for partnership with the private sector were geared largely towards private contractors building housing for sale on local authority land. By 1985 over 450 partnership schemes had been developed, with a further 400 under way or in the pipeline. However, as the 1980s progressed, the government's expectations of the role of the private sector had grown to encompass the disposal of council stock, particularly dwellings designated 'difficult to let'. These were often system-built or deck access estates in poorer localities, habitually used as dumping grounds for households with little choice or economic mobility. Between 1979 and 1985, over 6000 council dwellings had been disposed of in this way, representing 0.1 per cent of total local authority stock. By the end of June 1995 the number of disposals had risen to 34 940, although this has tailed off in later years. This figure is however small in comparison with the 1.8 million Right to Buy sales and over 180 000 disposals to housing associations over the same period.

One major reason for the relative decline in private sector interest in the purchase of local authority housing has been the collapse of the housing market since 1989. House prices have been steadily falling and private developers have therefore been less inclined to speculate, particularly at the cheaper end of the market. However, as a result of this downturn in the owner-occupied market, private builders have become increasingly interested in working in partnership with local authorities and housing associations. The recession has further benefited social housing by creating a situation in which the financial institutions have looked more favourably at investing in rented housing in the absence of attractive alternatives. This has created opportunities for the larger housing associations and organisations such as THFC to gain credible footholds in their search for private finance. The introduction of the Business Expansion Schemes (BES) which introduced tax breaks for rented housing, and the Building Societies Act 1986 which removed many of the constraints on building societies, also contributed to the interest in rented housing. The result of these trends is that social housing now has one foot firmly located within the private sector. This theme has been continued by the introduction of Housing Investment Trusts (HITs) within the Housing Act 1996.

The government has also promoted the public/private partnership via a number of policy initiatives. In 1992, the Private Finance Initiative (PFI) was introduced to promote partnerships between the public and private sectors on a commercial basis. In 1993 it was placed under the auspices of a quango, The Private Finance Panel, with a target of £14 billion worth of projects by 1999. In addition to generating investment, it was expected that PFI would also enable public sector organisations to learn from working with the private sector and by so doing to improve their own management styles. The Housing Corporation see themselves, together with housing associations, as 'being at the forefront of the government's Private Finance Initiative' (Housing Corporation, 1995a). By adopting this approach, they point to a substantial increase in the level of development finance available to associations, with over £1000 million being contributed from private finance in 1992/3, and over £750 million in 1993/4. Without such an extra injection of cash, the Corporation indicated that fewer homes would have been built.

Other private sector partnership initiatives have included:

- English Partnerships – launched in April 1994 'As a Government-sponsored agency . . . to bring together the private, public and voluntary sectors to create economic growth, employment opportunities and environmental improvement in areas of need throughout England' (English Partnerships Annual Report 1994/5). English Partnership had a budget of over £250 million in 1994/5 which included the management of projects taken over from the previous regimes of City Grant, Derelict Land Grant and English Estates.
- City Challenge – launched in 1991 as a competitive allocation for partnership schemes for urban areas. Fifteen cities were invited to bid, of which eleven received funding totalling £82.5 million, spread over five years. Allocations were dependent on the involvement of the private sector, in terms of both funding and expertise. The strategic objectives of the programme were related to the regeneration of the urban environment and social and economic infrastructure. Specific housing objectives were geared towards changing the tenure mix of public housing and encouraging tenant involvement in management. The funding for City Challenge was top-sliced from other existing budgets, including Estate Action. It was suspended in 1992 as part of the winding-up of the Urban Programme.
- Single Regeneration Budget – launched in 1993 as a consolidation of previous urban initiatives, it subsumed programmes such as Estate Action. It was designed to tackle all aspects of urban deprivation through a public/private sector partnership. Thus to be successful bids must attract private finance. Initiatives are required to meet certain guidelines, including: enhancing employment prospects and encouraging

economic growth; and improving the physical environment. There have been two rounds of bidding to date, in which housing projects have been relatively poorly represented.

• Compulsory Competitive Tendering/Voluntary Competitive Tendering – the introduction of competitive tendering is clearly intended to involve the private sector in the management of council housing. Even if in-house teams win the contracts, as has been the case in the first phase of tendering, there will inevitably be a cultural movement towards private sector operations.

It must also be remembered that both local authorities and housing associations have had close working relationships with the private sector for many years in terms of client/developer roles. Few housing associations have their own Direct Labour Organisations (DLOs), and have therefore relied on private contractors for construction and maintenance services. For many in the private sector, this is the type of relationship valued most. Few speculative developers feel the need to become more involved in the commissioning process or to become landlords themselves. They recognise a division of expertise which separates the construction trades from that of housing managers.

However, expectations have changed within recent years. Contractors have in a number of cases been expected to shoulder a greater burden of public responsibility by being receptive to recruitment and training practices which are sensitive to the needs of the locality. Thus in an area with a large ethnic minority community, contractors might be expected to recruit locally for their workforce rather than importing labour from elsewhere. Similarly, there has also been a growth in the number of training schemes linked to the construction industry, financed either by City Challenge/SRB funds or by contractors themselves, possibly assisted by the Construction Industry Training Board (CITB).

The public/private partnership can be highly productive. There is little doubt that cross-sectoral partnerships bring diverse and often complementary skills and expertise to any arrangement. Crudely speaking, public sector expertise represents and delivers on a moral commitment to social justice. The private sector, on the other hand, are generally good at making profits by delivering the type of products appropriate to their markets. These two areas are by no means mutually exclusive, offering a vehicle for marrying the concepts of effectiveness and efficiency discussed earlier in this book.

Summary

Partnership has undoubtedly become a key concept in the development of social housing since the mid-1980s. The 1990s in particular have extended partnership to encompass the growing relationship between public and private sectors. Whatever the ideological basis for encouraging intersectoral partnership, the effect has been to remove barriers and promote a greater degree of innovation and collaboration in the production of housing services.

However, the term 'partnership' tends to be used rather glibly. On a simplistic level it relates to the bringing together of two or more parties, sharing a common goal in order to achieve a productive relationship. The reality is that the process demands a great deal of management if success is to be guaranteed. Partnership involves encouraging, facilitating, innovating, and above all developing a level of understanding and trust between collaborators. As relationships will generally be unique, the success or failure of individual partnership arrangements will depend on the compatibility of its component parts and the circumstances in which they operate. However, experience indicates that certain factors, outlined earlier in the chapter, hold the key to a positive or negative outcome. The fact that they exist and need to be accommodated suggests the requirement for skills and expertise specific to partnership working. For organisations entering into the process believing the implications to be minimal, the outlook is bleak.

For local authorities, this is particularly relevant. Their position has changed from being able to provide housing largely in isolation, to the requirement that they operate strategically, providing services through third parties either as partners or contractors. As examined earlier in this book, such a transformation requires more than the physical establishment of mechanisms or even policies. The attitudes required to make it a success are often quite different from those traditionally adopted within the public sector.

Nor is effective partnership an easy option. It is often extremely time-consuming because of the problems of ensuring effective communications between the organisations involved. The greater the number of partners, the greater will be the complexity of interface. This relates not only to the logistics, e.g. arranging meetings, formalising legal arrangements and manoeuvring through the various organisational requirements of each partner. There are often even more difficult issues of status, personality, culture and political approach to massage and accommodate. Often, while the overall objectives of a partnership might be agreed, it may prove extremely difficult to find common ground on the process. Agreements forged in haste, largely in response to development opportunities, may not have the robustness to stand the test of time. Housing is a long-term investment which requires effective development and management if it is to provide the quality of environment required. For organisations inexperienced in the complexities of partnership, they must be aware of the pitfalls as well as the benefits.

In general, however, partnership should be viewed in a positive light. The exposure of organisations to alternative ways of working, skills and experience can only strengthen social landlords, who until relatively recently had operated within the narrow confines of political and bureaucratic

Social Housing Management

control. Nor is benefit merely a one-way process. Not only will public sector organisations learn from each other and from the private sector, but they will inevitably influence private sector attitudes to the potential of the public sector. The result has already been that billions of pounds of private finance has been invested in social housing. But the effect is about more than just resource generation. Partnership has created a professional attitude which is less introverted, which encourages a broader, external perspective. In many organisations this has also begun to encompass the perception of consumers as partners, to be consulted and involved wherever possible. However, some aspects of partnership are resource-intensive and are therefore not easy options. There is the danger that in the current financial climate, the quick-fix, short-term return partnership opportunities will proliferate, whilst the more in-depth, liberating type will appear difficult and unattractive. For housing management, the problem remains the same – the attractions of short-term returns over the potential of longer-term investment.

10 Housing Professionalism

'Soon the Institute [CIH] will be responding to policy initiatives against the backdrop of a much more pluralist housing world. Should the Institute reflect diversity and difference or should it try to mould a consensus? Diversity will bring a wider range of (sometimes conflicting) viewpoints within the housing world. How can the Institute form a viewpoint on an issue when there may be no consensus within the profession?'

(CIH, 1994a)

Throughout this book there is evidence of significant change in social housing, often appearing more revolutionary than evolutionary. Much of it has been in response to government policies promoting market competition and financial stringency alongside a greater emphasis on partnership, performance cultures, and a more influential role for the consumer. It has been difficult for any social housing organisation to avoid being affected and altered by these initiatives, no matter how they have tried to retain the status quo. Nor has such change been limited to organisations alone – practitioners have also felt the effects. Individual practice has increasingly come under the microscope in the drive for increased cost-effectiveness and customer care. The result has been the emergence of a new set of skills, approaches and expectations which have challenged many traditional practices and attitudes.

As is clear from the opening quote from the Chartered Institute of Housing (CIH) consultation document, *All Change for Housing* (1994a), the effect of these changes has been to fragment rather than consolidate the existing professional base. In many organisations, traditional public sector values and beliefs have been discarded, perceived as outdated and ineffective in meeting the managerial demands of the 1990s. Long-established ways of working have proved untenable and traditional skills have become obsolete. Significant numbers of housing practitioners have found the introduction of consumer rights, increased accountability and transparency both threatening and destabilising. Others have fallen short of the expertise necessary to deliver the appropriate standards of service required of the new public management. The result has been something of a 'shake-out' amongst social housing personnel, with early and medical retirements becoming common especially amongst senior staff. Those who have remained have often experienced steep learning curves in adapting to new styles of working appropriate to the threats and benefits of the brave new world.

The *housing profession*, if indeed such a collective body can be said to exist, has also experienced a rude awakening. Having entered the 1980s as a disparate, insular and rather reactionary collection of individuals, the 1990s have seen a more concerted attempt to establish a credible image for housing management. As the representative body for housing professionals, the CIH has raised the profile of the housing profession, establishing itself as a recognised source of expert advice and knowledge. Such a role has been largely supported by the government through the DoE and the Audit Commission, recognised as contributing to the better management of public housing.

However, promoting housing professionalism has not been without its problems, coming at a time when professional roles are more fluid than at any time in the past. The strongly ideological 'conviction politics of Margaret Thatcher' (Malpass and Means, 1993, p. 189) of the 1980s wrested initiative and control away from practitioners, trades unions and representative bodies in the pursuit of deregulation and centralisation of power. 'The government appears to be riding roughshod over professional standards when they find they conflict with their political interests' (Metcalfe and Richards, 1990, p. 130). In their place has been implanted a new, managerial approach having as its credo the belief that management is the primary function in ensuring organisational effectiveness. Inherent in this approach is the conviction that good managers can manage in any situation, whether in a hospital, school or commercial company. As a result, practitioners have been expected to become managers first, and professionals second. This has generally weakened professionals and their representative bodies in their ability to influence social policy agenda and dictate the parameters of change. The locus of power has shifted from almost complete professional autonomy over public services, to a position in which the policy agenda is now imposed largely by politicians. The professional role has therefore often become more reactive than proactive.

For many housing practitioners, the attempt to establish professional credentials comes too late to make any significant difference. Huge cuts have been made in social housing spending, while levels of housing need have increased. CCT is in full swing, having already resulted in housing officers transferring involuntarily to new employers following failed in-house bids. Sceptics will point out that professional input failed to resist such change, despite widespread opposition. However, they would also recognise that a number of major concessions were made by the government in implementing CCT. Professional influence has therefore appeared to be more effective at a detailed, operational level than in shaping policy. The ability to exercise absolute control over their discipline has diminished for many professionals, restricted to translating, rather than formulating policy (Cole and Furbey, 1994).

What then is the role for housing professionalism? Many housing practitioners have taken the view that professional status is neither important nor desirable. There is a body of opinion that professions have in the past been too exclusive, admitting a relatively narrow profile of members. Qualification for membership has usually been by the examination of technical skill and expertise demanded by professional codes, coupled with practical experience. This has traditionally favoured those with academic ability, which does not accurately reflect British society. Professions have often been slow to change, lacking the flexibility to keep pace with dynamic events in practice. It is perhaps to the CIH's advantage that its relative lateness on the professional scene has enabled it to develop from a more contemporary starting point. However, it is now faced with having to carve a recognisable and acceptable professional identity out of the current uncertainty. This can only be achieved by winning the hearts and minds of an increasingly diverse workforce many of whom may not naturally look to a housing professional body for guidance.

This chapter examines the effects of these changes from a practitioner's perspective. Many work in environments in which the ability to be reflective and impartial is hampered by strongly emphasised organisational objectives. There is often a thin dividing line between what is for the good of the organisation and what benefits consumers of services. This has been clearly highlighted in the District Auditor's investigations into Westminster's housing policy in which two senior housing officers were found to have colluded with politicians in gerrymandering. The dividing line between objective advice and collusion is often perched on a knife edge. It is therefore important for personal actions be evaluated within a broader context than the narrow confines of current employment. Even without incidents of impropriety, with such a variety of organisations, adopting such different policies and practices, there is an obvious need for professional bodies to fulfil the role of a stable and objective arbiter of good practice and professional standards.

A Housing View of Professionalism

In the hierarchy of professions, housing management has been a relatively recent, minor player. For many years, the process was considered a collection of low-level administrative tasks centred around the letting of property. Many of the more prestigious functions related to financial and technical expertise were carried out by practitioners from other, already established professions, e.g. accountancy, architecture, law and surveying. In addition, the absence of mystique or mythology in the practice of housing management resulted in much higher levels of political involvement and ideological influence than in other, established professions. Local councillors were often 'unwilling to relinquish such influence over housing and management issues' (Laffin, 1985, p. 108). Directors of Housing have been more likely to find that they have been forced out of jobs following changes in political control (LB Ealing, Tower Hamlets) than their counterparts in other service departments. The sources of potential conflict between 'professionals' and their employing bodies are perhaps more likely to arise among the social professions than, for instance, accountancy, law, or other technical services. As a result, the recognition of housing management as a complex professional function has been slow to gain widespread acceptance. Past images have therefore been relatively poor, so that unlike other professions, recruits to housing management posts have generally not been highly academically qualified. In the main, ambitious graduates with a social conscience have attained greater status, career development potential and job satisfaction within social work or planning. It is only within the last decade that this situation has effectively begun to change.

The legacy of this relatively late development has been the position outlined by the Audit Commission in its 1986 report *Managing the Crisis in Council Housing*:

'The professionalism of housing management needs to be enhanced generally . . .

- Fewer than 2500 staff within local government housing organisations have the recognised professional qualification in this field, from the IoH; this represents less than one qualified housing officer for every 2000 dwellings (worth some £50 million in replacement costs) . . .
- In-service training is limited. Even in one of the better managed housing organisations within local government, average training time for third tier managers amounts to less than two days a year per person.
- Typically estate management is the responsibility of relatively young and inexperienced people who are newcomers to the estate for which they are responsible, Only a very small fraction of estate management staff have a relevant housing qualification.' (Audit Commission 1986a, p. 15)

While the picture may have improved within the ten years since the Audit Commission's report, it is not hard to see that housing management has not naturally represented itself as a professional discipline. The responsibility for this does not lie solely at the door of housing practitioners, or even the Chartered Institute of Housing. As already discussed, there are numerous interested parties whose influence and power would inevitably be diminished if the status of housing managers was enhanced. There has therefore been a significant degree of self-interest involved in denying housing management its due recognition.

As a result, it has been harder to achieve the unanimity of purpose and commitment amongst housing managers which has existed in the traditional professions. Perceptions of housing professionalism have varied widely between individuals and organisations. While in the past this may have been inconvenient, it posed little threat to the existence of an albeit relatively low-key social housing profession. However, it has become more critical in a climate of organisational fragmentation in which the demarcation lines between public and private sectors have been fast dissolving under a welter of legislation and innovation. Social housing managers who were previously based within the public sector are now increasingly finding themselves employed by private sector companies. In tandem, business managers and developers who were once exclusively employed by the private sector are to be found in senior positions in the public sector.

This has presented the CIH with a number of dilemmas. The first harks back to the quote at the beginning of this chapter. Should the CIH become a broad church of opinions and attitudes for anyone working in housing, or should it attempt to establish a single professional approach based on consensus? If it chooses the former route, it faces the danger of becoming little more than a random collection of individuals with little in common save employment in social housing. If it chooses the latter route, it faces the danger that by shutting the door to an increasing number of potential recruits, the CIH will remain on the margins of professional influence while its competitors might develop further advantage.

However, the CIH are not alone in facing these dilemmas. The demand for all professions to adapt to the new public managerialism has been irresistible, forced by a frenetic pace of change. Such a challenge has not had a single focus, being mounted from both right and left of the political spectrum, consumers and related pressure groups alike. From the political right, the Public Choice School have launched an assault based on the belief that organised bodies have consistently contravened 'liberty and individualism' (King, 1987, p. 11). Commentators from the political left (Ward, 1985) have propounded the view that professions serve only to bureaucratise and centralise power, acting against the best interests of consumers who are effectively disempowered. Few voices have been raised in objection to the imposition of a New Right agenda in pursuit of deregulation, deprofessionalisation and consumer primacy.

What is Professionalism?

In considering future options for the housing profession, it is useful to establish a point of reference against which the concept of professional activity might be evaluated. A variety of definitions exist for the term 'professional', due largely to the diversity of functions and bodies needing to be covered. The social work profession differs significantly from that of barristers or accountants. However, there are common denominators which characterise existing professions: 'professions are occupations with special power and prestige. Society grants these rewards because professions have special competence in esoteric bodies of knowledge linked to central needs and values of the social system, and because professions are devoted to the service of the public, above and beyond material incentives' (Larson, 1977, p. x).

Professions are also generally accepted to be occupations requiring a prolonged and specialised period of training, often involving a theoretical base and resulting in a higher education qualification. There will also be

Table 10.1   Defining a professional

- The acquisition of specialist knowledge through a programme of education and training, regulated by a professional institute.
- The assumption that professionals have the exclusive right to advise their clients on matters within their spheres of professional competence and to expect their advice to be taken.
- The enjoyment of high public esteem, which will be protected and reinforced by the imposition of professional and personal codes of conduct which are intended to maintain the respect with which members of the profession are held.
- A greater or lesser degree of autonomy in their working lives.
- A professional will not owe his or her loyalty solely or even primarily to the organisation . . . He or she will be expected to conform to the demands of good professional practice.

Source: Elcock and Rose (1993).

an element of ethical responsibility – e.g. medical and legal professions have concepts of 'unprofessional conduct' which can lead to members being struck off a register and debarred from practice. Yet, as Larson points out, 'the implicit assumption that the behaviour of individual professions is more ethical, as a norm, than that of individuals in lesser occupations has seldom, if ever, been tested by empirical evidence' (ibid, 1977, p. xi). Professions are often considered to have a number of common character-istics such as those listed in Table 10.1. Although defining professionalism in this way has its limitations, it provides an insight into traditional values and structures which have developed within professional bodies.

Altruism has also been traditionally significant in distinguishing profes-sionals from other practitioners. The ethos of service delivery 'is the es-sence of professionalism . . . it is not concerned with self-interest, but with the welfare of the client' (Marshall, 1939, p. 58). However, clients do not always share professional interpretations of what constitutes acting in their best interests. By necessity public services do not always operate in ways perceived as beneficial by the client, e.g. taking children into care, plan-ning and environmental health notices, and homelessness decisions. Such actions are often controversial by their nature, rarely achieving universal acclaim, but nevertheless playing an important strategic role in safeguard-ing the wellbeing of the community.

Disabling Professions

Professions have long been viewed with suspicion by outsiders: 'All pro-fessions are conspiracies against the laity' (Shaw, 1907). Even apart from the direct victims of professional power, the perspective of professions as automatically beneficent is not universally shared. On the contrary, the influence of autonomous professional conduct has been seen by some as a negative rather than positive trend. They have challenged the notion that professional altruism always operates in the best interests of service consumers: 'Professionals tell you what you need and claim the power to prescribe. They not only recommend what is good, but actually ordain what is right' (Ilych, 1977, p. 17). In circumstances where the control of services lies solely, or predominately, in the hands of a single provider or group, quality and entitlement will inevitably reflect the perceptions of the deliverer rather more than the recipient. Professionals have in the past often exercised the power to decide the nature of services and entitlements regardless of, or in ignorance of, the wishes of the consumer. 'The assurance of knowledge and skills has led the professionals to assume that because they know what the public need, they do not require to know what the public wants. Professionalism can become a barrier for the public rather than a resource to be used' (Stewart, 1993, p. 52).

In reality, professionals are generally less autocratic than this might suggest. However, the lack of meaningful consumer consultation in the past reflects an established emphasis on decisions being taken on behalf of consumers. While, in the majority of cases, such decisions will have been taken in good faith, professional perceptions of need have not always kept pace with the change in consumer demands.

There are also those who point out that professions are by their nature exclusive, i.e. by setting minimum criteria for membership, therefore potentially acting against the achievement of diversity. Social disadvantage and discrimination experienced by certain groups in society affects their ability to do well academically. As a result, the emphasis on academic ability as a prerequisite for professional membership may disadvantage such groups. This has been a view particularly prevalent amongst Labour local authorities in London, where membership of the CIH does not hold significant currency. However, such concerns to a large extent have been addressed by the introduction of housing National Vocational Qualifications (NVQs) and certificated courses (described later). NVQs are competence-based qualifications which do not rely on academic ability, offering a route through to professional recognition to many who were previously ineligible.

Do Professionals Always Act Professionally?

Few housing practitioners would disagree with the need to cultivate behaviour and attitudes which conform to the highest standards of service delivery. However, there are disagreements over the direction that professionalism should take and where the focus of control and/or regulation should be located. Many would consider that professional conduct should closely adhere to a personal code of ethics and behaviour borne of common sense, consideration and commitment to a cause. To act in a 'professional' way often reflects the use of skills and qualities which individuals have developed over time through experiential reflection and training. There is therefore a view that regulation by an official body is less important than self-discipline and peer pressure.

This is founded on a reaction against the presumption that *'acting professionally'* is the exclusive preserve of *'professionals'*. The many housing practitioners choosing not to become CIH members would strongly assert that they are as professional as anyone in performing their jobs. Membership of a profession does not automatically endow an individual with personal and professional qualities regardless of training or qualifications. Some doctors have good 'bedside' manners while others do not, although both may be technically proficient.

What then is the substance of the difference between these two terms? Perhaps the crucial issue is the greater formality of *Professional*, i.e. related to a professional body, and the intuitive nature of *professional*, i.e. personal behaviour. While the one does not necessarily exclude the other, they are not necessarily synonymous. Is it sufficient to have one without the other or are both essential to be effective?

Acting *professionally* assumes a behavioural emphasis, relying more on personal approach. It has as its basis the identification of human qualities and motivations which distinguishes good behaviour from bad. Thus, the type of qualities which might form a checklist for generic *professional* behaviour are: discretion, reliability, honesty, compassion, commitment, responsibility, maturity, trustworthiness, loyalty. To act in a professional manner reflects an approach which owes a duty of care and loyalty to both employer and consumer, while also providing self-fulfilment through job satisfaction. It also involves an inherent expectation that individuals will behave in a manner appropriate to their position and responsibilities. These attributes will also undoubtedly mirror the behavioural expectations professional bodies will place on their members. However, the key point is that they are not exclusive to the accredited members of such bodies.

Being a *professional* has already been defined in the terms outlined in Table 10.1. While incorporating the behavioural expectations outlined earlier, it is based on a degree of regulated formality centred on status, activity and conduct. There is also a high degree of conformity, both to the ethos of the profession and to the image projected by the professional body. Formal professionalism therefore takes the concept into a more structured and wide-ranging arena, reflecting more than the immediate interests of organisation and consumer.

Arguably, the best practitioners will be those combining a professional approach with membership of the housing profession. Such individuals will not only serve the immediate interests of their employers and consumers, but will also contribute to the development of good practice across the profession. This has become increasingly important as the shift towards managerialism has resulted in a tendency to interpret professional behaviour in terms of the organisational outputs rather than contributions to either consumers or the wider profession. This is particularly true of the public sector, where the claims to professional status of occupations such as housing management and social work are based on expertise in meeting the needs of clients (Stoker, 1993). However, such claims become vulnerable to the imposition of political ideologies dictating clients' needs and entitlements.

The New Professionalism

The traditional model of public sector professionalism is becoming a thing of the past. In its place is emerging a new approach to professionalism which has greater emphasis on managerialism, possibly to the detriment of the traditional core value of altruism. This change has been linked to the new style of local governance which has emerged for both local authorities and housing associations, influenced by a combination of financial constraints, the centralisation of control and the growth in customer choice. The social welfare backcloth against which priorities were decided and performance judged has been replaced by a more commercial approach which often values quantitative outputs above qualitative outcomes. Professional pedestals have been whittled away by the forces of competition, supplanted and amended by new imperatives.

There is therefore a dynamic for change which has placed many professional bodies in an unfamiliar position: 'Professional structures have an almost inevitable inertia, which can lead to a reluctance to change' (Stewart, 1993, p. 49). This has in part resulted from a commitment to maintain established standards, defending them against what might be perceived as erosion and diminution. Such a defence has often been adhered to even in the face of the changing needs of a dynamic society. While such an approach may have been sustainable in a less customer centred environment, it has become untenable in the light of a political commitment to citizen-customers.

However, despite demands for change, reliance on the technical skills and expertise of professionals, often attained through complex training and education has remained undiminished. On the contrary, without such skills many services in both the public and private sectors would become seriously undermined or of poor quality. For example, there would be little confidence in any process of property development not involving qualified architects, surveyors and engineers. However, not all professionals have found their claim to indispensability supported within the expectations of the new public sector managerialism. Some have anticipated change and consolidated their position; others have experienced a clear loss of autonomy. These two extremes represent a continuum which Stoker (1993) divides into five categories (Table 10.2)

Stoker's analysis offers a picture in which many professionals have found their positions compromised in the new order of local governance. Others

Table 10.2   Professional relationships within the new governance

---

1. *The De-Skilled Professionals:* have become subservient within their
   employing organisation by virtue of a simplification of their work to routine
   and repetitive tasks, systems of performance measurement which limit
   discretion, and the separation of work tasks from policy-level decision-
   making.
2. *The Constrained Professionals:* have been obliged to accept some limitation
   of their autonomy, usually by accepting clearly defined guidelines for good
   practice (e.g. teachers and the National Curriculum) and external quantitative
   measurement of performance.
3. *The Contracting Professionals:* have moved to a private sector-style model of
   providing their services on the basis of a contract. This is likely to become
   an increasingly common position as CCT extends throughout the public
   sector. The nature of a contractual relationship requires such professionals to
   demonstrate value-for-money whilst delivering an acceptable level of service.
   They will become less directly involved in determining policy development
   other than at arm's length.
4. *The Technocratic Professionals:* 'are the advisors to the lay non-elected elite
   that are assuming a large role in the new governance'. The proliferation in
   the number of quangos which have assumed power at the expense of
   locally elected politicians has provided a vehicle for professionals to exercise
   considerable autonomy. Limited public redress has been provided via the
   establishment of specialist Ombudsman schemes to investigate complaints of
   maladministration.
5. *The Managerial Professionals:* have 'become converts to management . . .
   [defining] themselves by reference to their ability to deliver organisational
   performance'. In such examples, whilst accepting political and professional
   perspectives, the focus of activity is in meeting performance targets and
   producing outputs.

Source: Stoker (1993, pp. 7–8).

have benefited by joining the managerial bandwagon, but in so doing
have adopted a different approach to professionalism. There are also significant numbers of professionals benefiting from the transfer of power
away from local government to government quangos. These non-elected
bodies have often provided considerable power bases within which professional autonomy may be exercised subject to less public scrutiny and
accountability.

The relative fortunes of professions and their members have therefore
been rather mixed. In some cases there has been a deprofessionalisation
of specific functions, while in others there has been a shift in the interpretation of what constitutes professional activity. This has been perceived by
some as constituting an attack on professionalism *per se*. Others consider
that it has provided a challenge to which professionals must respond if
they are to retain their potence. According to Stewart (1988), the *new
professionalism* should be located within an environment which emphasises the following:

Table 10.3   *Management qualities for the new manager*

The new manager will be . . .
* skilled in working with and through others, and in enabling others to do the work
* open to learning, and to developing themselves and others
* sensitive and determined to meet the needs of those for whom the service is directed
* aware of discrimination in themself and others and determined to eradicate it
* tolerant of uncertainty
* experienced in diversity
* flexible in style to meet the needs of others
* able to recognise, value and utilise these attributes in others
* entrepreneurial in approach
* politically sensitive and aware
* effective in contract management
* capable of strategic management
* good at reading and understanding the organisation
* effective in staff management, motivating, counselling, listening and communicating
* skilled in analysis, not least financial analysis.

Source: Stewart (1988).

* dynamic knowledge and skills with less emphasis on basic training, and more on a changing repertoire of knowledge and skill
* external focus – on the customer and client rather than on the profession
* adherence to the values of the local authority as well as the professional values, so that new professionalism sustains rather than denies the diversity of local government
* authority given by those whom the profession serves rather than assumed by qualification alone (Stewart, 1988).

However, to achieve such a position will require a movement away from the reliance on bureaucratic procedures which have in the past cocooned practitioners from the reality of managing a customer-centred service. Such a legacy has resulted from an administrative orientation which had become institutionalised within many housing organisations, often serving the organisation more than its consumers.

For social housing management to remain a sustainable profession, it must be through an attitude which recognises and embraces the need for controlled change. Such an objective can only be achieved on the back of the coordinated efforts of staff committed to change and qualified to implement it. The qualities considered by Stewart (1988) to be crucial in achieving such a transformation are contained in Table 10.3.

Few managers would dispute the worth of any individual who could meet such a person specification. However, rarely would such a diverse range of personal skills and qualities be encountered within a single individual. As Stewart points out, this range of attributes should be present within an organisation rather than in each and every individual manager.

The transition to this new vision of management-centred professionalism cannot occur overnight. There will inevitably be a period during which old practices have to coexist with the new, giving rise to potential tension and conflict. Some organisations are better equipped to handle this than others, emerging from the process with a common commitment among staff to core values and objectives. Others, perhaps with a less clear vision of the future, may require the reassurance of the continuity and support provided by an external source to help them through. Such a role might uniquely be provided by the professional body, i.e. the CIH, providing it can offer the credibility and expert credentials to inspire trust and confidence.

The Chartered Institute of Housing

Through this protracted period of change, the Chartered Institute of Housing (CIH) continues to be identified as the body representing housing professionals. It markets itself as 'the professional organisation for people who work in housing' (CIH, Code of Professional Conduct, undated), its objective being to 'promote the science and art of housing' (ibid). The need to develop greater credibility within and outside of its membership has been a major problem for the CIH. It has commenced from a relatively weak base, undermined by the range of alternative professions and numbers of non-CIH personnel already working within the housing field. This has been further complicated by the lack of stability within many of the organisations and environments in which housing management operates.

The CIH was awarded a Royal Charter in 1984, ironically at a time when the outlook for council housing, the traditional stronghold of CIH membership, was one of retrenchment rather than expansion and development. The level of influence which had accrued to housing professionals by virtue of their control over a much-sought-after resource, had already been seriously undermined by government intervention. Thus, if the attainment of the Royal Charter was to have any meaning, the CIH was therefore faced with little choice other than to adopt a proactive approach to carving out a new, sustainable niche for the housing profession. The resulting strategy has been to raise the profile and image of housing management across a broad political and professional canvas. New developments, some of which are described in the following sections, have been designed to enhance the status of housing training and education, establish standards of behaviour and practice, and increase general consciousness about the housing management function.

Professional Membership

Since receiving its Royal Charter, the CIH has achieved notable success in increasing its membership, currently numbering over 12 000, and growing at a rate of 6 per cent per annum. However, despite this significant expansion, professional membership as a proportion of all housing staff (approximately 100 000 core housing staff) remains relatively small, accounting for less than 15 per cent of the housing workforce. The decline in local authority staff relative to those in housing associations has also meant that the traditional power base of the CIH has diminished. The number of members working in housing associations has continued to increase in recent years from 21 per cent in 1993, to 23 per cent in 1994, and 24.5 per cent in 1995 (CIH Year-books). However, in the current year, this translates into a figure of approximately 3000 staff representing only 5 per cent of the total workforce of nearly 60 000 employed within housing associations (source: HAR 10, Housing Corporation). However, this proportion has been sustained despite substantial increases in the number of staff employed by associations, indicating that the CIH may have a growing appeal in this sector.

The local authority/housing association divide is not the only distributional issue for the CIH to address. Membership is particularly patchy within London, where many organisations place less value on professional qualifications for reasons outlined earlier in this chapter. This clearly constitutes a notable gap in representation, particularly as London-based housing organisations face many of the more intractable problems in social housing. The membership profile of the CIH therefore remains a selective representation of the total social housing workforce. To some extent this is inevitable, with many staff employed in the technical areas of housing belonging to other professional bodies. However, there remains a significant number of eligible practitioners, particularly in lower graded positions who choose not to take up membership. This has had an unfortunate effect of perpetuating an image of elitism and exclusivity which the CIH has tried hard to overcome.

There are several reasons why the CIH has enjoyed a limited appeal in the past, not all of which have been within their direct control. They reflect, in part, the traditional position of housing within local government and its status within the professional hierarchy:

1 *It has been largely biased towards local authority representation*   This remains true despite some increase in the numbers of housing association members and the growing mobility between the two sectors.
2 *It has been too exclusive, restricting full membership to entrants of relatively high educational attainment, i.e. A-levels and above*   Changes in the structure of professionally recognised training and education have gone some way towards redressing the restrictions to membership. The development of an HNC course for non-graduate entry, level-4 NVQ, and the establishment of a series of certificated courses has paved the way for a much more diverse membership of the Institute.

3 *It has been unrepresentative of the housing workforce, being largely white-male-dominated* The extension of professional qualifications to include HNC, NVQ and Certificated courses should, in time, lead to greater representation of black and women members at all levels. Fewer than half the corporate members are women and only 12.2% are non-white, which compared with the race and gender profile of the housing management workforce, is unrepresentative.

4 *It has had only limited influence over housing employment opportunities* An increasing number of employers are beginning to require CIH membership, particularly for senior posts. This is particularly true outside of London. Professional qualifications are also becoming useful yardsticks for local authorities in assessing the quality of the CCT bids from private companies. However, in the final analysis, professional membership can neither guarantee nor prevent an individual obtaining housing-related employment.

5 *'Housing' is too diverse a field, with many practitioners already being members of other professional bodies* In the past, housing has not been an attractive option to qualified practitioners with the opportunity to opt for higher-status professions. This has also, until quite recently, had the knock-on effect of creating a poor image of housing to potential high-calibre recruits. The position has, however, improved, with DoE-funded studentships attracting more highly qualified entrants into a career in housing.

An additional barrier to increasing CIH membership is that many staff have reassessed the source of their professionalism guidance, looking to their organisation to define the expectations of the professionals they employ. The prospect of external regulation holds little appeal when the driving forces behind many social housing organisations are increasingly geared towards performance expectations and output measures.

Standards of Behaviour

Professional officers have, in the past, been afforded enormous influence and control over the lives of members of the public. For such power to be justified it must be based on conventions of good practice, which must be demonstrated to act in the best interests of the public. As part of the development of a professional culture for housing professionals the CIH issued a Code of Professional Conduct in November 1992. The code was intended 'as a move towards promoting the highest standards of professional practice amongst its members' (CIH, 1992b). It applies to all members of the Institute as a condition of membership, the purpose being to give CIH members clear guidance about how to conduct themselves. 'It is also of value to employers, customers and the community by demonstrating the standard of behaviour they can expect of Institute members' (ibid).

Byelaw 18 of the Institute's constitution provides the power to suspend or disqualify members found to be 'guilty of dishonourable or unprofessional conduct or of conduct prejudicially affecting the welfare of the Institute'. There is little doubt that professional bodies must establish standards of behaviour against which its members will be judged. However, to have any real meaning, this must also be accompanied by a credible sanction if behaviour were to fall outside of accepted standards. A question-mark remains over the effectiveness of such a sanction, when membership of the CIH is not essential to gain employment. Clearly the stigma of expulsion from one's professional body would be great, but technically would not stand in the way of an individual retaining their job, or even seeking promotion elsewhere.

In addition to the Code of Conduct, the CIH have also sought to raise standards by following the practice of other professional bodies in introducing Continual Professional Development (CPD) for existing and potential fellows. This requires a minimum level of defined professional activity over the course of a year to encourage practitioners to foster new skills and remain apprised of current developments.

Other key developments by the CIH in recent years have been:

1 *The Test of Professional Practice*   Required for corporate membership of the CIH. This requires a minimum level of practical experience based in the workplace which has been both properly supervised and thoroughly tested.

2 *Training and Education*   The extension of the portfolio of education and training courses offering recognised professional qualifications has also produced benefits. First, by introducing a range of Certificated Courses it has had the effect of offering recognition to a large number of previously undervalued housing workers, e.g. wardens and caretakers. Second, by introducing entry via Further Education, i.e. the HNC in Housing Studies, it has opened the way for groups normally underrepresented within the higher education sector (e.g. mature entrants, ethnic minorities and many women) to become fully qualified and achieve senior positions within both the CIH and housing organisations. The introduction of a Certificate in Tenant Participation has extended the educational boundaries in other ways by offering a professional qualification to recognise the skills of tenant activists and workers.

   The CIH has also promoted other certificated courses in more professional areas, i.e. finance, management and development. These are aimed at practitioners wishing either to focus on a specific area of housing work, having perhaps achieved qualifications from a different professional body, or to update their knowledge in the light of recent changes.

3 *The Good Practice Unit*   This was established in 1995 with the aid of a DoE grant to coordinate, promote and develop good practice in housing management. The unit publishes regular bulletins on specific

housing management themes and commissions manuals and practice guides for housing practitioners.

4 *The Housing Management Standards Manual*   First published in 1994, the CIH have established a set of definitive standards against which housing management might be judged. The Manual has been widely welcomed, as offering a framework for consistency and a comprehensive information resource.

5 *Housing NVQs*   Following on from the development of NVQs in other fields, the CIH has been the lead body in a consortium involved in introducing housing NVQs. These are competence-based qualifications, achieved within the workplace. They have had the undoubted benefit of offering opportunities to many housing staff who would never have considered themselves suited to the more traditional CIH qualifications.

Future Issues for Housing Professionalism

In light of the changes outlined in this chapter there must be a question-mark about the future nature of professionalism within the housing management context. Many practitioners continue to remain outside of CIH membership either by choice or by default. Even for those supporting the professional line, the defining characteristics of professionalism have been dominated by organisational expectations of managerialism and performance outputs. The reducing job security in the public sector, coupled with the effects of competition, has considerably diminished the ability of professionals to operate independent of the wishes of their employers. This is reflected in Stewart's description of the *new professional*, directed more towards organisational loyalty than professional allegiance.

For most people, professionalism is essentially about the delivery of consistently high standards in terms of expertise, judgement and probity. There is evidence (Pearl, 1993) that many housing practitioners consider such attributes to be synonymous with their professional body. Most believe a 'professional' approach to be beneficial in virtually all aspects of housing management, improving relationships with stakeholders while at the same time increasing performance and credibility. However, what is also clear is that perceptions of what constitutes 'acting professionally' vary significantly. It is in this divergence that the seeds for a potential rift between practitioners has been sown. The increasing fragmentation of the social housing sector has resulted in a variety of approaches to the task of housing management. While standards have never been universal, differences lay largely in interpretation and implementation rather than intent. With the growth in private sector companies, predatory housing associations and minimalist local authorities, the variety has become much greater.

For the CIH, this has presented a new dilemma: 'Changes in the housing world could bring a conflict of interests within the Institute. How much support should we give members working for private companies competing aggressively under CCT?' (CIH, 1994a). A view has been taken within the CIH's Five Year Action plan, that the potential for such conflicts should not deter the broadening of the membership base to cover 'housing professionals working in the independent and housing association sector, local authority, private housing sector and all other areas of housing activity, e.g. housing benefit, housing consultancy and contractor services' (CIH, 1995b). However, while professional influence may be extended by widening the membership, there may be other, less beneficial outcomes:

1 The CIH might become too 'broad a church' with so diverse a range of interests, views and expectations that it will be able to represent none effectively.
2 There could be a fragmentation of the CIH itself, with small cliques forming around certain interests, e.g. private contractors, LSVT associations, housing companies, etc.
3 Dialogue within the profession may become more guarded as members become wary of sharing information with potential competitors.

However, for each of these potentially damaging outcomes, it is equally feasible that the outcome of an extended CIH would be to encourage more constructive dialogue, remove existing barriers and lead to greater understanding, diversity of skills and expertise, and a more united housing profession. To its credit, the CIH has recognised the need to look forward rather than backwards in planning its future. It has produced a five-year action plan to cover perhaps the most crucial period of its history. Whether it achieves its primary goal, which is to 'encourage, promote and secure the provision and management of good quality affordable housing for all' (CIH, 1995b, p. 1), remains to be seen. It will certainly have its work cut out to preserve a recognised housing management profession which continues to work 'in the service of the community at large' (CIH, ibid) when every conceivable pressure appears to be working against it.

Summary

The exact nature and role of the housing profession continues to generate considerable debate amongst those most closely associated with it. The view that 'Professionalism is now on the wane in British society . . . professions in general have suffered a decline in status and influence in our society' (Laffin and Young, 1990, p. 32) is counterbalanced by another perspective that 'Professionals have acted collectively to influence policy-making, to assist in implementation and to ensure the disciplined operation of public services within local government during a period of immense change' (Travers, 1993, p. 48). Yet, whatever the perceptions about its value and effect, professionalism cannot be discounted as a significant factor in influencing the delivery of housing management. Despite variations in belief about the focus of professionalism, there is little dissent amongst practitioners that a professional approach to service delivery is important. The major issue is the growing divergence in understanding of what exactly the term 'professional' should mean.

'There is no clearly identified professional role in housing... The diversity of knowledge it calls upon makes it difficult to establish professional identity... Is housing management best seen as a management or as a professional task?' (Stewart, 1988, p. 16). This situation has been heightened by the increasing diversity within social housing of organisational types and cultures, coupled with an intensification of consumer choice and expectation. Changes in policy and practice have led to a widespread reassessment of the core values and relationships traditionally forming the foundation of housing management. From a position of insularity and paternalism, housing managers have been exposed to the probing scrutiny of an extended range of stakeholders, forcing a major reassessment of the mechanics of the professional approach. Much of this has focused on the increasingly evident tensions emerging between the competing demands of the contractual and welfare models of housing management (see Chapter 2).

This hiatus has generated something of an identity crisis amongst housing practitioners. The interpretation of professionalism has been thrown into the melting-pot by a greater externality adopted by the professional body, and the increasing diversification of the housing sector. Issues such as quality and performance have become high on the practice agenda, motivated by professional pride, but also concern for job security. While there is doubtless a common acceptance by housing staff of the need to achieve high standards at all times, there is a divergence in approach on how to ensure this is achieved. For some, it bears little relationship to affiliation to any professional body, stemming instead from individual core values and personal commitment. Others choose to channel similar motivations through the CIH or equivalent body, believing the existence of an expert body, removed from the operational milieu, is vital to maintain standards and sponsor good practice.

However, negative perceptions of formal professionalism persist. Concerns have been voiced in terms of both equal opportunity and managerial perspectives. Within the former context, professionals have been seen by many as innately conservative, slow to reflect diversity, too often resistant to change. Few have ruling bodies which reflect the gender profile of its members, and even fewer have membership profiles reflecting the multi-cultural nature of the communities in which they operate. There is a danger that without such diversity professions may not be equipped adequately to reflect the views and perspectives of underrepresented groups.

Professionalism might also been seen as imposing a cultural straight jacket within which 'The "professional" answer is often seen by the professional as the "only approach"' (Brooke, 1989, p. 60). To its critics, housing management has already suffered from too little innovation and creativity coupled with a reluctance to offer credibility to the expertise of non-professionals, i.e. consumers of services. Within this scenario professionalism has also been perceived as preserving traditional skills regardless of public demands (Pearl, 1993). This has been borne out in the difficulty experienced by a number of housing personnel in adapting to managerial responsibilities having been primarily administrators. This is also discussed in Chapter 5, i.e. the manner in which experienced practitioners have adapted to releasing traditionally held power, thus empowering tenants to exercise control. For many, years of hands-on control has proved difficult to relinquish.

The increasing involvement of the private sector in providing housing management services will inevitably produce greater diversity in the profile of housing staff. It is possible that in the future housing staff could be generic managers who just happen to deal in social housing. As the divide between the rented tenures becomes less evident, perhaps the demand will be for generic rented property management skills rather than specialist ones. Whilst this may be less apparent in the short term as experienced housing managers are recruited by private companies attempting to get a foot in the door, this may change over time. It is unlikely that such organisations would carry out housing management in the same way as their social housing predecessors. They will seek to introduce new methods, perspectives and approaches which will deliver greater cost-effectiveness, crucial to their profitability. Such change will almost certainly involve redefining the expectations of staff and their professional skills.

It may be seen as the sign of a healthy profession that it is able to accommodate such a wide range of perspectives. However, uncoordinated diversity can also result in a fragmentation of purpose which might prove destructive where there is no common agreement about broad objectives. Where social housing organisations are pitted against each other in the interests of competition, efficiency and economy, there is the danger that the focus of professional enterprise becomes more organisational than consumer oriented. If housing management is to establish a sustainable professionalism, it must constitute a hybrid of modern and traditional values. The task is therefore to create a culture within which altruism can be integrated alongside the changing managerial demands of a 'performance culture', producing an acceptable balance between the needs of the profession, organisations and consumers.

11 The Shape of Things to Come

'The government is committed to maintaining a strong social rented sector in which subsidy is given to landlords to provide housing at rents below market levels. This is the most cost-effective way of making sure that people on long term low incomes have access to a decent home.'

(DoEb, 1995)

Approaching the new millennium, the future of social housing remains far from clear. Despite reassurances from the government, there is a prospect that the social housing sector, as it has come to be known, could have its birth and demise within the same century: 'just as housing could be viewed as the sector to be "first in" to the welfare state . . . so it might be the "first out"' (Cole and Furbey, 1994, p. 235). The absence of the constitutional right to housing which exists in some other European states, renders subsidised housing vulnerable to ideological swings. This has been evidenced by the creeping privatisation of social housing fuelled by the commitment to market forces and the adoption of private sector approaches to service delivery. The management of the stock remaining in public ownership has either been contracted out to private companies, or is due to be tendered within the near future.

Consecutive Conservative governments have consistently reiterated their ultimate objective, to promote owner occupation at the expense of subsidised renting. In parallel, they have attempted to revive the private rented sector as a viable alternative for those unable or unwilling to purchase their own home. Local authorities have had a limited role in this grand design, assuming an exclusively strategic input to the housing process. Housing associations have been promoted in their place as providers, perceived by Conservative politicians to be the more acceptable face of social housing. However, this new-found status threatens to be short-lived. Associations have faced increasing competition for Housing Association Grant (HAG), which may further increase should the government implement their White Paper proposal to extend eligibility to private developers. Already, reduced HAG rates, coupled with increased competition for private finance, have forced active associations to become more commercial in their outlook.

Even without such measures, the noose has begun to tighten around many smaller associations, as HAG funding appears likely to be restricted to their larger counterparts, most able to guarantee lower rents for new developments. This requirement contradicts all previous policy trends since

1989, the rationale lying not in any substantive shift in housing policy, but rather as the result of pressure from the Treasury. 'The overall objective is to ensure that those bidders who offer lower rents, and hence lower housing benefit subsidy requirements, than their competitors, gain an advantage in the bidding process' (Housing Corporation, 1995c). Associations have also increasingly been expected to fund reductions in rent levels via efficiency savings, which tends to favour larger associations which inevitably have higher overhead expenditure to cut back. Yet even in these cases, there is a limit to the savings which can be made without compromising viability. In general, only those able to subsidise rents from surpluses, or cut costs through lower standards, could sustain such an objective over any length of time.

Since 1988, a number of new organisational types have emerged in response to the changing housing environment (see Chapter 8). Whatever the future political hue of the government, it is likely there will be a much greater diversity of social housing landlords. Perhaps less certain is the extent to which these organisations will compete for resources and customers or will be able to offer complementary services, catering for a range of different needs and aspirations. The answer will largely depend on whether future housing policy remains determined principally by financial objectives or ever attains its rightful position at the heart of coherent and integrated social and economic policy.

This final chapter examines the future prospects for social housing, referring to the issues facing housing practitioners and their organisations. Many have already been outlined over the course of the book. However, they have to some extent been compartmentalised within topics for the purposes of presentation. In reality, the practical implications of issues such as CCT, community care and tenant participation are inextricably linked. It is within these inter-relationships that housing management assumes its specific characteristics and quality.

Looking Backwards to the Future

It is, of course, impossible to predict with any certainty the manner in which future events will unfold. The majority not possessing clairvoyant powers are forced instead to speculate, informed by the experience of hindsight. The past usually holds clues towards future patterns although it is clearly impossible to predict random events so calamitous or beneficial as to break the existing policy mould. Predicting political futures is a highly imprecise art as many so-called experts have found to their embarrassment in the recent past. However, sharp swings both locally and nationally against the Conservatives during the first half of the 1990s engineered a situation in which electoral defeat appeared a distinct possibility. While Britain remains a two-party state a change of government would almost certainly result in a Labour administration, with either an absolute majority or in a loose coalition with the Liberal Democrats. In either event, such a change would be accompanied by an alternative political agenda. What this might mean in practice is examined later in this chapter, as the housing manifestos of the three main political parties are compared.

The ideological differences which have traditionally dogged housing policy in the United Kingdom have been one major reason why strategic planning has often proved so difficult. This has been true at both national and local levels. Policies and funding mechanisms have been established and dismantled at depressingly regular intervals since the war. The result has been that four or five-year planning cycles have been the maximum envelope of time that can be relied on by politicians. For officers, even such a relatively medium-term period would often be more useful than the year-by-year existence to which they have become accustomed. Even though the 1980s and early 1990s were marked by an element of political stability under the Conservatives, there was little stability for social housing. Instead, constant reform coupled with gross underinvestment left a legacy of disrepair and unmet need.

This was largely predictable from a party committed to rolling back the state and reducing public expenditure. Not even the most ardent municipalist would have expected a Conservative government to support the public sector in the way a Labour government might have. Assuming 'more of the same', i.e. the continuation in power of a Conservative government, a number of key tenets which have featured strongly in the past seem likely to dominate future government policy. These are:

1 Competition
2 Customer care
3 Increased diversity
4 Performance
5 Value for money.

Each has achieved a considerable impact in its own right. However, together they have created a dynamic which would be difficult to reverse in the short term, They remain therefore the shape of the future to a greater or lesser extent. Under a Conservative administration they would be further developed to the benefit of the private sector, at the cost of public landlords. One might speculate that a Labour government would adopt a different approach, reducing the emphasis on these market-oriented mechanisms, and offering support to the public sector. However, 'it is easier to predict the housing problems of the future than to predict the policies that governments will adopt' (Malpass, 1995). Perhaps a crystal ball should become essential equipment for all social housing managers.

Into the Millennium?

The immediate future was presaged by the issue of a White Paper, *Our Future Homes,* in June 1995 which 'sets out a comprehensive framework of policies taking us into the next century' (DoE, 1995b, p. 9). There was little contained within it which deviated from the policy path trodden by successive governments since 1979. However, some developments proved particularly controversial, most notably the proposed changes to the home- lessness legislation and the effect of the sale of housing association dwell- ings on rural communities. In both instances, sustained lobbying and political pressure from opposition parties secured significant concessions from the government.

At the forefront of the vision set out in the White Paper remained the continued commitment towards promoting home ownership. The govern- ment indicated their intention to increase the number of home owners in England by 1.5 million over ten years, noting that households were pro- jected to increase by 1.7 million over the same period. In policy terms, such a commitment appeared ambitious in the light of a depressed hous- ing market which showed little evidence of improvement in the short term. However, this target was dependent on the extension of the Right to Buy for future housing association tenants and the introduction of *Voluntary Purchase Grant* for tenancies commencing before the legislation was enacted. While this justifiably extended the rights enjoyed by council tenants to the tenants of housing associations, it also potentially further reduced the stock of social rented housing. Although local authority restrictions on the re-use of capital receipts would not apply to housing associations, the ability to provide replacement housing in specific locations or built to particular standards or designs would be limited.

The White Paper also contained a government commitment to a social rented sector, 'alongside a healthy private rented sector'. This did not indicate a new level of support for local authorities. On the contrary, the diversification of council housing via transfers to new landlords would continue to be encouraged with a new emphasis on inner-city transfers. In supporting the model of housing companies, the government appeared confident that urban transfers could become a reality and be financially viable. Virtually all previous transfers had been in shire districts involving relatively well-maintained stock. The main disincentive for urban transfers has been the level of negative equity which the transferring authority would have to fund. Thus, rather than receiving a capital receipt for the stock, an authority would have to pay a dowry to the receiving organisation to take the dwellings, clearly an unattractive prospect. If the finances could be made to work, local authorities would then be encouraged to transfer run-down estates which could then be regenerated in partnership with the private sector.

A new means of diversification was proposed by the extension of HAG (or Social Housing Grant as it has become) to the private sector. Although this did not appear within the Housing Act 1996, the Housing Minister, David Curry, reiterated a commitment to introduce this measure in future legislation. This would enable commercial companies to bid for capital grant, with ownership and management remaining either with the developer, or passing to a housing association or management company. All new social landlords would be expected to meet the same standards of service as existing housing associations, with statutory regulation by the Housing Corporation.

Implicit in the White Paper was the view that competition born of diversity would improve performance and efficiency amongst social landlords. The document acknowledged that subsidised rents improves the incentive to work, proving cheaper than personal subsidies over a period of years. Grant rates began to stabilise in 1996, but it was expected that efficiency savings would contribute to producing lower rents. The Housing Act 1996 has also included sweeping new powers for the Housing Corporation in its regulation of housing associations. These extend to the ability to disqualify officers and members and nominate replacements. As a bill it also proposed providing the Corporation with the right to transfer the assets of a housing association to another of its choosing with no reference to the financial institution providing the non-HAG funding. However, this generated a strong reaction from funding institutions, prompting the government to back down.

Environmental awareness also featured in the government's agenda for the future. This was emphasised in both the identification of suitable development sites and the approach to designing new housing. The problems caused by the inappropriate location of new social housing on remote and isolated sites has already been examined (see Chapter 4). Many greenfield sites chosen in the recent past have been pursued because of availability and lower cost rather than suitability. The emphasis on re-using brownfield sites is often a better use of resources in terms of available infrastructure, existing facilities and amenities and access to transport. For social housing managers, effective design strategies are crucial, not only in pursuing responsible and sustainable development programmes, but also in improving the lot of tenants. Energy efficiency is not only environmentally friendly, but crucial to low-income households who need low heating bills.

The contents of the White Paper and Housing Act 1996 have followed the path taken by previous Conservative governments. The support for diversity, including the involvement of the private sector in social housing, suggests a further step along the road to total privatisation of housing management. This is undoubtedly born of an ideological commitment to the private sector rather than any substantiated rationale of the ineffectiveness of the public sector. It is a view contested by the majority of local authorities and by the main opposition parties. However, such a position is nothing new to social housing, having been subjected to political ping-pong for many years.

The Party Political Divide

Over the years, social housing has been at the sharp end of political ideology. Few public services have engendered such polarisation in the policies promoted by political parties at both local and national level. On the left of the political spectrum, longstanding beliefs have centred on a commitment to municipalisation and public service, whilst on the right, private ownership and the primacy of the market has been the overriding priority. The result has been that publicly funded housing has endured a damaging tug-of-war in which long-term investment has been undermined by a constant reversal of policy and funding mechanisms.

In general, Conservative governments have been more radical in their housing policies, being more prepared to break the mould of previous practice. This was particularly true of the Thatcher administrations of the 1980s. The Labour Party has in contrast appeared more content to work within existing policy frameworks, adopting an amending rather than a reforming brief. Under Tory control, there has been a marked centralisation of controls over spending and the role of the public sector, but less evidence of significant interference in the detailed implementation of housing policy. In contrast, the Labour approach has seen significant levels of intervention in the detail of local implementation whilst 'tinkering' with national housing policy.

In the past, the ideological differences between the two main parties have been substantial. The Conservative Party has long been seen as the party of owner-occupation, while Labour has championed the cause of public sector tenants. For many years there has been little common ground between these approaches, although this has appeared less true in the 1990s. Despite having vehemently opposed the introduction of the Right to Buy, Labour and Liberal Democrat politicians have come to accept it in an attitude of electoral pragmatism. Disagreements about owner-occupation have therefore increasingly centred on degrees rather than principles.

As the period of John Major's second term in office drew to an end, April 1997 marked the last possible date for an election. However, the government's majority in the Commons continued to reduce following a series of by-election defeats, giving rise to speculation that this date might have to be brought forward, effectively making 1996 the prelude to the general election. It might have been assumed that in an electoral campaign to overturn an established Tory dynasty, the Labour Party would promise wholesale changes to a decade and a half of right-wing housing policies. However, six months into 1996 there were few indications that this would be the case. Senior Labour Party figures instead emphasised an overriding commitment to responsible financial management, with a reluctance to commit the party to any public spending which might be perceived as increasing taxes. Housing also appeared relatively low down on the political agenda, hardly featuring in electioneering publicity. Labour housing policy documents consistently lagged behind other service manifestos, most notably health and education, indicating perhaps that a future Labour government might not consider a programme of housing reform to be an urgent priority.

The contents of a possible Labour housing manifesto were divulged by key Labour politicians, Messrs Dobson and Raynsford, Shadow Environment Secretary and Housing Minister respectively :

1 Local authorities would be allowed to build again.
2 Capital receipts held by local authorities would be released on a phased basis.
3 Competitive tendering would become optional rather than compulsory.
4 Partnership between the public and private sectors would be encouraged, generating additional finance to build new homes.
5 Support would be provided for housing companies.
6 The return to bricks-and-mortar subsidies, i.e. subsidising building costs rather than relying on personal subsidy such as housing benefit and income support.

These issues had all been highlighted for action during the Labour Party's Social Justice Commission which reported in 1994. Further recommendations included the need to reform housing benefit and mortgage benefits, curb the rise in housing association rents, extend the homelessness legislation, and improve tenants' rights. However, specific commitments were downplayed, reflecting a politically pragmatic approach to their election campaign, and the lessons learned from earlier election defeats. The exact nature of a future Labour government's housing policy remained imprecise, although 'Labour's housing policy is based on the belief that every family should have somewhere decent to live and that they should be able to afford to live there' (Dobson, 1995). In reality, such a statement differed little between any of the three main parties, offering hardly any 'clear blue water' between the established Conservative approach and the alternatives.

In the past, the debate about social housing policy has often centred on the commitment of the government during the 1980s and 1990s to reduce public expenditure to keep down the PSBR. The Labour Party was highly vocal in promoting the removal of housing spending from such constraints particularly through the creation of housing companies. However, this position subsequently softened, amid indications that Labour would not amend the accounting regulations for public spending. This effectively ties a future Labour government to working within existing spending constraints. Thus any increase in housing expenditure would have to be paid for by either increasing taxes or reducing spending on other services.

Of the three main political parties, the Liberal Democrats were alone in their commitment to change the public sector borrowing rules, treating housing as a long-term investment rather than ordinary public borrowing. A cynic might reflect that as the Liberal Democrats stand little chance of forming a government in their own right, they are relatively safe in promising such radical reform. However, in the event of a hung parliament, such a commitment might attain higher currency. In most other aspects of social housing policy, little separates the opposition parties. Both oppose much of the ideological stance adopted by the Tory government in relation to homelessness, housing benefit and the promotion of owner occupation, perhaps defining the real differences between the parties.

In reality, whichever political party attains power, there is little to suggest that social housing management would revert back to the position occupied prior to 1979. In a Conservative future, continued emphasis would be placed on increasing owner occupation, the emasculation of local authorities and the involvement of the private sector, including housing associations. A Labour government would continue to support owner occupation but not promote its extension, would offer local authorities a more active role in developing and managing housing and would seek to develop partnership with the private sector rather than depend on it. If the Liberal Democrats were to hold the balance of power in a hung parliament, they would support much of Labour's approach but push more strenuously for a reform of housing finance. The prognosis for the social housing manager is therefore to expect much of the same medicine, but with the potential for a variance in the strength of the dosage. While offering little in the way of additional resources, a Labour government or Labour Liberal coalition might prove easier to work with, being more receptive to innovative means of developing social housing, and perhaps offering some additional flexibility.

The Social Housing Product

Should the political position remain unchanged, there are clear indications that the privatisation of social housing will continue unabated – privatisation not only in the sense of transferring ownership from public to private sector, but also the shifting culture amongst public sector organisations reflecting their exposure to competition and commercial practice.

The tensions between the contractual model and welfare models have been examined earlier in this book in Chapter 2. However, the evidence strongly supports a continued trend towards the establishment of a narrow definition of social housing management solely in terms of bricks and mortar. This has already been set in train by past actions such as ring-fencing the Housing Revenue Account (HRA) and the introduction of CCT. The publication of *Our Future Homes* (DoE, 1995b), served to continue this momentum, proposing an extension of the eligibility for HAG to include private developers and seeking to continue the transfer of council dwellings to alternative landlords. This not only envisaged the involvement of registered housing associations, but also profit-making landlords based in the private sector.

To reflect the need for acceptable standards across a mixed economy of housing management, the government introduced the term *Social Housing*

'*Product*' to establish a common denominator against which to judge the performance of organisations with different constitutions and objectives. The key elements of this 'product' are defined as:

- development and maintenance
- allocations
- rent levels
- the provision of rights and services to tenants (DoE, 1995c).

The government's definition of the term 'Social Housing Product' (later redefined as the 'Social Housing Standard') indicated a further shift towards an emphasis on efficiency. 'Taken together this package of "outputs" defines the social housing "product" which Government is "buying" either with grants to subsidise new-build or rehabilitation or by approving the transfer of local authority stock at a price designed to enable purchasing landlords to deliver this "product"' (ibid, 1995c). This leaves little doubt that social housing is moving towards being reconstituted as a commodity rather than a 'need' or a 'right'. In such a scenario, resources become the prime determinants of service delivery with *outputs*, i.e. quantity, displacing concerns over *outcomes*, i.e. quality and effectiveness. Such a concern has been articulated by the CIH in its response to an NFHA consultation paper on this issue. 'The term social housing product is causing a certain amount of concern amongst our members. On one hand, it is generally felt that the term sounds very commercial and impersonal and on the other, that it rather stigmatises the housing itself as something inferior' (CIH, 1996). While the provision with the Housing Act 1996 stop short of formally endorsing a defined 'product', it has introduced much broader powers for the Housing Corporation and more radically, the Audit Commission, to influence and dictate the standard of service delivery.

It is without doubt a legitimate objective for governments to ensure that social housing provides value for money for taxpayers in general and rentpayers in particular. The interpretation of value, particularly in the light of increased competition, has tended to focus on the reduction of costs by efficiency savings. However, while some savings have been possible, there is a point at which economy becomes counter-productive in terms of achieving objectives: 'if the standards to which ... housing is built, maintained and managed are not adequate, competition will result in a social housing product that fails to meet the needs to which it is addressed' (NFHA, 1995c). Many social landlords have become more innovative, responsive and sensitive to the needs of their consumers, motivated in part by the need to compete for their futures. But, 'there is a risk that the drive to reduce costs will determine the level of service that can be delivered and that objectives are adjusted (consciously or not)' (NFHA, 1994).

The adoption of a defined *social housing product* may have its advantages. If it has the effect of establishing standards which uphold the aims and objectives of the social housing sector, it will be welcome. However, it appears more likely that the recasting of a welfare service as a commercial product signals a further movement along the path of a property management model within which tenant interests are separated from asset management.

The Future for Local Authorities

It would be unusual for local authorities if the future did not hold the prospect of further change. They have faced a constantly moving policy agenda since the beginning of the 1980s, which has seen many of them change out of all recognition, most notably as the result of CCT. By 1999 all eligible authorities will have tendered their services at least once. If the results of the first round of CCT are mirrored in later phases, the vast majority of housing management contracts will continue to be delivered by local authorities. However, it is possible that the private sector will view the first round as a learning experience, mounting a more credible threat in future phases. Even if in-house teams are successful in retaining the management function in the first instance, victory may be only short-lived. Most contracts are awarded for a maximum five-year term after which time they will be open to renewed competition. The onus is therefore on contractors to remain competitive with an eye to the future.

Only time will tell whether the successful in-house teams were prudent in their projections. Many officers involved in the bidding process had little or no experience in commercial costing or the housing 'market', often submitting significantly lower bids than their competitors. Staff and consumers have carried the burden of the consequential cost savings in reduced standards of service and poorer conditions of employment. Staff employed in the contracting capacity have already experienced reductions in working conditions and rates of pay. The position has been even worse for some staff transferred to external contractors despite the apparent protection of TUPE (see Chapter 7). Whoever wins the competitive tenders, a commercial culture is the inevitable consequence of contracting services. It is therefore difficult to envisage any scenario other than a more cost-oriented approach to employment and service delivery.

Choices do remain open to local authorities should they consider the consequences of CCT too unpalatable. The most established 'escape route' is to pursue the option of large scale voluntary transfer. Already fifty authorities, managing 250 000 dwellings, have trodden this path, and the government remains committed to supporting LSVTs in the future. An alternative route is the unknown and untried transition to housing company, which offers a different set of threats and opportunities. The main attraction has been the potential to access additional funds denied to the public sector by PSBR restrictions. However, this has been called into question as neither the Conservative nor Labour parties appear willing to change the borrowing rules. Even without changes to public sector accounting methods, the company model might still offer benefits for local authorities. The opportunity would exist to create organisations flexible enough to deliver a much wider social housing product than the limited role allowed within government constraints. It appears likely that housing companies will prove popular, having been endorsed by all main political parties and by the CIH. The proponents of companies have gone to great lengths to reassure local authorities that they are not simply another route to privatising public housing. But whatever the benefits of transition, that is what they amount to. In one sense, housing companies would simply replicate the position already experienced by the fifty local authorities which have pursued LSVT, i.e. a lack of direct control over their housing. However, they may prove to be different, having the scope to operate in a more innovative, collaborative and accountable manner.

The above scenario would probably change if a Labour government were to be elected. They have already indicated that local authorities will be able to build again, that they would release capital receipts on a phased basis and that CCT would become voluntary. Under such circumstances, there would be little incentive for councils to change the way they currently operate. Some, of course would still take the opportunity to adopt a minimalist position, preferring to work though housing associations. Others may have already gone too far down the road of dismantling the apparatus for the direct provision of housing, making such an option medium term rather than an immediate one. It may be that issues other than CCT and stock transfer will ultimately define the future of local authority housing. The growing momentum for tenant involvement and control should not be underestimated. Already, one local authority, Kensington and Chelsea, has set up a tenant management organisation to which it has transferred its entire stock. Having been offered a taste of responsibility and influence, tenants are unlikely to relinquish such a position lightly. This is particularly true as the relationship between the cost of service delivery and rent has become more sharply focused in recent years. Although Tenants' Choice has now been abolished, the Right to Manage still offers considerable power to tenants' groups. Perhaps the consumer will ultimately have the final say.

The Future for Housing Associations

The 1990s began with considerable promise for housing associations. From a stable but restricted role, they were quickly thrust into the position of the main providers of social housing. The ADP rose from £1 billion in 1989/90 to £1.8 billion in 1993/4, almost doubling within five years. However, such growth has been acquired at the expense of the security enjoyed by the movement and a certain loss of diversity, previously considered to be a significant strength. The result has been that many smaller associations have disappeared, swallowed up by larger, more robust associations. Attitudes to development and management have changed, reflecting a more commercial and performance-oriented approach to social housing. In addition, associations are operating within an increasingly competitive environment in which interpretations of value and quality have frequently related more to quantitative outputs than qualitative outcomes.

What would the future hold should the current political picture remain the same? Certain trends which have emerged in the past appear likely to continue:

1. Competition

There is enormous competition between housing associations for funding and development opportunities. This has been exacerbated within recent years by the establishment of fifty additional associations following large scale voluntary transfer. The effect has been to create a position in which available HAG was overbid by 400 per cent in the 1995/6 ADP bidding round. This is despite the continued protestations by many associations that they are unable to develop high-quality affordable housing with such low levels of HAG. The reality appears to be that a culture has emerged in which developing associations feel locked in to a continued programme of development. There is a concern that to step off the treadmill for an instant will result in losing out on development opportunities for good, resulting in the ultimate demise of the association. Such approaches often result in associations adopting development-led strategies with housing management taking second place.

There is little evidence that competition will lessen in the future. Indeed, proposals contained in *Our Future Homes* increase it further:

- The continued commitment to LSVT and other forms of stock transfer, resulting in additional associations.
- The opportunity for non-profit making private companies, including housing companies, to register with the Housing Corporation as Registered Social Landlords and thus apply for Social Housing Grant.
- The promise that at some future time, non-registered private developers might be able to apply for Social Housing Grant.

If competition is increased, the criteria for success will become more focused and the margin for error reduced. Those associations likely to continue receiving development subsidy are those able to demonstrate that they are strong enough to sustain risks, efficient enough to deliver the promised goods, effective in involving tenants in managing their housing and secure enough to be able to keep rents to within acceptable limits. Other factors such as the strength of relationship with local authorities, and a commitment to Housing Plus, may also prove important. However, the Housing Corporation will probably offer the greatest support to associations most favoured by financial institutions. Without such arrangements, development is impossible, and concerns have grown that the financial sector does not offer a bottomless pit of investment for the social housing market.

There has also been evidence to suggest that many associations will go where the money is to be found. This has led to an increased interest in the area of special needs in recent years as money for community care has proven attractive. There must, however, be a worry that entering into such areas without the expertise or understanding of the potential problems may spell disaster in the future. The same may be true of CCT, where associations are being tempted to take on the management of some of the most difficult local authority housing stock – e.g. Hyde HA in Lambeth. It may be that they are equipped to do a better job than has previously been achieved. However, bids for such contracts are not based on direct experience, and there must always be a possibility that an association has underestimated the task. There is a danger that such a miscalculation could lead to the demise of the association concerned.

A spin-off from CCT has been the inevitable comparison between the housing management costs of local authorities and housing associations. In general, associations are consistently more expensive than local authorities, spending up to 20 per cent more on their management (Housing Corporation, 1995d). While direct comparisons are often inappropriate because of the different nature of the stock, service levels and financial regimes, the differing levels have worried many associations. Concerns relate to their ability to bid for CCT contracts, a situation borne out by the relatively poor performance in the first round of tenders. A further worry is that CCT may at some future time be extended to housing associations. While this is not an immediate danger, it would appear a logical extension to local authority CCT. The result is that many of the larger, ambitious associations are reviewing their management costs with the objective of decreasing them where possible. This often means increasing patch sizes and creating leaner staffing structures.

2. Affordability

One of the outstanding issues still to be resolved is that of affordability. The relatively high cost of new housing association dwellings has contributed to the creation of unbalanced communities (see Chapter 4), often complicating relationships with local authorities many of whom are committed to keeping rents low. Even though council rents have also risen significantly in recent years, they generally remain much lower than their association counterparts. This difference is often exacerbated by the higher management costs of associations than those of local authorities. The result is that local authority tenants are often reluctant to transfer to more expensive housing association dwellings when they need a transfer. Many councils therefore place considerable pressure on associations to keep rents as low as possible, favouring larger associations able to subsidise rents from reserves.

The affordability dilemma promises to become even more problematic in the future. The 1995/6 ADP bidding round for the first time used rent levels as an indicator in deciding allocation of HAG. The corporation indicated that rent levels must be kept as low as possible, reversing past trends. This corresponds with government intentions to reduce the level of expenditure on benefits. Rent levels in the private sector have already been capped, and this will also apply to housing associations. Lower rents may impede the ability of some associations to secure new development facilities, potentially causing concern amongst funding institutions keen to be assured that associations' rental streams are sufficient to guarantee the repayment of loans. While HAG levels have stabilised, there is no indication that they will rise again, maintaining the gap between scheme costs and public subsidy. Lower rents could therefore prove a gap too far for smaller associations in particular to contend with.

3. Governance

The issue of governance has featured highly amongst housing associations in recent times. The NFHA published a Code of Governance (NFHA, 1995b) following a year-long enquiry, and the Nolan Committee has also investigated the association movement. Whilst there have been few major scandals to date, the more that associations are drawn into commercial competition, the greater will be the motivation and opportunity to reduce the standards of probity currently sustained.

There are also unresolved issues about the way that associations are managed and by whom. Increasingly boards of management are dominated by those with sufficient professional expertise to hold sway over crucial financial decisions. Attempts to recruit balanced boards which reflect communities have been undermined by the increasing complexity and demands of association work. Considerations of equal opportunities and voluntarism will continue to take second place to financial and development oriented expertise.

The danger is that this position will become more entrenched as competition increases and resources reduce. Some associations may consider that a move to housing company status may offer greater flexibility than their current constitutions. While housing companies will be regulated by the Housing Corporation, their remit will inevitably be wider and less constrained than housing associations. One area in which there will be less constraint will be in the payment of board members. The NFHA governance review indicated a clear preference amongst existing board members not to be paid a salary for their efforts. However, a strong lobby for payment remains, believing that only by acting thus will boards attract and retain members of sufficient calibre to ensure they are properly run. The route to housing company status may offer an attractive proposition to boards supporting such a view.

If there were a change of government, the prognosis for associations would change, but to what extent is unclear. A Labour government would permit local authorities to build their own homes again, many for the first time since 1989. They would also allow accumulated capital receipts to be spent in a phased manner, although this may not prove to be the panacea widely expected. These two situations offer both good news and bad news. On the one hand there may be additional funding for social housing, but on the other local authorities may choose to use the money themselves. There are already indications that some Labour-controlled local authorities are preparing themselves for just such an opportunity. In addition, if the compulsion were removed from CCT, so too might a number of opportunities for associations to bid for contracts.

On the positive side, Labour have indicated continued support for associations albeit possibly in a special-needs role rather than in the mainstream role they enjoy at present. In many situations local authorities may have gone too far down the enabling road to contemplate reviving their development aspirations. In such cases, associations may enjoy a windfall of capital receipt funding to further extend their programmes. Because of the pattern of council house sales, it is probable that large amounts of capital receipts are held by authorities outside the Metropolitan areas. These are more likely to be the type of authority happy to continue the funding relationship with associations.

The future for associations is almost certain to be volatile whichever political party is in power. The dynamic environment in which they find themselves offers little respite for those unable to keep up with the pace. The requirement is to adapt or drop out of the role of active developer, which may ultimately lead to merger or takeover. Indications are that circumstances will favour larger associations. Out of a 1995/6 ADP of £1.02 billion, 57 per cent was allocated to associations of 2500 or more dwellings, with those owning fewer than 500 dwellings receiving only 9 per cent of the allocations. Associations owning more than 2500 dwellings represent less than 0.5 per cent of associations registered with the Housing Corporation although together they own almost 25 per cent of the total association stock. The top twenty associations increased their share of the allocation from £236 million to nearly £319 million, an increase of 35 per cent. This, coupled with the advantage that larger associations have in generating private finance, places them in the forefront of social housing provision. This may not mean that smaller associations will completely disappear in the future, but their role will tend to be a localised one, responding to specialist needs and filling niches at a local level.

Housing associations have also had to come to terms with the growth of tenant involvement, with many larger, inner-city ones reacting positively to establish appropriate mechanisms. While all developing associations have been required to implement tenant participation as a condition of receiving HAG, this is likely to be more strongly enforced in the future.

The Nolan Committee appears set to recommend greater transparency and public accountability in the way that housing associations operate. Associations would be well advised to work closely with their tenants; their support may be critical to sustaining a social housing sector.

Under the current political environment, associations are increasingly caught between a rock and a hard place. Grant rates may be stabilising, albeit at a low level, but the amount allocated to rented housing is decreasing in favour of ownership initiatives. This has created a dilemma for many associations following an expansion of their development capacity in the light of the enormous promise of the early 1990s. Some associations have already 'downsized' their development staffing levels, although by so doing they may be compounding their difficulties by being unable to react to unexpected opportunities. The result is that associations are increasingly looking to diversify their operations, such as taking on special-needs projects and/or building housing for students. Perhaps the future possibilities for housing companies may provide a lifeline for associations struggling to find a role as their development programmes are cut. Whether associations are increasingly forced to compete with the private sector for land, loans and housing management remains to be seen. However, 'At the end of the day whether social housing can be provided by the private sector in this country will be a political decision. But associations will have to adjust to a more competitive, pluralistic regime whatever happens' (Stansfield, 1996).

The View from the Bridge

What does the future hold for those employed within housing organisations? Faced with the new public sector management and changing perceptions of professionalism, they have had to adjust to substantially different ways of working. The 1980s and 1990s have been difficult years for the public sector at large, but housing in particular. Even housing associations, considered by the government to be private sector organisations, have experienced significant problems. Housing staff generally have had to deal with the changes flung at them and to make the best of often difficult circumstances. Some staff have clearly suffered as a result of the CCT process, yet there is little evidence of a widespread disenchantment with housing management as a career. Employment remains relatively buoyant, and the standard of new entrants into professional housing courses has been high. So, is the future perceived as bright or dismal from the inside, and do those 'at the coalface' consider social housing to have a future?

The housing magazine, *ROOF*, conducted two surveys of local authority housing directors, in 1993 and 1995 (Table 11.1). The survey results indicate a mood of optimism amongst local authority directors despite the difficulties endured. There is a widespread belief that councils continue to

Table 11.1   ROOF surveys of local authority housing directors

1993	1995
1. 80 per cent disagree with the proposition that there is 'no future for council housing as we now know it'.	1. 92 per cent disagree that council housing is a spent force with no real future in building homes.
2. 62 per cent expressed an interest in setting up 'local housing companies'.	2. 82 per cent think a local housing company would benefit their area.
3. 67 per cent find the job of being a director less satisfying than it used to be.	3. 75 per cent think their job has become less satisfying, 15 per cent it has become more satisfying, 10 per cent feel it has remained the same.

Source: ROOF surveys, 1993 and 1995.

have reasonable future prospects. However, although senior staff have been crucial in achieving such a position, it has been at significant personal cost, with almost three-quarters considering their job satisfaction to have reduced. It is an interesting reflection on these two sets of responses, that housing companies became increasingly attractive over the two-year period within which the surveys were conducted. Confidence in the future role of councils is perhaps based on an expectation that a change of government would change their fortunes. If this fails to materialise, housing companies may prove an increasingly popular option.

There has been a growing belief amongst senior local authority and housing association staff that the millennium may hold less comfort for housing associations than for council housing departments. In the 1995 *ROOF* survey, 68 per cent of housing directors believed that associations stood little chance of retaining their role as main provider of new social housing, whichever political party holds power. The current trends towards increasing competition, reduction in the ADP and tightened regulation for associations may lead to a period of decline in which mergers and takeovers are accelerated.

On a broader front, senior housing staff will probably be expected to possess generic business management skills alongside housing-specific ones. With so much subsidy, scrutiny and expectation invested in social housing organisations, it is likely that, 'The skills of financial management and strategic planning will be more highly prized than housing management' (Passmore, 1995). Further pressures towards genericism will be generated by the growing trends towards merging professional disciplines within a single directorate. The increasing linkage between housing and social services as the result of community care is a prime example of this (Waddicore, 1995).

The view from the 'captains' of social housing is that the future appears to hold potential alongside uncertainty. Many feel that local authorities have reached their nadir, with some prospects for an improvement in their fortunes, whilst housing associations have passed their zenith, with a more difficult road ahead. A common response from staff across both sectors is that the strain is beginning to show, caused mainly by the effects of competition. Some believe that this has had the positive effect of sharpening the involvement of staff, and of overcoming apathy and disengagement from the task to be completed. Others take the view that such pressure has taken its toll, creating a negative effect on staff already overburdened with work. The view from the bridge is for more stormy seas ahead.

Winners and Losers

The 1980s and 1990s have been marked by the rich getting richer and the poor getting poorer. The opportunities for good-quality housing have generally hinged on ability to pay. Far from the 'one nation' approach propounded by some conservatives, the *Zeitgeist* for the Major era has been to focus on the 'deserving' and 'undeserving' poor. The Back to Basics campaign sought to promote orthodox family values while vilifying the 'irresponsibility' of single parenthood. Other groups have also fallen victim to government attack including young single people, refugees, the unemployed, and gypsies.

In general, financial policies since 1980 have worked against those in low-paid employment or who are unemployed. The withdrawal of HAG and HRA subsidy has had the effect of driving up rents in the social sector, creating benefit ghettos which offer little hope to their occupants. The constant erosion of benefit levels and eligibility has in parallel removed under-18-year-olds from the system entirely, and extended the poverty trap for many households on the breadline. This has particularly affected new tenants of housing associations who are forced to pay rents at least 40 per cent higher for the same property as neighbours whose tenancy was secure, having commenced prior to 1989.

Housing practitioners have also felt the pinch, having to work under increasingly pressurised conditions with diminishing resources. As a result, not only do they face having to contend with growing levels of dissatisfaction and violence, but they also face the prospect of being privatised or becoming surplus to requirements. The perception that housing management offers secure, lifetime employment has been truly banished by the commercialisation of the public sector.

However, there have also been winners within this scenario. Over 1.5 million council tenants bought their homes under the Right to Buy provisions, many at large discounts of between 50 and 70 per cent. In a number of cases, dwellings were purchased by the children of elderly tenants, subsequently being sold at a significant profit on the death of the parent. Such an outcome has achieved little in respect of alleviating housing need, serving only to enrich a number of fortunate individuals. Yet such a picture might conceivably be repeated, albeit at a reduced level, by the extension of the Right to Buy to housing association tenants. Although discounts will be lower, the opportunity to purchase good-quality dwellings in a depressed property market may prove extremely attractive.

Tenants in general have been both winners and losers. Since 1980, council tenants have been endowed with a series of 'rights' in addition to the opportunity to purchase their council dwellings. These have included the right to repair, access to information, right to manage and, under the ill-fated Tenant's Choice, the right to switch landlords. In addition, as a result of the various Citizens' Charters, including a Council Tenants' Charter, the consumer has been offered greater influence and status. However, while these rights may be enshrined in statute, many tenants remain unable to derive significant benefit from them. Many factors serve to marginalise households and individuals from entitlement, including language barriers, discrimination, poverty, cultural and religious requirements and institutional inefficiency. These are often the same groups housed in the poorest housing, receiving the lowest incomes and with the poorest experience of education, training and health provision. There are also losers in the owner-occupied sector. Many people were attracted into owning by the prospect of capital accumulation through an ever-increasing property boom, only to find themselves with negative equity or the experience of repossession. This has included Right to Buy purchasers who over-extended themselves on the promise of a better future. Owner occupation, for poorer households who can afford only to purchase at the cheaper end of the market can mean becoming trapped within often poor-quality dwellings which may turn out too small for their needs and are expensive to maintain.

There is little to suggest that these 'victims' of the housing market will experience any eventual improvement to their lot. Personal benefits continue to be tightened, unemployment continues to remain high, and fewer good-quality, affordable houses are being provided by social landlords. Future winners will remain those able to exercise choice and influence, usually because of access to financial resources. Housing practitioners may find their salaries and conditions of employment deteriorating as competition takes hold. Many may also find that they have little affinity with contractual housing management which will offer less quality to both providers and recipients of services. However, perhaps the ultimate losers are those for whom poverty, ill health and unemployment have become facts of life, a virtual throwback to a Victorian past.

Summary and Reflections

This book was conceived as a resource to both inform and stimulate discussion among students of housing about the 'real world'. There is perhaps a danger that having painted a sometimes grim picture of the reality of housing management some may be discouraged. If this happens, perhaps it is for the best – social housing is not for the faint-hearted. However, the vast majority of individuals employed in the field will usually testify that although there are frequent problems, housing management offers unique rewards. It may be a modern cliché to choose a career which involves 'working with people', but it is this which continues to provide the motivation for many new entrants and experienced officers alike. There are times when the clients/tenants/customers will prove difficult to work with. Increasingly, housing officers have to cope with violence, abuse and personal threats. This partly reflects the change in societal behaviour, but also illustrates the importance of housing to those who are not adequately housed – it may literally be a matter of life or death.

The more that resources for housing are reduced and demands for housing increase, the greater is the requirement for housing staff to be committed to the consumers they serve. For while a large proportion of the community may be able to accept the role of customer, significant numbers need and would choose to be supported and have their causes championed by well-trained and informed practitioners. The ultimate high-quality service is one which provides a range of service options catering for a broad range of needs and expectations. To this end, housing officers need to possess a number of personal qualities and skills which equip them to work in such an environment. Perhaps the most important is the ability to reflect on experience. It is only by learning from others and from personal mistakes that practitioners can improve and become competent. This has been a strength of professional initiatives such as the Test of Professional Practice which have required the maintenance of a reflective log over a period of time. To some, this process may appear a time-consuming and irritating distraction from practice. However, without it, social housing management becomes no different from selling cars or providing estate agency services. While services in these areas may meet very high standards, they are geared towards selling a commodity to those able to afford it.

Social housing rarely offers such choice, is frequently over-subscribed and consequently usually rationed by bureaucratic process. All too often allocations policies are about placing those with least choice in the worst property. This can either be performed as a mechanistic, routine function or infused with compassion, sensitivity and innovation. Some may consider that idealistic attitudes no longer have a place in modern housing organisations judged on performance rather than good intentions. However, a service based on achieving output targets alone is poorer than one which retains a clear commitment to its wider responsibilities to the community. Approaches to CCT which demand productivity at the expense of quality and equality stand little chance of survival against the financial muscle of the private sector. Local authorities stand a greater chance of retaining the housing management function in-house by offering a service which differs from that provided by the private sector rather than competing on price alone. The flexibility to achieve this may be limited by the progressive tightening of the CCT guidelines on issues such as anti-competitiveness and quality requirements. However, if it remains a government priority to remove management from the public sector, this will be achieved no matter how well local authorities perform.

It is perfectly conceivable that within the foreseeable future, social housing management will no longer be a public sector function. 'There is a distinct possibility within the next decade that social housing provision will not be organised as it is today. Instead we might see local housing management companies (combining associations, authorities and arm's length companies) and regional housing development companies, all within the private sector' (Williams, 1993). This is perhaps less important than the framework within which services are delivered. Housing associations are already considered to be private sector organisations, but are non-profit-making concerns. This is important, in that it eliminates much of the motivation to reduce costs solely to pay share dividends. The expectation that services are cost-effective remains, but surpluses (rather than profits) can be reinvested to provide additional housing or improve existing housing. The difference is that commercial organisations facilitate an outflow of funds from the service to pay shareholders, while non-profit organisations recycle money to improve services.

If housing management should ultimately be located within the profit-making sector, the scope for reflection and compassion will be limited to what can be afforded within company cost projections. At that stage, welfare motivated practitioners will be faced with dilemmas about the role they are able to play and the satisfaction gained from their jobs. In the meantime, over five million homes remain to be managed by public sector/housing association landlords. While these organisations may not be perfect, they continue to preserve an attachment to 'the cardinal principle of service delivery that there should be equality of access and treatment for all – regardless of their social status, gender, ethnicity, sexual orientation, age, disability, etc.' (Palmer, 1995). This provides a strength rather than a weakness by delivering services which are both cost-effective and provide value for money. The good practice which has already begun to develop around initiatives such as Housing Plus and care in the community underlines the role the social sector has to play in the future. The real world offers a challenge to housing practitioners to square the circle which links social values with performance, equality with economy and efficiency with effectiveness. The prize for success is a sustainable system of high-quality, affordable housing for all who need it. The cost of failure is the commoditisation of housing at the expense of the social welfare ethic.

Bibliography

Aldbourne Associates (1993) *The Management of Neighbour Complaints in Social Housing,* Aldbourne Associates, Wiltshire.

AMA (1994) *Preparing for CCT: Specifying Housing Management,* AMA.

Anlin, S. and Lush, P. (1994) 'Hanging On In There', *ROOF,* March/April, p. 8.

Anonymous (1995a) 'Minister to Rethink Rules Which Hamper Tenant Participation', *Inside Housing,* 30 June.

Anonymous (1995b) 'Right to Manage Hits Partnerships', *Inside Housing,* 7.

Arnold, P., Bochel, H., Brodhurst, S. and Page, D. (1993) *Community Care: The Housing Dimension,* Joseph Rowntree Foundation.

Association of District Councils, Association of Metropolitan Authorities and National Federation of Housing Associations (1984), *Housing Associations and Local Authorities,* NFHA.

Association of District Councils (1987) *Closer to the People,* ADC.

Association of District Councils (1990) *The Enabling Authority,* ADC.

Association of Metropolitan Authorities (1994) *Preparing for CCT: Specifying Housing Management,* AMA.

Audit Commission (1986a) *Managing the Crisis in Council Housing,* HMSO.

Audit Commission (1986b) *Making A Reality Of Community Care,* HMSO.

Audit Commission (1988a) *Performance Review in Local Government: Action Guide,* HMSO.

Audit Commission (1988b) *The Competitive Council,* Management Papers No. 1, HMSO.

Audit Commission (1993a) *Putting Quality on the Map: Measuring and Appraising Quality in the Public Service,* Occasional Paper No. 18, HMSO.

Audit Commission (1993b) *Who Wins? – Voluntary Housing Transfers,* Occasional Paper No. 20, October, HMSO.

Audit Commission (1994) *Taking Stock: Progress with Community Care,* HMSO.

Audit Commission (1996) *Balancing the Care Equation: Progress with Community Care,* HMSO.

Barker, A. (1991) 'Putting Housing Out to New Management', *Inside Housing,* 27 March, pp. 8–9.

Bayley, R. (1992) 'The Tender Agenda', *Inside Housing,* 12 June, pp. 8–9.

Bickler, S. and Hood, M. (1991) 'Voluntary Transfers: The Need for Independent Advice', *Housing and Planning Review,* October/November, pp. 21, 24.

Billis, D., Ashby, J., Ewart, A. and Rochester, C. (1994) *Taking Stock: Exploring the Shifting Foundations of Governance and Strategy in Housing Associations,* Centre for Voluntary Organisations, LSE.

Black, J. (1993) 'High Hopes', *ROOF,* January/February, pp. 20–1.

Bright, J. (1995) 'Millions Wasted As In-House Teams Find No Competition', *Inside Housing,* 3 November, p. 1.

Brimacombe, M. (1989) 'Beyond Design', *Housing,* September, pp. 11–15.

Brooke, R. (1989) *Managing the Enabling Authority,* London: Longman.

Brown P. (1995) *Homing in on the Public Sector,* Guardian Society, 8 February.

Catterick, P. (1992) *Total Quality Management in Social Housing,* Institute of Housing.

Centre for Public Services (1995) *Calculation of the National Costs and Savings of CCT,* Centre for Public Services, Sheffield.

Chartered Institute of Housing (undated A) *More Than Bricks and Mortar,* CIH.

Chartered Institute of Housing in Scotland (undated B) *Can We Afford to Care?,* CIH (Scotland).

Chartered Institute of Housing (1992a) *Response to DoE Consultation Paper: Competition in the Provision of Housing Management,* CIH.

Chartered Institute of Housing (1992b) CIH Code of Professional Conduct.

Chartered Institute of Housing (1993a) *Housing Standards Manual,* CIH.

Chartered Institute of Housing (1993b) *Response to DoE Consultation Paper: Compulsory Competitive Tendering of Housing Management,* CIH.

Chartered Institute of Housing (1994a) *All Change for Housing? A Discussion Document on the Future Direction of the Chartered Institute of Housing,* CIH.

Chartered Institute of Housing (1994b) *Out of the Shadows: Housing's Place in the New Authorities,* CIH.

Chartered Institute of Housing/Tenant Participation Advisory Service (1994c) *Tenant Participation in Housing Management.*

Chartered Institute of Housing (1995a) *Challenging the Conventions: Public Borrowing Rules and Housing Investment,* CIH.

Chartered Institute of Housing (1995b) *The Future of the Chartered Institute of Housing – a Five Year Action Plan: 1995–2000,* Chartered Institute of Housing.

Chartered Institute of Housing (1996) *Response to NFHA Consultation Paper: The Social Housing Product,* CIH.

Clapham, D. (1989) *Goodbye Council Housing,* Unwin Hyman.

Clapham, D., Kemp, P. and Smith S. (1990) *Housing and Social Policy,* London: Macmillan.

Clapham, D. and Franklin, B. (1994) *Housing Management, Community Care and Competitive Tendering – a Good Practice Guide,* CIH.

Clarke, M. and Stewart, J. (1986) *The Public Service Orientation – Developing the Approach,* Local Government Training Board.

Clarke, M. and Stewart, J. (1989) *Challenging Old Assumptions,* Local Government Training Board.

Clinton, A. (1990) 'Explaining Effectiveness', *Housing,* February.

Cole, I. (1993) 'The Decentralisation of Housing Services', in *Implementing Housing Policy,* eds P. Malpass and R. Means, Buckingham: Open University Press.

Cole, I. and Furbey, R. (1994) *The Eclipse of Council Housing,* London: Routledge & Kegan Paul.

Cole, I. and Goodchild, B. (1995) 'Local Housing Strategies In England: An Assessment of Their Changing Role and Content', *Policy and Politics,* vol. 23, no. 1, pp. 49–60.

Coleman, A. (1985) *Utopia on Trail: Vision and Reality in Planned Housing,* Hilary Shipman: London.

Commission for Racial Equality (1984) *Race and Council Housing in Hackney,* CRE.

Commission for Racial Equality (1985) *Race and Mortgage Lending,* CRE.

Conway, J. (1995) 'Housing as an Instrument of Health Care', *Health and Social Care in the Community,* no. 3, pp. 141–50.

Crossley, R. (1995) 'Time to Give Tenants a Hearing', *ROOF,* May/June, Shelter.

Cullen, J. (1995) 'The Risks of Moving into a Gray Area', *Inside Housing,* 1 December, pp. 12–13.

Cullingworth Report (1969) *Council Housing: Purposes, Procedures, Priorities,* London CHAC, HMSO.

Darke, R. (1995) 'Partnerships, Local Authorities and Housing Associations', unpublished background paper.

Department of the Environment (1987a) *Housing: The Government's Proposals,* HMSO.

Department of the Environment (1987b) *The PEP Guide to Local Housing Management: The PEP Model,* HMSO.

Department of the Environment (1989) *The Nature and Effectiveness of Housing Management in England,* HMSO.

Department of the Environment (1991) *Estate Action – New Life for Local Authority Estates,* DoE.

Department of the Environment (1992a) *The Scope for Competitive Tendering of Housing Management,* HMSO.

Department of the Environment (1992b) *Competing for Quality in Housing,* HMSO.

Department of the Environment (1992c) *Empirical Study into the Costs of Local Authority Housing Management,* HMSO.

Department of the Environment (1992d) *Evaluating Large Scale Voluntary Transfers of Local Authority Housing: An Interim Report,* HMSO.

Department of the Environment (1992e) *Tenant Involvement and the Right to Manage: Consultation Paper*, HMSO.

Department of the Environment (1993a) *Managing Social Housing*, HMSO.

Department of the Environment (1993b) *Estate Based Housing Management: An Evaluation*, HMSO.

Department of the Environment (1993c) *Compulsory Competitive Tendering of Housing Management*, HMSO.

Department of the Environment (1993d) *Priority Estates Project Cost-Effectiveness Study: Summary of Findings*, HMSO.

Department of the Environment (1993e) *A Consultation Paper on Probationary Tenancies*, DoE.

Department of the Environment (1994a) *The Housing Revenue Account Ring-Fence*, HMSO.

Department of the Environment (1994b) *Learning to Manage*, HMSO.

Department of the Environment (1994c) *Preparing to Manage*, HMSO.

Department of the Environment (1994d) *The DoE Modular Management Agreement for TMO's*, HMSO.

Department of the Environment (1994e) *The Guide to the Right to Manage*, HMSO.

Department of the Environment (1994f) *Training for Tenant Management*, HMSO.

Department of the Environment (1994g) Local Government Act 1988 (Defined Activities) (Exemptions) (England and Wales) (Amendment) Order 1994, SI 2296, HMSO.

Department of the Environment (1995a) *Evaluating Large Scale Voluntary Transfers of Local Authority Housing*, HMSO.

Department of the Environment (1995b) *Our Future Homes: Opportunity, Choice, Responsibility*, HMSO.

Department of the Environment (1995c) *More Choice in the Social Rented Sector – Consultation Paper Linked to the Housing White Paper Our Future Homes*, HMSO.

Department of the Environment (1995d) *Tenants in Control: An Evaluation of Tenant-Led Housing Management Organisations*, HMSO.

Department of the Environment (1996) Circular 5/96 – *Guidance on the Conduct of Compulsory Competitive Tendering*, HMSO.

Department of Health (1994) *Implementing Caring for People: Housing and Homelessness. Report of the Community Care Monitoring Special Study, October 1993–April 1994*, DoH.

Department of Health (1995) *Community Care Development Programme – Consultation Document*, DoH.

Department of Health/Department of the Environment (1995) *Draft Joint Guidance – Community Care, Housing and Homelessness*, HMSO.

Dobson, F. (1995) 'Frank Dobson MP: Shadow Secretary of State for the Environment', *Housing and Planning Review*, December 1995 and January 1996, pp. 10–11.

Dwelly, T. (1991) 'Too Much Trust', *ROOF*, March/April, pp. 22–5.

Dwelly, T. and Blake, J. (1995) 'Long Live Council Housing!', *ROOF*, July/August, pp. 25–8.

Elcock, H. and Rose, A. (1993) 'The Future of Professionalism in Local Government: Training for the Management of Change', *The Belgrave Papers, No. 10 – The Future of Professionalism in Local Government*, Local Government Management Board.

Forrest, R. and Murie, A. (1988) *Selling the Welfare State: The Privatisation of Housing*, London: Routledge.

Fraser, R. (1991) *Working Together in the 1990s*, Institute of Housing, Coventry.

Gastor, L. (1991) *Quality at the Front Line*, School of Advanced Urban Studies.

Gaudion, N. (1995) 'Discreet Charm of a Lib-Dem', *Housing*, December 1995/January 1996, pp. 22–3.

Geddes, M. (1994) 'The Role of Partnerships in Promoting Social Cohesion', Discussion Paper for The European Foundation for the Improvement of Living and Working Conditions, November.

George, V. and Wilding, P. (1976) *Ideology and Social Welfare*, London: Routledge & Kegan Paul.

Ghosh, S. (1994) 'Community Care – or Careless?', *ROOF*, March/April, p. 11.

Goodlad, R. (1993) *The Housing Authority as Enabler*, Longman/Institute of Housing.

Goss, S. and Rosser, J. (1996) 'Never Mind the Cost, Feel the Quality', *Inside Housing*, 26 January, pp. 14–15.

Gregory, S. and Brownill, S. (1994) 'The Housing/Care Divide: Community Care and the Management of Single Person Housing in Oxford', Oxford Brookes University Working Paper.

Gregory, S., Brownill, S. and Pearl, M. (1995) 'Filling the Gaps: The Management of General Housing and Community Care in Oxford', Oxford Brookes University Working Paper No. 162.

Griffin, C. (1995) 'Nick Raynsford MP, Shadow Housing Minister', *Housing and Planning Review*, June/July, pp. 6–8.

Handy, C. (1985) *Understanding Organisations*, Harmondsworth: Penguin.

Hatchett, W. (1995) 'Labour's Heresies', *Housing*, July/August, pp. 22–4.

Health Committee (1993) *Community Care: The Way Forward*, Sixth Report of the Health Committee, Session 1992–3, vol. 1, HMSO.

Health Committee (1994) *Better Off in the Community? The Care of People Who Are Seriously Mentally Ill*, First Report of the Health Committee, Session 1993–4, vol. 1, HMSO.

Hoggett, P. (1991) *A New Management in the Public Sector'*, Policy and Politics, vol. 19, no. 4, pp. 243–56.

Hood, C. (1991) 'A Public Management for All Seasons', *Public Administration*, vol. 69, no. 1 (Spring), pp. 3–19.

Hood, M. (1993) 'Question Time', *ROOF*, November/December, p. 11.

Hood, M. (1995) 'Tenants Can't Participate on Their Own', *Inside Housing*, 19 May.

Housing Corporation (1990) *Into the Nineties: Opportunities and Challenges for the Housing Association Movement*, Housing Corporation.

Housing Corporation (1995a) *Fact File – The Housing Corporation's Statistical Bulletin*, no. 2, February.

Housing Corporation (1995b) *Performance Audit Visit Manual*, HMSO.

Housing Corporation (1995c) *Competing for Grant – Rents, Subsidies, Standards and Efficiency*, Housing Corporation.

Housing Corporation (1995d) *Homing in on Performance: Social Housing Performance in 1994 Compared*, Housing Corporation.

Housing Corporation (1996a) *Future Directions for Housing Associations*, Housing Corporation.

Housing Corporation (1996b) *Future Directions for Housing Associations – Insight*, Housing Corporation.

Hutchins, T. (1990) 'Beyond the Big Switch', *ROOF*, November/December, pp. 38–9.

Ilych, I. (1977) *Disabling Professions*, London: Marion Boyars.

Institute of Housing (1987) *Preparing for Change*, IoH.

Institute of Housing (1990) *Social Housing in the 1990's: Challenges, Choices and Change*, IoH.

Institute of Housing (1991) *Position Statement on Compulsory Competitive Tendering for Local Authority Housing Management*, IoH, 15 November.

Isaac-Henry, K., Painter, C. and Barnes, C. (1993) *Management in the Public Sector: Challenge and Change*, London: Chapman & Hall.

Jackson, V. (1993) 'A New Breed of Association', *Housing*, July, pp. 43–4.

Jevons, R. and Madge, J. (1946) *Housing Estates – A Study of Bristol Corporation Policy and Practice Between the Wars*, University of Bristol.

Joseph Rowntree Foundation (1995) *Foundations – Action on Estates*, Joseph Rowntree Foundation, March.

Karn, V. (1993) 'Remodelling a HAT: The Implementation of the Housing Action Trust Legislation 1987–92', pp. 74–90 in *Implementing Housing Policy*, eds P. Malpass and R. Mean, Buckingham: Open University Press.

Karn, V., Lickless, R., Hughes, D. and Crawley, J. (1993) *Neighbour Disputes*, Institute of Housing.

Karn, V. and Sheridan, L. (1994) *New Homes in the 1990s*, University of Manchester and Joseph Rowntree Foundation.

Kean, D. (1995) 'Homing in on a Labour Victory', *Municipal Journal*, 23–29 June, pp. 24, 27.

Kearns, A. (1994) *Volunteering Views – Report of an Opinion Survey on Housing Association Governance*, Centre for Housing Research and Urban Studies.

Kelly, P. (1995) 'Antisocial Antidotes', *ROOF*, July/August, pp. 38–9.

Kirklees Federation of Tenants and Residents Associations (KFTRA) Annual Report 1993/94.

Kirklees Federation of Tenants and Residents Associations Newsletter (March 1995) *Home Truths*.

KFTRA (March 1995) *KFTRA's Background Information Sheet*.

Kirklees Metropolitan Council/KFTRA (1991) *Getting Together* (Video).

Kirklees Metropolitan Council/KFTRA (1995) *Tenant Consultation Charter Procedure Manual*.

Labour Housing Group (1989) *Guidelines for Tenant Involvement*, Labour Party.

Labour Party (1992) *It's Time to Get Britain Working Again*, Election Manifesto, Labour Party.

Laffin, M. (1985) *Professionalism and Policy*, Avebury.

Laffin, M. and Young, K. (1990) *Professionalism in Local Government*, Longman.

Larson, M. (1977) *The Rise of Professionalism*, University of California Press.

Ledgerwood, N. (1995) 'Getting What You Pay For', *Housing*, July/August, pp. 41–2.

Lupton, M. (1993) Correspondance dated December 1993.

Malpass, P. (1992) 'Housing Policy and the Disabling of Local Authorities', pp. 10–28 in *Housing Policy in the 1990s*, ed. J. Birchall, London: Routledge & Kegan Paul.

Malpass, P. (1995) 'What Future for Social Housing in Britain', *Housing Review*, vol. 44, no. 1 (January–February), pp. 4–7.

Malpass, P. and Murie, A. (1993) *Housing Policy and Practice*, 3rd edn, London: Macmillan.

Mason, S. and Sopp, L. (1988) *Partnership Schemes: Manual of Guidance for Local Authorities and Developers*, HMSO.

McKnight, J. (1977) 'Professionalised Service and Disabling Help', in I. Ilych, *Disabling Professions*, London: Marion Boyars.

Means, R. (1993) 'Perspectives on Implementation', in *Implementing Housing Policy*, eds P. Malpass and R. Means, Buckingham: Open University Press.

Means, R. and Smith, R. (1994) *Community Care – Policy and Practice*, London: Macmillan.

Metcalfe, L. and Richards, S. (1990) *Improving Public Management*, London: Sage.

Millar, K. (1993) 'Tender Moments', *Housing*, April, pp. 15–18.

Morris, H. (1994a) 'Braving the New World of IT', *Inside Technology*, CIH, 28 Jan., pp. 2–3.

Morris, H. (1994b) 'Fishing Around for the Right Association', *Inside Housing*, 29 April.

Morris, H. (1994c) 'A Harrowing Experience', *Inside Housing*, 18 Nov.

Morris, H. (1996) 'Councils Clean Up 96 per cent of Contracts in Round One', *Inside Housing*, 26 January, p. 2.

Mullins, D., Niner, P. and Risborough, M. (1993) 'Large Scale Voluntary Transfers', pp. 169–84 in *Implementing Housing Policy*, eds P. Malpass and R. Means, Buckingham: Open University Press.

Murphy, E. (1991) *After the Asylums*, Faber & Faber.

National Federation of Housing Associations (1987) *Standards for Housing Management*, NFHA.

National Federation of Housing Associations (1989) *Housing: The Foundation of Community Care*, NFHA.

National Federation of Housing Associations and East London Housing Association (1991) *Housing Consortia for Community Care*, NFHA.

National Federation of Housing Associations (1993) *BS 5750: A Tool For Improvement*, NFHA.

National Federation of Housing Associations (1994) *Value Added: A Discussion Paper about Housing Management*, NFHA.

National Federation of Housing Associations (1995a) *Competence and Accountability*, NFHA.

National Federation of Housing Associations (1995b) *Code of Governance*, NFHA.

National Federation of Housing Associations (1995c) *The Social Housing Product: A Discussion and Consultation Paper*, NFHA.

National Federation of Housing Associations (1995d) *Managing Vulnerability – The Challenge for Managers of Independent Housing*, NFHA.

National Tenants' and Residents' Federation/National Tenants' Organisation (1992) *Tenant Participation Charter*.

National Voluntary Committee Members' Forum (1994) 'A Discussion Paper for the NFHA Inquiry into Housing Association Governance', HACAS.

Office of Population Censuses and Surveys (1995) *Housing in England 1993/4*, OPCS.

Page, D. (1993) *Building for Communities: A Study of New Housing Association Estates*, Joseph Rowntree Foundation.

Page, D. (1994) *Developing Communities*, Sutton Hastoe Housing Association.

Palmer, J. (1995) Response to a Survey Questionnaire distributed by M. Pearl.

Pankhurst, J. (1993) 'CCT – Can the Comprehensive Housing Service Survive?', *Housing and Planning Review*, August/September, pp. 7–10.

Passmore, J. (1995) Response to a Survey Questionnaire distributed by M. Pearl.

Passmore, J. and Fergusson, S. (1994) *Customer Service in a Competitive Environment*, Chartered Institute of Housing.

Pearl, M. (1993) *The Professionalisation of Housing Management*, Oxford Brookes University Working Paper No. 142.

Perry, J. (1994) 'Fruits of Labour's Thinking on Housing', *Housing*, December, p. 18.

Pinto, R. (ed.) (1995) *Developments in Housing Management and Ownership*, Manchester University Press, Manchester.

Power, A. (1987) *Property Before People*, London: Allen & Unwin.

Power, A. (1991a) *Running to Stand Still*, London: PEP.

Power, A. (1991b) *Housing: A Guide to Quality and Creativity*, London: Longman.

Power, A. and Tunstall, B. (1995) *Swimming Against the Tide: Progress or Polarisation on 20 Unpopular Estates*, York: Joseph Rowntree Foundation.

Priority Estates Project (1994) *Involving Tenants in CCT: A Simple Guide*.

Priority Estates Project (April 1994) *PEPtalk*, issue 37.

Priority Estates Project (undated) Leaflets on: Options for Tenants; Tenant Involvement in CCT of Housing Management; the Right to Manage.

Provan, B. and Williams, P. (1991) 'Joining the Professionals? The Future of Housing Staff and Their Work', ch. 13 in *The Housing Service of the Future*, eds D. Donnison and D. Maclennon, London: Longman/IoH.

Rao, N. (1990) *The Changing Role of Local Authorities*, Joseph Rowntree Memorial Trust.

Raynsford, N. (1995a) 'A Recipe for Revival', *Inside Housing*, 8 December, pp. 16–17.

Raynsford, N. (1995b) Speech at the Annual Review Presentation of Bromford Carinthia Housing Association, Wolverhampton, July 1995.

Ridley, N. (1988) 'The Local Right: Enabling Not Providing', Centre for Policy Studies, pp. 17, 22 and 25, quoted in J. Gyford, 'The Enabling Council – A Third Model', *Local Government Studies*, January/February 1991, pp. 1–5.

Schriesheim, J., von Glinow, M.A. and Kerr, S. (1977) 'Professionals in Bureaucracies: A Structural Alternative', in P.C. Nystrom and W.H. Starbuck (eds), *Prescriptive Models of Organisations*, Amsterdam: North-Holland.

Smith, A. (1995) 'Backdoor', *ROOF*, September/October.

Smith, S. (1989) *The Politics of 'Race' and Residence*, Cambridge: Polity Press.

Spray, W. (1992a). *Taking the Reins: A Case Study of the Hornsey Lane Estate. Management Board*, PEP Ltd.

Spray, W. (1992b) 'The First Estate Management Board in London', *Local and Government Policy Making*, vol. 19, no. 2.

Stewart, J. (1988) *A New Management for Housing Departments*, Local Government Training Board.

Stewart, J. (1993) 'In Conclusion – Issues to be Explored', *The Belgrave Papers, No. 10 – The Future of Professionalism in Local Government*, Local Government Management Board.

Stewart, J. and Walsh, K. (1989) *The Search for Quality*, Local Government Training Board.

Stewart, J. and Walsh, K. (1992) 'Change in the Management of Public Services', *Public Administration*, vol. 70 (Winter), pp. 499–518.

Stoker, G. (1993) 'Professions, Accountability and the New Local Governance', *The Belgrave Papers, No. 10 – The Future of Professionalism in Local Government*, Local Government Management Board.

Tenant Participation Advisory Service (1994a) *CCT Factsheets*.

Tenant Participation Advisory Service (1994b) *Involving Tenants in Housing Associations. A Training Guide for Staff and Committee Members*.

Thompson, L. (1993) 'The Ealing Judgement', *Housing Review*, vol. 42, no. 5 (September–October) pp. 80–3.

Travers, T. (1993) 'Professionalism and Local Government Reform: Not So Much Villains As Saviours', *The Belgrave Papers, No. 10 – The Future of Professionalism in Local Government*, Local Government Management Board.

Trippier, D. (1989) 'The Housing Act 1988: Looking to 1990', speech given at Institute of Housing Seminar.

Waddicore, C. (1995) Response to a Survey Questionnaire distributed by M. Pearl.

Wadhams, C. (1994) 'Running a Social Housing Business – Executive Control or Voluntary Effort?', paper to NFHA Committee Members Conference, January 1994.

Walker, R. (1994) 'Putting Performance Measurement into Context: Classifying Social Housing Organisations', *Policy and Politics*, vol. 22, no. 3, pp. 191–202.

Walsh, M. (1994) 'Housing Associations As Managing Agents – A Local Authority Perspective', Briefing Note.

Walsh, K. and Spencer, K. (1990) *The Quality of Service in Housing Management*, Institute of Local Government Studies, University of Birmingham.

Waltham Forest HAT (1994a) *Corporate Plan – 1995/96 – 1997/98*.

Waltham Forest HAT (1994b) *Annual Report and Accounts for 1993/94*.

Ward, C. (1985) *When We Build Again – Let's Have Housing That Works*, London: Pluto Press.

Wates, N. and Knevitt, C. (1987) *Community Architecture – How People Are Creating Their Own Environment*, Harmondsworth: Penguin.

Watson, L. and Conway, T. (1995) *Homes for Independent Living: Housing and Community Care Strategies*, Chartered Institute of Housing.

Watson, S. with Austerberry, H. (1986) *Housing and Homelessness: A Feminist Perspective*, London: Routledge & Kegan Paul.

Wilcox, S. (1993) *Local Housing Companies: New Opportunities for Council Housing*, Joseph Rowntree Foundation.

Wilding, P. (1982) *Professional Power and Social Welfare*, Routledge & Kegan Paul.

Wilding, P. (1994). *Maintaining Quality in Human Services'*, *Social Policy & Administration*, vol. 28, no. 1 (March), pp. 57–72.

Williams, P. (1993) 'Allies or Adversaries', *ROOF*, January/February, pp. 28–9.

Wolmar, C. (1992) 'A Tender Dilemma for Labour', *The Independent*, 9 April, p. 20.

Young Sir George (1992) 'Speech at ADC/AMA Conference on CCT'.

Young Sir George (1993) 'LSE Housing Lecture' 4 March.

Index

quality 26, 44–9, 84, 114, 121, 141–3, 157, 160, 162, 224, 234, 245
quality assurance
see also total quality management 27, 40, 41, 47, 121

racial harassment 31, 70–1, 79, 87, 142
racism 36, 37, 87, 127
rents 5, 7, 56, 66, 75, 139, 164, 174, 178, 179, 189, 195, 198, 226, 227, 230, 238, 239, 243
repairs 17, 36, 82, 103, 104, 105, 107, 139, 140, 142, 161, 162, 173, 179
residualisation 63, 64–6, 67, 87, 111, 128, 191
Right to Buy 3, 4, 5, 28, 63, 67, 91, 105, 131, 132, 135, 155, 169, 173, 174, 177, 202, 229, 231, 243, 244
Right to Manage 95, 98–100, 102, 236, 244
ring fencing 8, 30, 166, 173, 233

Safe Neighbourhoods Unit (SNU) 77
Single Regeneration Budget (SRB) 85, 86, 141, 166, 181, 199, 201, 203
social businesses 18, 46, 56, 160, 161, 187
Social Housing Grant 229, 232
see also Housing Association Grant
Social Housing Product 233–5
Social Housing Standard 234
see also Social Housing Product
Social Justice Commission 232
social security 21
social services departments 32, 113, 114, 117, 119, 122–5, 129, 167, 189, 242
special needs housing 31, 54, 118, 120, 123, 165, 193, 238, 240, 241
consortia 196–7
stakeholders 20, 45, 46, 53, 222, 224

tenant management organisations (TMOs) 92, 95, 98, 100, 107, 134
tenant participation 55, 89–109, 190, 221, 227, 240
prerequisites 93, 95, 106, 107, 180
s16 grants 96
Tenant Participation Advisory Service (TPAS) 28, 45, 91, 94, 95, 171
tenants
and CCT 134, 135, 150–1, 157
collective power 38, 39
and community care 119, 127–9
as customers 49, 244
and HATs 6, 167–8, 171
on management committees 57
problem tenants 67–70, 79, 80, 87
and residualisation 63, 68
rights 6
see also tenant participation
Tenants' Charter 96, 244
Tenants' Choice 4, 5, 28, 97, 104, 132, 173, 181, 189, 236
Tenants' Guarantee 7, 97, 178
total quality management (TQM) 41
trading-up 65
training 38, 43, 46, 52, 60, 85, 95, 100, 110, 122–4, 150, 169, 173, 200, 204, 210, 212, 219, 221
trickle transfer 163, 194

waiting lists 80, 192, 193, 195
Waltham Forest HAT 85, 168, 169, 170, 171–3
Wandsworth 26, 73, 152, 155
welfare state 1, 13, 17, 46, 226
Westminster 12, 77, 97, 135, 151–5, 209
White Papers
1975 *Better Services for the Mentally Ill* (DHSS) 112
1987 *Housing – The Government's Proposals* (DoE) 5, 113, 167, 184
1989 *Caring for People: Community Care in the Next Decade and Beyond* (DHSS) 113
1995 *Our Future Homes* (DoE) 16, 72, 75, 86, 177, 180, 226, 229–30
women 36, 59, 60, 149, 220, 221